D1136889

DESMOND
HAYNES

By the same author

Sportswatching (*with Steve Pinder*)
Spring Summer Autumn
Sonny Boy
Britannic Assurance Guide to County Cricket

DESMOND HAYNES

Lion of Barbados

ROB STEEN

H. F. & G. WITHERBY

First published in Great Britain 1993
by H. F. & G. Witherby
an imprint of Cassell
Villiers House, 41/47 Strand, London WC2N 5JE

© Rob Steen 1993

*All rights reserved. No part of this publication may be
reproduced or transmitted in any form or by any means,
electronic or mechanical including photocopying, recording or
any information storage or retrieval system, without prior
permission in writing from the publishers.*

The right of Rob Steen to be identified as
author of this work has been asserted by him in
accordance with the Copyright, Designs and
Patents Act, 1988.

A catalogue record for this book is available from
the British Library

ISBN 0 85493 221 6

Photoset in Great Britain by
Rowland Phototypesetting Ltd, Bury St Edmunds, Suffolk
and printed in Great Britain by
Butler and Tanner Ltd, Frome, Somerset

To Jeremy: all you have to do is win

Contents

Acknowledgements

Researching this book made it imperative that I visit the Caribbean, probably the most enjoyable obligation of my life so far. It also allowed me to pester the following kind people: Carlisle Best, Steve Camacho, Tony Cozier, Michael Findlay, Mike Gatting, Gordon Greenidge, Arletha Haynes, Dawn Haynes, Keith Holder, Michael Holding, Windle Holmes, Kenny Hutchinson, Clive Lloyd, Isaac Paris, Hartley Richards, Idrina Richards, Keith Richards, Mike Roseberry, Cammie Smith, Ezra Stuart, Stephen Thorpe, Courtney Walsh, the members of the Barclays Sports Club in Barbados, the regulars at Marshall's Bar in Holders Hill, the shady Mini Moke agent in Holetown, the jolly catering staff at Kensington Oval. My thanks to all.

I am grateful, too, to Richard Wigmore and John Pawsey for their encouragement and inordinate patience, to Simon Hughes for proposing that an English hack was the right man for this job, to Stephen Green for permitting me to plunder the MCC Library, to Patrick Eagar for his visual splendours, and to Sir Garfield Sobers for introducing me, and so many more of my generation, to the soul food of Caribbean cricket. To the friends and family, Anne and Woody above all, who have suffered the backlash of my affair with a rather shapely PCW 9512 – sorry.

Finally, to Desi, a good sport in every sense.

I

The Pride of Lions

Emancipate yourself from mental slavery
None but ourselves can free our minds.

Redemption Song, Bob Marley

The innovator has for enemies all those who have done well
under the old conditions and lukewarm defenders in those who
may do well under the new.

Machiavelli

'Take Your Licks Like Men, England.' So cajoled a banner fluttering in the Queen's Park Oval stands during the third Test of the 1989–90 Wisden Trophy series. Trouble is, scurrying around like mice, straining to evade second-class status, has become an area of English expertise. No matter how accustomed we grow to being licked, an alibi can always be dredged up from somewhere, and nowhere are these straw-clutching skills practised with greater tenacity than on the cricket field.

On Channel 4 last autumn, Tony Parsons, one of a raft of self-styled social commentators currently earning a crust by lamenting the decline of the English working classes, complained that his country's self-esteem dried up in 1945. To a degree he had a point. The Germans, with the assistance of some decidedly useful American reserves, had been roundly thrashed. Having waived the rules for centuries while she built up her empire, Britannia once again ruled the waves. The flagship, unfortunately, has been shipping water ever since. Now the Bundesbank rules, the ultimate slap in the face. As the pound dives and morale sinks, the only lingering vestiges of pride are to be found wallowing in the quicksand of old glory. Yet such is the national aptitude for self-deception and self-magnification that defeat, whether in Strasbourg or Edinburgh, can always be attributed to some chicanery perpetrated by the opposition. Hell hath no fury like an ex-Empire scorned. The last line of *The Great Gatsby* captures the futility of it all: 'So we beat on, boats against the current, borne back ceaselessly into the past.'

In the Caribbean, all eyes are on the morrow. The days of curtseying to Mother Whitehall are over. Yesterday has little to commend it. Like Jay Gatsby, its inhabitants believe in that green light, that 'orgiastic future that year by year recedes before us'. Though still dependent on IMF handouts, these descendants of the Barrancoids, Arawaks and Caribs bristle with pride, and rightly so. Whitey, after all, is no longer so mighty. Nowhere, again, is this more apparent than on the cricket field, that last bastion of Commonwealth harmony, a realm the English still feel it is their innate right to command. 'All the senior players', wrote Viv Richards in his autobiography, *Hitting Across The Line*, 'accept that it is our responsibility to instil this feeling into the newcomers. It is like handing down to them our pride.' It is this pride that has spurred Richards and his comrades to shrug aside the shackles of economic deprivation and social hardship and harness their ball skills on behalf of some idealized concept of inter-island solidarity. Should such a collective consciousness ever evolve in the accepted political sense, one nation under a groove, these love's labours will not have been in vain.

If Lloyd ran the kingdom, Roberts, Holding, Marshall and Garner supplied the power, Richards the glory, Greenidge and Haynes the eternal spirit. Dujon personified elegance, Gomes ice, Croft fire. This book is about the only one of these demigods still commuting regularly between wicket and Mount Olympus: Desmond Leo Haynes, the Lion of Barbados, Desi to his friends, and, variously, Budgie, Comedian and Hammer to his work colleagues. A man whose philosophy dangles from an ample neck in the form of an inscription on a glinting gold pendant: 'Live, Love, Laugh'. Since the two are so interwoven, it would be remiss to embark on his story without first touching on that of the lands he has served with such impassioned intensity, and on the bitterness incited by their expertise with bat and ball.

Over the past dozen years, Desi and his colleagues have forged the most durable force the bat-and-ball world has ever seen. But sport is chock-a-block with boggling statistics: Bob Beamon's Mexican jumping beano, Jim Laker's n-n-n-n-nineteen, Dixie Dean's sixty pearls for Everton, Joe DiMaggio's fifty-six-game hitting streak. Stretching back thirteen years and twenty-three rubbers prior to the start of Pakistan's visit in the spring, the West Indies' record run of unbeaten Test series is way up there. Arguably the most profound tribute came from *Sports Illustrated*, which named the West Indies, Liverpool FC and the San Francisco 49ers as the teams of the eighties. No mean accolade from an American magazine more inclined to give column space to cricket-racing than leather and willow. To those with a broader perspective and a deeper understanding of the difference between maintaining a standard of excellence at national level and lording it on the home front, Anfield and Candlestick Park would never be mentioned in the same breath as Georgetown, Bridgetown and Kingston. Think of all the great conglomerations who have stitched their insignias into sport's rich tapestry, of Puskas's Hungary, Di Stefano's Real Madrid and Pele's Brazil (1970 model), of Whineray's All Blacks and Dawes's Lions, of Lombardi's Green Bay Packers and Stengel's New York Yankees. Now think of the West Indies of Lloyd and Richards for defying the machinations of the International Cricket Council.

One of the performance fuels has been a profound love of the game itself, a passion that has always appeared to flow deeper than among any other members of the international circuit: partly for the opportunities cricket affords for escape and self-expression (for West Indians who choose not to emigrate, no other sport offers comparable possibilities), partly for the opportunity to present a united Caribbean front. This sense of community is not apparent elsewhere in this far-flung collection of diverse nations.

Even so, attempts at integration have been made, and continue to be made. 'Whether federation is more costly or less costly, whether federation is more efficient or less efficient, federation is inescapable, if the British Caribbean territories are to cease to parade themselves to the twentieth-century world as eighteenth-century anachronisms,' said Eric Williams, leader of Trinidad and Tobago's ruling People's National Party, shortly before the formation of the West Indian Federation in 1958, a brave but ultimately forlorn enterprise. For one thing, the Queen retained authority to legislate on matters of defence, finance and external affairs. Her Governor-General, furthermore, could act 'in his own discretion' and so veto any federal law he chose. Jamaica, one of the power brokers, had bauxite, farms and tourists, and could quite happily carry on regardless. Some of the other seven islands were similarly unenamoured by the prospect of sharing their hard-earned, albeit relative, wealth. But the game was up almost as soon as it had kicked off, and within a year plans for the end of the Federation were already being hatched. When the second and final Inter-Governmental Conference took place in London in June 1960 Williams and Norman Manley, the leader of the People's National Movement in Jamaica, were at each other's throats. The Windward and Leeward Islands, believing they were being used as bait in the perennial struggle between Trinidad and Jamaica, were not best pleased either. By the time they left Lancaster Gate, few of the delegates were on first-name terms.

The desire to repair the damage was strong, and moves to revive the federation followed. Two years later a constitution was accepted at another London conference. Reginald Maudling, the British Secretary of State, caused a stir by making it plain that political independence would go arm-in-arm with financial independence, then angered the so-called Little Eight by taking twenty-one months to agree on a formula whereby grants-in-aid would continue for five years. But by the time everything had been sorted out, a British Commissioner, Dr O'Loughlin, had calculated that the new federation would need three times the amount of support originally envisaged. The Little Eight's Council of Ministers, not unreasonably, demanded the new amount. Frustration, insularity and jealousy seeped back in. Grenada opted out. Antigua announced that she wanted to keep control of her post office and followed suit when this request was rebuffed, pulling her Siamese twin, Montserrat, with her. St Lucia rejected the Draft Federal Scheme. The tenth and last meeting of the Council of Ministers in April 1965 saw them lock horns with Barbados, whose prime minister, Errol Barrow, took exception to some remarks from his St Lucian counterpart and stormed out of the meeting, which was adjourned. In the words of the founder of the University of Barbados, Sir Arthur Lewis, 'mutual hatred and contempt' had once again proved too lethal a combination.

Since then, despite the seemingly imperative needs for political bonding, a common passport, a single currency, arising from the size of the Little Eight constituents, antipathies and self-centredness have repeatedly conspired against any all-embracing federal state. Admittedly, the level of co-operation has improved markedly. CARIFTA, the Caribbean Free Trade Area, was formed in 1968, CARICOM, the Caribbean Community, five years later. CARICOM subsequently took CARIFTA under its wing and paved the way for a co-operative approach to foreign policy. But Trinidad still has oil, Barbados sugar and tourism, Guyana unfashionable left-wing politicians, Jamaica her reggae. They all have their own commodity, their own means of survival, their own flag, their own identity and their own pride. As the xenophobic path to European federation has emphasized, this, sadly, is the way of the world. Differences tend to be accentuated rather than blurred when disparate peoples are flung into the melting pot, even when the nature of that disparity is more geographical than spiritual.

On a 22-yard strip of turf, at least, gulfs are bridged, an example set. 'When a Test match is being played, that is the only time that the people of the Caribbean come together as a cohesive whole,' stresses Viv Richards. 'That is why, to a West Indian, a Test match is so special. It is the only time that the true power of the islands comes to the fore. To see this makes me proud, but it also saddens me, once a Test series finishes, to watch this power evaporate.' What annoys and frustrates Richards is what he perceives as overt island nationalism. 'When the West Indies have accomplished a victory, each West Indian looks towards his own flag. What I long to see is one flag. Sometimes I get very embarrassed when someone asks me what is the colour of my flag. You look up and see all those different colours, all those different flags from all the Caribbean nations displaying to the world the nature of our problem.'

But by the mid seventies, it was the opposition that had a problem. The calypso had been displaced by a more militant beat, driven by the acquisition of independence and the growing American influence. The nations that had for so long derided the West Indian team for lacking the steel to turn talent into success now began, with enormous reluctance, to develop a taste for humble pie. Between March 1976 and 1993 (discounting the years of Packer-induced second-stringers) the West Indies won 63 and lost 16 of their five-day encounters, though this was something of a misnomer: more often than not, the opposition regarded survival until the fifth morning as a feat worthy of celebration. Of those 63 wins, eight were accomplished within three days, 20 inside four. The spirit imbued by this apparent omnipotence was never better illustrated than when South Africa entered the final day of their comeback Test in Bridgetown last spring requiring a perfunctory 78 with eight wickets intact, whereupon a weakened, inexperienced West Indian XI, inspired by Curtly Ambrose and Courtney Walsh, but above all by pride, swept to a 52-run victory before the beaming kitchen ladies had finished cooking the lunchtime *rôtis*.

That historic inaugural clash with Kepler Wessels and his born-again charges was a significant one. If we ignore the changes forced on them by the Packer Revolution, the West Indian selectors awarded three new caps in one game for the first time since Haynes's own début fourteen years previously. During that time, the promotion of Carlisle Best and Patrick Patterson for the first Test against England at Sabina Park in 1986 had provided the only instance of two freshmen being introduced simultaneously. At one settled stretch in 1979 and 1980, fourteen games went by without a newcomer breaking through. In the 1991 Worrell Trophy rubber, the same eleven featured in all five Tests. In the whole of the eighties, no more than thirty-nine men were honoured to don the maroon blazer; in the 1989 Ashes rubber alone England honoured twenty-nine members of the county set. The sense of continuity has been such that, from the end of the Packer era until the last ball of the century's penultimate decade, Australia capped forty-four new boys, England fifty-six and the West Indies twenty-one.

Partially necessitated by the comparative lack of options open to the Caribbean selectors, these figures are more a reflection of superiority on the field and the consequent capacity for giving talent time to breathe and so find its feet. The selectors' patience and judgement must also be given their due. Would any other country have persisted with Carl Hooper for so long for such erratic reward? Mark Benson, the Kent captain whom England dumped after one cap, predicted before the outset of the Guyanan's first county campaign last summer that Canterbury's latest import would soon be one of the world's top five batsmen. Hooper submitted a more than useful case for the defence over the succeeding months and now, five years after his début, is beginning to repay the faith so rightly shown in him. A struggling side, even an average one, would have had him out long ago.

Evidence of the extent of this unprecedented era of Caribbean dominance can readily be gauged by the following analysis of Test matches played between 12 December 1930, the day Bill Woodfull and George Copeland Grant led their respective homelands into the first-ever meeting between Australia and West Indies, and the end of the eighties. The reason for the cut-off? Simply that that Adelaide affair represented the first time West Indies had played someone other than England; from then on, they were part of the furniture.

Best performers decade by decade since first-ever Australia–West Indies Test, December 1930 (not including 1940s):

			P	Won	Lost	Win–loss ratio
1930s	AUSTRALIA	(Tests*)	33	21	9	2.33
		(Series†)	8	6	1	6.00
1950s	AUSTRALIA	(Tests)	47	23	10	2.33
	ENGLAND	(Series)	19	12	3	4.00

1960s	ENGLAND	(Tests)	97	29	15	1.93
	AUSTRALIA	(Tests)	67	23	14	1.64
	AUSTRALIA	(Series)	14	7	2	3.50
	W. INDIES	(Series)	10	5	4	1.25
1970s	AUSTRALIA	(Tests‡)	56	24	15	1.60
		(Series)	13	7	3	2.33
1980s	W. INDIES	(Tests)	83	44	8	5.50
	W. INDIES	(Series)	20	14	1	14.00

* Tests finished in decade
† Series of at least two games and ending in that decade
‡ Tests played with full-strength squad, ie not involving Tests played in Packer era

WIN/LOSS RATIO (Tests)
1. WEST INDIES 5.50–1980s
2/3. Australia 2.33–1930s and 1950s

WIN/LOSS RATIO (Series)
1. WEST INDIES 14.00–1980s
2. Australia 6.00–1930s
3. England 4.00–1950s

At first, the coup responsible for ousting the long-standing Anglo-Australian regime was blamed on the generosity of the English in allowing the likes of Lloyd, Richards and Roberts to hone their skills in the county game, a theory that disregarded the inherent benefits both to the club coffers and aspiring young locals. However, as time progressed and the upstarts declined to return from whence they came, things grew a little tenser. By their reliance on brutal pace to the exclusion of subtle spin, the West Indies, or so the party line went, were offending the notion of cricket as a genteel pastime, for pink-ginned plutocrats to watch and for gentlemen, not players, to play.

To some, the end did not come remotely close to vindicating the means. The West Indies were paid that most dangerous of back-handed compliments – envy. Fear bred loathing. Lloyd, Richards and their co-conspirators were found guilty of the crimes of bowling fast and making batsmen hop about, and sometimes even hitting their well-armoured bodies. When half a million Victorians thronged the streets of Melbourne to bid a tickertaped adieu to Frank Worrell's gay blades in 1961, they were doubly happy: delighted that these black chappies had injected some much-needed verve into a game fast losing its nerve, relieved that Richie Benaud and the rest of their boys had still put them in their place. 'West Indians at that moment', wrote C. L. R.

James, 'had made a public entry into the comity of nations.' When the West Indies peddled their wares at the MCG during Christmas 1992, they had long since entered the enmity of nations. Being valiant losers, enchanting the white folk without threatening their sense of superiority, was all fine and dandy; the aura of the ruthless winner was insufferable. Given that this is a land where the descendants of its earliest citizens are robbed of their homelands and shunted off to townships, where the plight of the Aboriginals is perceived as a wart on Waltzin' Matilda's neck more than a stain on the national character, the dearth of tickertape now was not unexpected.

A great deal is made of the four-pronged pace attack, more often than not by those who find it convenient to forget that England and Jardine, not the West Indies and Lloyd, own the patent. The second instalment of the infamous and shameful 1932–3 Bodyline series saw Allen, Voce, Larwood and Bowes unite as, for the first time in 186 Tests, England took the field without a spinner. Unfortunately, this was on a turning wicket that ultimately yielded 15 wickets for O'Reilly, Grimmett and Ironmonger, and Australia's only win of the winter. Jardine brought back Hedley Verity to stop the harrumphing at Lord's and unleashed the full force of his master plan in the next game at Adelaide, bringing the whole show to a discordant crescendo. Verity remained in tow for the remainder of the tour, and not until the Brisbane Test of 1954 did an England selection panel dare to deal its captain a similar hand. Again, the move did not so much backfire as trigger self-immolation. Len Hutton elected to field, Australia racked up 601 – the biggest haul yet managed by an international team after being inserted – and romped home by an innings and 154 runs. By the time the combatants had adjourned to Sydney, stealth was back on the agenda. On the morning of the match, however, Hutton, upon deciding the pitch was greener than one of Granny Smith's finest, not only left out Alec Bedser, his most accomplished weapon in such conditions, but neglected to inform him in person, choosing instead to communicate the news via the heartless piece of paper he eventually pinned to the dressing-room door detailing the final XI. Mercifully, Hutton had not gone completely potty, and Frank Tyson ensured that the end came close to justifying the means.

For a while all went a bit sleepy. Still, there was a taster of inconsistencies to come when Charlie Griffith's unwitting impersonation of Eric Bristow stirred up a right old hoo-ha in the mid-sixties, this after Ian Meckiff and a veritable chorus line of Australian chuckers had been allowed to get through the 1958–9 Ashes series without a single no-ball call. Then came the Year of Living Dangerously. At Brisbane in 1974, Ian Chappell and his Ugly Australians unleashed a howitzer attack on Mike Denness's hapless, un-helmeted Englishmen, apparently in response to some bumpers from, among others, the considerably less than ferocious Tony Greig. On this occasion it was not so much the manpower as the mode of delivery and the identity of the premier postmen, Jeff Thomson and Dennis Lillee. 'I enjoy hitting a batsman more than getting him out,' Thommo claimed with his customary flair for sound bites. 'I like to see blood on the pitch.' And so he did. 'None of us enjoyed going out to bat,' recalled Keith Fletcher. 'The knowledge that one needed to move very fast to keep one's body intact was not a pleasant way to spend a day in the sunshine, and there were times for all of us when a few weeks in frozen England seemed quite a palatable alternative to yet another session of ducking the stream of short balls.' The game would never be the same again.

Duly encouraged, Australia took the field in Perth the following winter with Messrs Lillee, Thomson, Gilmour and Walker supplemented by the off-breaks of Ashley Mallett. Once again, the excess of pace proved imma-terial: Andy Roberts's match bag of 9-119 was more impressive than the combined spoils of the Aussie quartet, 9-453, and the Windies breezed into port with an innings and almost a day to spare, thus levelling the series. Again, the reversion to a less top-heavy offence worked wonders: Australia won the next four Tests. The message seemed obvious enough: why get four men to do the job of three, especially when the trio concerned could wreak such havoc? As Richards and Lloyd have constantly reminded their critics, this was the watershed, the tour that gave West Indian cricketing pride its biggest prick. Never again would they be so humbled, so ridiculed. Richards, in particular, bore a deep scar. 'We are basically very calm, very peaceful people. I do not know of any West Indian cricketer who swears at the opposition in the way that those Aussies did. We came up against extreme savagery, what many people would call extreme racism.'

Racism is an issue more potent in cricket than other sports for the simple reason that the game's leading participants are split so evenly between white and non-white. That this is now a greater cause for concern than ever before is equally explicable: the balance of power has changed. Where England and Australia once dominated the roost, West Indies and, more recently, Pakistan have been doing the crowing for some time. Crouched over a coffee table in his bedroom at the Embassy Hotel in Bayswater, Clive Lloyd proffered the balanced overview one might expect of one of Lancashire's finest, and

best-loved, adopted sons. The book lying on the dressing table certainly gave
an insight into man and muse: *Inward Hunger – The Education of a Prime Minister*
by Eric Williams. Lloyd's own inward hunger rages as strongly as any. At the
age of twelve he lost his father. At the Adelaide Cricket Ground, in December
1972, he suffered a back injury when diving for a catch and was at one stage
close to death. The following July he was scoring a feline 132 against England
at the Oval; two years later he was captaining the West Indies.

'I've never tried to look at things in a black and white manner,' he averred.
'I never had a heated argument with anyone over that in twenty years. In my
first Test against England in 1968, Jeff Jones called Wes Hall 'black bastard'
or something. Wes got uptight at first then realized that he shouldn't let it
get to him. You mustn't let these guys get through to you. The minute they
upset you they've done their job because you're going to give away your
hand. You're going to want to hit that ball so hard you're going to hit it too
hard, so you're not going to time it. The best thing is to stay there and grind
those fielders into the dust. That was the West Indies of old, calypso, Carry
On Flamboyant, not putting a lot of thought into your cricket. That's how
they used to get us out years ago, probably call out some racist remarks and
then you get uptight and give your hand away.

'After that trip to Australia we began to change, to get it together. People
think it's payback time but that's just stupid. It's not a matter of paying back.
People don't understand the importance of cricket in the West Indies. We
were showing people, we were showing the world that we can be just as good
as anyone else. That's all. It's a quiet demonstration, if you like. When Tony
Greig said they'd make us grovel I don't know if he understood the meaning
of the word, but here you had a white South African telling you he was
going to make you grovel and the sort of pride that is in players today made
people just go out there and make him eat his words. That's all we did. We've
got more professional, more disciplined – that's how we've done it. Look at
that 300-odd target we chased at Lord's in 1984. I would love to have had the
whole video of that. I'd keep it for all time. Years ago, if we'd had that sort
of target we'd have been seven down and plenty short. The guys said to me,
"How should we play?" I just said, "Play your normal game." We won hands
down.'

If cricket is the Caribbean's in-house window-dresser, the precision and
impact of the display a barometer of strength and pride, of unity and purpose,
it must be seen to its best advantage at all times. Yet in the past, once this
hybrid collection began to slip from its pedestal, many of the age-old inter-

necine frictions began to resurface. The corporate identity eroded. Jamaicans and Trinidadians, as ever, blamed each other, Africans accused Indians. Like Frank Worrell before him, Lloyd recognized this divisiveness and acted on it, decreeing that fellow islanders were not to be permitted to share the same hotel room. Communication was encouraged, cliques discouraged, collectivism *de rigueur*. Here was a chance to broaden horizons, not restrict them, to set an example. To Lloyd, the greatest challenge was to construct a team that could be held up as a microcosm of a homogeneous Caribbean state. His greatest triumph, and satisfaction, lay in fulfilling that aim. 'I had people from different islands sharing so they could get to understand each other. That was very important. A guy would never talk about "my Trinidadian mate"; it would be "my roommate", who could be from St Kitts or wherever. That bred a sort of conviviality, got rid of the insularity that had existed before. By playing together, by doing so well for so long, all the politicians now have to realize that this is something we can do with the islands. Cricket has been a catalyst and now they're getting it together. We now have a West Indian commission talking about doing things together. That's what cricket has done for us: it has brought us together. We were unified through cricket.'

Few of his detractors are likely to recall that, for Lloyd's first match at the helm, against India at Bangalore in 1974, he carried two spinners in his holster. Things went swimmingly, so much so that, short of lashing England by an innings at Lord's, 'Paddington' could hardly have asked for a more auspicious initiation. The West Indies had lost their previous Test to England, or, more specifically, to Tony Greig's craftily flighted off-spin. That was Sobers's last Test, and Rohan Kanhai's. The roof, though, did not cave in. In marched a couple of freshmen in I. V. A. Richards and C. G. Greenidge, the latter a new opening partner for Roy Fredericks. Andy Roberts, the first Antiguan to be picked at this level, was making his second appearance. Greenidge promptly became the first Caribbean batsman to score a Test century on début overseas, Lloyd himself prowled to a vivid 100 off 85 deliveries, Roberts's 3–24 helped scuttle India for 118, their lowest total yet on home turf, and sealed a 267-run victory.

In Lloyd's estimation, however, it was the three purveyors of tweak, Imtiaz Ali, Raphick Jumadeen and Albert Padmore, who let the side down at Port-of-Spain in 1976, when India launched the greatest Test chase of all to make 406–4 and so triumph against virtually all odds. 'The point was', explains Lloyd, who maintains that there was no conscious decision to divest his team of spin, 'there simply weren't any spinners good enough after Lance Gibbs retired. We just had guys who bowled spin, not got people out. As a third-world country we were trying to use our resources, and we had good fast bowlers. But because everyone would tell us to play two quickies and two spinners we never won any Test matches, so we reverted to four fast bowlers and we started winning. And not to the detriment of spin. I used fourteen spinners as captain.'

The first whiff of a new deal had wafted in from Adelaide earlier that winter, when three brisk strike bowlers, Keith Boyce, Roberts and Holding, took up cudgels alongside the knock-kneed nous of Vanburn Holder. Yet again, the results were dispiriting, Boyce, Roberts and Holding mustering one victim apiece. After that, however, the battle plan was resurrected. Bernard Julien, Wayne Daniel, Holding and Holder were all pitched into the deciding round at Kingston. Gaekwad spent two days in hospital after being clattered on the ear; Viswanath capitulated to a ball that fractured and dislocated one of his fingers *en route* to slip; Patel had three stitches inserted in a mouth cut; at one stage all seventeen members of the touring party had been called into the ever-gaping breach. Angered by what he interpreted as intimidatory bowling, Bedi declared in protest with only six wickets down. Some construed his decision to close the second innings at 97–5, and thus concede defeat, as being similarly motivated. He denied this, insisting that he and Chandrasekhar had both picked up injuries while attempting to take return catches. Hmm. Having escaped facing the music first time round, neither can have had much enthusiasm for confronting it now.

That said, the Four Horsemen of the Apocalypse imagery did not truly enter the picture until the West Indies' first post-Packer outing, at Brisbane in 1979, wherein each rider chosen was capable of cranium-crushing hostility. Cue Roberts, Holding, Croft and Garner – and another failure, albeit a minor one, as stalemate ensued on a comatose pitch. Refusing to be deflected, Lloyd drew strength from the memory of Roberts, Holding, Garner and Daniel juggernauting through Ian Chappell's WSC Australians in the Second 'Super-test' at the Sydney Showground in 1977. The next two Tests were won at a canter, the foursome sharing 40 wickets at 17.78 a shot and so bringing home a particularly tasty rasher of bacon. At last, West Indies had won a series Down Under, and against a powerful Australian combo at that, this just a year after Thomson, Lillee and Pascoe had put the West Indian World Series Cricket batsmen through their own highly efficient mincer. With four pacemen life was so much simpler: sensible rotation, after all, can ensure two fresh bullets at any one time. As a blueprint it was hard to ignore. As a moral issue it didn't get past first base. To be or not to be – four quickies or three? Is it nobler in the mind to suffer the slings and arrows of outrageous fortune or complain about the number of arrows?

From then on the song remained much the same. For the rest of the cricketing fraternity the tune was, in comparison to what had gone before, frequently loony. Between the Sabina spine-chiller against India and the end of the 1992 season thirty-seven batsmen were compelled to retire hurt in Tests against Lloyd and his wrecking crew, of whom Croft and Marshall, with six victims each, were the most accomplished demolition artists. Was this down to sadistic bowling? Inadequate technique? Weak umpires? Bad pitches? Bad luck? Opinions varied. For most, the musings of Thomas Gray were all too appropriate: 'Now fades the glimmering landscape on the sight,/And all the air a solemn stillness holds . . .' Others could point out that the nearest Test cricket had ever come to claiming a casualty in this manner was in sleepy Auckland on 25 February 1975, when Peter Lever forced Ewan Chatfield, the New Zealand number 11, to deflect a rising ball into his left temple. Technically, Chatfield died. For several seconds his heartbeat stopped, and only mouth-to-mouth resuscitation and heart massage from the ever-alert England physio, Bernard Thomas, saved his life. Of the thirty-five who retired hurt – Sadiq Mohammad and Peter Toohey were put out of action twice in the same match – only two could be described as coming anywhere near Chatfield in the rabbit hole: Abdul Qadir (shoulder injury) and Geoff Lawson (fractured jaw after foolishly disdaining a visor), and they shared seven Test 50s to Chatfield's zenith (in 43 Tests) of 21 not out. OK, forget the violence. What about the cynicism? Nothing the old game has ever come up with has been as cynical as the daisy cutter Greg Chappell and brother Trev pulled out of the bag to prevent New Zealand's Brian McKechnie hitting a six off the final ball of a one-day international.

Eventually, the International Cricket Council – in which England and Australia still retain a dictatorial right of veto despite recent worrying trends, decreed that the answer was to restrict bowlers to one bouncer per batsman per over, and deny them altogether in the one-day game. So there we were, back in the playground, England and Australia the school bullies, swaggeringly used to getting their own way. Now that they were losing, the rules had to change. Fat lot of good it did. The offending article was deemed to be a ball that passed above shoulder height; the West Indies, however, had long since perfected the 'underarm' ball, discomfiting the batsman by angling balls into his upper torso with such accuracy that he had no room to breathe. Lloyd sticks to realism: 'You've got to scare batsmen. The umpires are there to protect them. It's a hard game.'

If the knives have been out ever since Holding and Daniel bombarded the creaking ribs of John Edrich and Brian Close in the Old Trafford twilight in 1976, parrying them is still no easy matter. Before the onset of hostilities in the 1991 Wisden Trophy series, David Frith, the editor of *Wisden Cricket Monthly*, a fierce lover of the game and one of its most knowledgeable and literate historians, composed an editorial headlined 'An Unappetizing Tour'. The first paragraph read: 'Another invasion is upon us by a West Indies team which is the most fearsome, the most successful, and the most unpopular in the world. Their game is founded on *vengeance and violence* [my italics] and fringed by *arrogance* [my italics]. The only mercy is that they're not bringing their umpires with them.' Ouch. The *Daily Mirror* swiftly edited the piece, decked it out in suitably 'shock horror' tabloidese and the writs flew. 'I thought the original editorial was racist, but then the *Mirror* made it worse,' recalls Desi, who promptly popped off a lawyer's letter to Frith.

At a Leeds hotel during the first Test a few weeks later, the litigants met in a lift. For a few moments the silence was electric. Desi defused it. 'Very disappointing, man,' he said, quietly. 'There's a lot of it about,' retorted Frith. Desi eventually decided not to proceed – 'It was a long process' – although Frith maintains this was because there could be no proof of racism. 'I just wanted to make him realize that he couldn't say these things and get away with it. I've never experienced racism. No one has ever called me a black bastard. So I can't talk about vengeance. I'm not sure how I would react, but you'd know if I was abused in that way, I can assure you of that.'

On a Channel 4 programme last August, *Devil's Advocate*, Frith was the inquisitee when Lloyd was granted the chance of a public riposte. 'It's not that I'm vengeful or arrogant, but what's wrong with being arrogant?' he mused. 'If I'm a top-class sportsman I want to be arrogant because I want to be the best – and if you want to be the best at something you gotta be arrogant at some stage. This is pride at stake here, country against country. I don't think anyone wants to kill anybody because you can't do that now with helmets and that sort of thing. The point is you're trying to get someone out. I just want to know whether Mr Frith was writing that time at Edgbaston when Iqbal Qasim, a nightwatchman, was in, and Bob Willis bowled a bumper, hit him smack in the mouth, blood all over the place. I don't remember a furore then.' Frith, a purist rather than a racist, admitted that the incident had, in fact, sickened him, and that 'maybe retribution would have been a better word' than vengeance. Less emotive. 'For fifteen years they've ruled cricket,' Frith continued. 'They're very difficult to criticize because it'll just sound like sour grapes. I'm just not all that enchanted by it.'

Frith is neither alone in, nor unentitled to, his distaste, but it is instructive to note how few contemporary players, they who live the realities as opposed to merely observing them, share it. Ian Botham, among many others, reinforced the notion that, given the ammunition, the gamekeepers would have turned poachers at a shot: 'Don't tell me if England had the fastest attack of four bowlers in the history of the game, as West Indies did, we or anybody else wouldn't use them in the same way. Of course we would. When West Indies are winning, they bowl fourteen overs an hour, when they're losing, they bowl eleven and I suppose you can't blame them. Test cricket is Test cricket and if we're out there only to entertain the public, give us rubber noses and funny hats.' Written shortly before his *annus mirabilis* of 1981, that last sentiment may come across as a touch odd for the Indomitable Showman, but the thrust of his argument cannot be obscured. In fact, England departed for the Caribbean early in 1990 with the chairman of selectors, Ted Dexter, vowing to fight 'fire with fire' – an unfortunate choice of cliché which nearly matched that infamous 'I intend to make them grovel' declaration by Lord Ted's erstwhile Sussex colleague, Tony Greig, as the emptiest, not to say silliest, threat in cricket history. Not once in the four Tests was an English spinner selected, yet for all Devon Malcolm's brimstone, Gladstone Small, David Capel and Phil DeFreitas were more treacle than fire.

'One of our problems is that we don't have enough sportswriters in the Caribbean,' laments Lloyd. 'We need them to back up our team.' Some feel they are better off without the press: apart from the near 250,000 drop in their home attendances that ensued, the Pittsburgh Pirates were blissfully happy that the city's newspapers were on strike for the last five months of the 1992 Major League baseball season. No papers, no comment – and no punctured egos. Lloyd, conversely, bemoans the lack of support from that direction – virtually every direction. 'We achieved what we had without a lot of help and I'm fiercely proud of what we've done. We don't have the monetary wealth, nor a Cricket Academy, nor artificial turf wickets. We have no excellent stadia and no great coaching scheme for young players. Yet through all this we have become the best team in the world for a long, long time. When I saw in *Sports Illustrated* that we were bracketed as the team of the decade with Liverpool and the 49ers, I said, "Well, we've made it, then." So when I see Frith writing his shit I feel bitter. Give credit where credit's due. Why not in our case? You can call it all sorts of things, call it prejudice, call it racism, I don't know. As far as I was concerned, when I became captain, if you didn't make runs against England or Australia you were not termed a very good cricketer. But I turned all that around, or we did. You had to make runs against *us* to be accepted. That was an achievement. It's like the Japanese. All of a sudden they're up with the big boys. What the yen is doing is now as important as what the Deutschmark and the dollar are doing.'

Had Darcus Howe, Channel 4's eponymous Devil's Advocate, taken the argument to its logical conclusion, he might have asked *why* Lloyd and his teams may have been seeking vengeance, or even retribution. Racial abuse? Past humiliations on the field? Generations of subjugation off it? You want more? Richards, a haughty, sensitive man whose reserves of tact and diplomacy do not quite match those of the gangling, genial Guyanan, has certainly never felt inclined to tone down the fury he felt after his initial experience of Australian cricket. The aggression, verbal and physical, disgusted him as much as it astonished him. To him, and quite rightly so, racism is indefensible and, more significantly, hard to ignore. Ditto the incessant carping over his side's achievement. If, on occasion, a vengeful glint was detectable in those burning eyes, can one honestly blame him? Not me.

Sport is the competitive art, supposedly the zenith of friendly rivalry, of fair play and generosity of spirit, characteristics needed now more than ever as an antidote to the prevailing winds of greed and heartless indifference that gust through the late twentieth century. Remarkably, given the advent of big money, agents, sponsors and TV deals, not to mention man's perennial inhumanity to man, sport exudes these noble qualities more regularly than any business I can think of. To ask any more of it would be unreasonable.

By the same token, it is unreasonable to lay cricket's ills at the Caribbean door. Desi and his accomplices may have changed the complexion of the game, and not necessarily for the better, but they were only completing a process that others had initiated. The scalpel he co-wielded with Greenidge, the clinical grace of Richards, Dujon, Holding and Bishop have injected a sorely needed dose of exhilaration into a traditionally sombre business. Some may have OD'ed a couple of times but no more than any of their peers. More concerned with career opportunities than the delusion of image, these Third World graduates are too conversant with the art of survival to be preoccupied with vendettas, petty or otherwise. Clive Lloyd saw to that. He taught his charges that anger was a dangerous emotion in a profession requiring so much control and reason. He taught them not to give their hand away, how to take their licks like men – and kick butt.

The career of Desmond Leo Haynes, the Lion of Barbados, the ultimate team man, the only remaining member of the original butt-kicking élite, is inextricably entwined with that process. What follows within these pages, by logical extension, can only be a story within a saga.

2

The Lunging Heart

I have only one theme:
The bowsprit, the arrow, the longing, the lunging heart . . .
The Schooner Flight, Derek Walcott

Of the West Indian team that opened the eighties by giving Greg Chappell
and company a 10-wicket drubbing in Melbourne, only Desi is still ticking
away, a perpetual pulse. After playing two Tests early in 1978, he was dropped
for joining the Packer Circus, then made seventy-two consecutive appearances
once the major turns had been readmitted to the official big top. The sequence
ended when a hamstring injury ruled him out at Old Trafford in 1988, but
he was back for the following game at Leeds, and remained in the saddle for
each of the West Indies' next 34 Tests up to this February. Neither Sobers
(85 consecutive Tests out of an official total of 93) nor Gundappa Viswanath
(87 consecutive out of 91) can match that sort of consistency to the same
volume, leaving only Allan Border (138 in a row out of his 141 Tests to
this summer) and Sunil Gavaskar (106 running out of 125) ahead of Desi.
Behind all that steadfastness, however, lies a longing, a lunging heart.

It is this which has enabled Desi to stay at the front rank of Test cricket's
most powerful army. Rigorous resolve and innate stubbornness, allied to an
exemplary technique, have helped him conquer the mental demands of being
the most put-upon worker in the world's most laborious sport. The job of
opener is a dirty one, but someone's got to do it. You and your partner are
cricket's most important team-within-a-team, a two-man advance party into
untrammelled territory, expected to scan the terrain, negotiate any would-be

ambushes and clear the path towards complete control. Succeed – add 50 or more, see off the first cavalry charge – and you're simply doing your job. Fail and you are responsible for sapping the morale of the whole side. How you react to the first bouncer, how you take that first single, can set the tone for the entire innings. A fine balance must be struck, between defence and attack, restraint and assertiveness, the carefree and the careworn. Schizophrenia might be considered an asset.

If it is, Desi, a man of immense zest and drive, has made the most of his. Prizing his wicket as if it were that pear-shaped, mixed-cut diamond for which Robert Mouawad shelled out nearly $13 million, he had emerged unscathed from, on average, one in every nine (or 11.66 per cent) Test innings up to the end of that tilt with South Africa in April last year. Among openers with 50 caps or more, only Geoff Boycott (11.92 per cent) can claim a stronger instinct for survival. Both have achieved the rare feat of carrying their bat in a Test, Desi breathing the sanctified air of those who have done so twice, namely Len Hutton, Glenn Turner and those two Aussie Bills, Woodfull and Lawry. Sir Frank Worrell and Conrad Hunte are the only other West Indians to have accomplished a similarly defiant tour of duty. Furthermore, on five occasions Desi has stood firm to the bitter end, since he has thrice been the last man out. All the same, here was the quintessential character actor, a Sterling Hayden to Lloyd's Gary Cooper and Richards's Brando. He nevertheless deserved lead billing, and got it, albeit for an inexplicably brief period, which is another story we must save for later.

On the surface, then, despite the sixteen years that divide them, the friendship Desi has forged with Boycott appears natural, a meeting of like minds, of common spirits. They faced each other in nine Tests, the relative strengths of their respective teams vividly illustrated by the fact that the Yorkshireman had 18 innings to the Bajan's 11, scoring 663 runs at an average of 41.44 to Desi's 542 at 49.27. While Desi's star was in the ascendant, however, Boycott's official international career was nearing eclipse. He nonetheless inspired a degree of awe in the youthful Desi.

During the 1985–6 Wisden Trophy series Boycott's search for adequate practice facilities in Barbados brought the pair together while, as the *Mail on Sunday*'s star columnist put it, 'Gower and the rest of the players enjoyed another day off in paradise.' Boycott was keen to get in trim for his last county season so Desi arranged for a local groundsman to prepare a wicket slap bang in the middle of an unkempt expanse of rough ground a few miles from the Kensington Oval, then called up a few of his mates. The curator

got some handy cash and every afternoon during the build-up to the Test
the two swots got in some extra homework against the likes of Franklyn
Stephenson, Hartley Alleyne and Ricardo Ellcock alongside a batch of agog
youths. 'It was good fun,' Desi remembers, 'good for the area, a great lesson
for the kids. He still changed his gloves every time they became damp because
he insisted on feeling right in every sense. Such attention to detail. Even
when he was commentating he would come up to me after a day's play and
make a few comments. Although I can't remember anything specific now, I
always listened. He's never been short on theories, and I don't care how big
you get in a sport, you can always learn something. You also learn so much
after you finish because you are examining the game more dispassionately.'

Yet the similarities between Boycott and Desi mask marked differences in
character and approach, differences fundamental to an appreciation of the
true spirit of sporting conflict. At the crease, Desi is by some distance the
more adaptable. His stroke range is wider, his willingness to switch between
attack and defence as the situation dictates considerably greater, assets borne
out by that record haul of sixteen 100s in one-day internationals. He radiates
enjoyment with that inimitable dazzling Colgate smile. Amid all that earthy
discipline there also soars a streak of rebellion, a shaft of humour, a shower
of colour. Boycott, on the other hand, was pure monochrome. Studious
application, to be sure, made him one of only five batsmen to collect 150 or
more first-class centuries, the only one to average 100 in a season twice and
possessor of the second highest career mean among those amassing at least
25,000 runs. But while the Yorkshireman had the wherewithal to broaden
his mind and expand his repertoire, that immaculate forward defensive, even
those precise clips through square leg were shrouded in that terribly English
blanket of fear-ridden conservatism. A great player, runs the popular bottom
line, but a poor team player. Having played alongside Boycott for nigh-on a
quarter of a century, John Hampshire is better placed than most to bear this
out: 'Brian Close's dictum on captaincy was that you had to *give* – to give
everything of yourself to your team. Boycott could give nothing of himself.
He was just made that way, a loner, desperately wanting to be liked but
finding himself unable to achieve popularity except through his ability to
score runs. I am absolutely sure he believed, and still believes, that massive
scoring is in itself a passport to universal popularity.'

Desi offers an alibi. 'People talk about Boycott being unpopular but he *is*
a loner, and you don't find many people associating with loners. Opening
also happens to be the most pressurized job in cricket. People say cricketers

are selfish, always worrying about their averages, but the first priority of an opener is to get a start for his *team*. I've been in situations with Gordon [Greenidge] and Mickey [Roseberry] when we've done all the hard work, the spade work, planting the seeds, then people like Viv or Gatt come in and start blooming like prize begonias, smashing the ball all over the place and making big scores. So you say to yourself, "Why didn't I hang on a bit longer?" Then you reassure yourself that they couldn't have played that way if you hadn't first made sure life would be a lot easier when they came in – shine off, spinners on. You are there to occupy the crease, prepare the ground, be a bomb detector. Time is often more important than runs in that context.'

Of course, Desi also derives a strong sense of self from his craft. 'Batting is a way of expressing myself, of getting myself across to people. I feel great when I'm batting well. People always compare Haynes and Greenidge with Greenidge and Fredericks and Rae and Stollmeyer when it comes to West Indian opening pairs. OK, so I might not be as good as Fredericks or Hunte, but I'm here. I'm good enough, I've got my own flair.'

Desi's approach at the crease mirrors the way in which he has incorporated that flair into his duties. 'Tempering that flair wasn't hard because I came from a good school. You *had* to learn to temper it. I was also batting with a senior member of the side in Gordon, so I knew that if anyone was going to be dropped it wouldn't be him. There was greater onus on me to maintain the partnership. As an opener you also have to temper any inclination to belt the living daylights out of the ball. You should caress the ball, use what we call the push-drive. I keep telling Mickey Roseberry that he has to make love to the ball instead of raping it. If you don't use that bit of finesse, especially against the ball leaving you, you cannot readjust.

'When people say things like "openers should never cut before tea", I see that as negative thinking. It depends on how you feel. If you are coming off a good score it doesn't matter. If you see a ball to cut, you cut. The best policy is to bat sessions. Try to survive and then perhaps consolidate before lunch, then capitalize when the going gets easier. Analyse the bowlers, the pitch, the overall conditions, before deciding on your most profitable strokes. It's no good leaving home and vowing to yourself not to cut, then some guy bowls you two long-hops. If the ball is there to be hit, be positive. It all comes down to how you feel, and that depends in part on how comfortable you feel at the crease. A lot of fuss is made about stances. I've changed mine a few times, and some say I don't look comfortable, but so what? If you are comfortable in yourself that's half the battle. I had a side-on stance originally, just as the textbooks recommend, but I sometimes found that I was playing across my front, left, leg. So I opened up a bit and I've been fairly successful. By having the leg a little open I found I could bring the bat down straighter and therefore play straighter.'

The ability to cope with pressure is all-important, mental serenity the key. 'One-day games are different because you play so many and the plots are pretty standard, but I always feel pressure at the start of a Test series. I like to feel it coming on too, because deep down within myself I need to conquer that fear of failure. Everyone does. I never worry about negatives. I do certain breathing exercises, try to get cool, inhale, exhale. It's a way of calming myself. Sometimes you set yourself goals for the day, for the game, for the series. There are always targets. Some batsmen set themselves two centuries a series or an average of fifty. They break down those goals, aim to start with a big score, get two centuries, and end up with 450 runs or whatever. I'm more interested in how I feel, and feeling good comes through preparation and application. If I feel in good nick I'll get runs. When you start looking at figures you put too much pressure on yourself. Just go out and play.'

In common with the best openers, Desi goes in for self-analysis. 'When I first came into county cricket I used to make notes about how I was getting out. For the first time in my career I was playing every day, so I realized I was bound to play bad shots at times, bound to get myself out. There are times when you know you can't do anything about it. I might have been in good nick but still got two good outswingers in successive innings in June. I can't remember the exact breakdown, but at the end of the season I had a list detailing how often I'd been dismissed in a certain way, which gave me an idea of any technical errors. I told Mark Ramprakash to do the same. That analysis also showed that I had given it away a certain number of times and my aim was to cut that number by half the following year.' All of which might help – though not wholly – to explain why Desi's Championship average for Middlesex in 1989, 47.36, rose by nearly 35 per cent the following summer.

Like Boycott, Haynes is powered by gallons of pride, yet while the former runs on vanity, the latter fills up on community fuel. At the end of each tour, Desi assumes the role of charity organizer, hustling for spare or unwanted bats and other bits of kit from friend and foe alike, then takes the proceeds back to Barbados for distribution among the less well-heeled. Every time he spends a summer in England he organizes sponsorship and makes all the necessary arrangements for a promising youngster from the neighbourhood to make the trip by his side and link up with either a League club or a county second XI. There is nothing he craves more than a Caribbean commonwealth, a common market and a common direction.

He has certainly played his part in creating one in the West Indies dressing-room. 'He always kept the guys going, always looked for the positive,' Michael Holding recollects. 'I've seen him when he's been disappointed with his form, especially during that rough patch he had around 1983 and 1984, but that never stopped him from enjoying life. He would come in, kick off his pads and sit down, and you knew he'd be trying to forget it from that moment. That's a very rare ability. Some guys get really moody, and there's nothing you can say to them until they've scored some runs again. Not Desi. He's a man who enjoys life. He's always looking forward. If the day went badly, he was always convinced tomorrow would be better.' Here, clearly, is a player only too happy to put team before self, a dedication re-flected in his voluntary transition from gambler to accumulator. 'What I admire about Desi', marvels Holding, 'is his ability to play the sheet-anchor role one day then let fly the next in a limited-overs match. When he first came into the side we called him Hammer Haynes because of the force he put behind his shots. But he was obviously a fighter too. Packer helped instil that.'

It was there already. Desi hails from that most active of cricketing conveyor belts, Barbados, birthplace to fifty-seven of the 213 players capped by West Indies up to the start of the 1992–3 rubber against Pakistan. Think about it: 26.54 per cent. Not bad for an area spanning a mere 166 square miles (by comparison, how many world-class performers have sprung from the Isle of Wight?) and incorporating a population of 250,000. Guyana has 600,000 residents, Jamaica 2.5 million, 600,000 in Kingston.

Desi was born in the parish of St Michael, high on Holders Hill, on 15 February 1956. The 20th Communist Party Congress had just commenced in Moscow; Britain had finally agreed to grant Malaysia independence; West-minster MPs were preparing to vote out the death penalty; the UK's first provincial commercial TV station was getting ready to open up shop; the West German army was on the verge of banning the goose step; in Alabama on the last day of the month, Autherine Lucy had to dodge a barrage of eggs and rocks as she tried to become the first black student to attend the state university. In England, Muffin the Mule defected from the BBC. The steady postwar stream of immigrants from Barbados to Britain was fast becoming a torrent as the Macmillan administration sought to offset a shortage of willing orderlies and bus drivers with the double-barrelled carrot of self-advancement and better pay (teachers and civil servants on the island were starting at £10 a month; sugar plantation workers earned £4 a week during the crop season, £2 for the remaining eight months of the calendar). The times they were a-changin', but some stubborn stains persisted.

Everton Weekes, the Bridgetown blitzkrieg, was in the middle of a run of three consecutive Test centuries against New Zealand when fifteen-year-old Arletha Haynes gave birth to her first child, Desmond Leo, all 9 pounds 8 ounces of him. 'He was a fat child,' she chuckles. Arletha and the father, eighteen-year-old Leon Hope, then embarking on a career in the burgeoning hotel industry, did not marry. Desi's arrival swelled to twelve the Haynes family circle, a claustrophobic but jolly clan of aunts, uncles and cousins crammed into a two-roomed wooden dwelling opposite the St John Baptist Church and its adjoining school. Bedtime hours were carefully staggered. There was no electricity, illumination provided by an oil lamp. Thirty-six years on, perched on a stool in the feed store Desi finances, Arletha remembered her eldest son's birthplace. An amply built woman with mirthful eyes and a Grand Canyon of a smile, she recently overcame cervical cancer and now resides in the smart modern home of bricks and mortar that Desi bought for her about half a mile further up Holders Hill. 'And no water. Desi had a big head and we used to send him up the hill with a bucket on it. We didn't even have a streetlight outside. Now everything's decent.'

In its original incarnation Holders Hill formed part of the Black Rock estate before Thomas Noel sold it on to Major Timothy Thornhill in 1656, the major's son in turn selling it on to the Honourable William Holder half a century later. The Holders were prosperous landowners in the seventeenth and eighteenth centuries, owning Joes River and sundry other estates, and both William and his eldest son are buried near the plantation house. More recently, Lord Beaverbrook's daughter, the late Janet Kidd, occupied Holders House before passing it on to her son. It was here that the present Duke of York first came to rest following his naval labours in the Falklands.

The Barbados general election of 1956 amounted to a seal of approval for the ruling Labour Party. Under the stewardship of Grantley Adams, the first black prime minister of Barbados, the BLP had implemented wide-ranging reforms since ending its coalition with the National Congress Party. Innovations included paid holidays, profit-sharing in the sugar industry and greater benefits for workers through amendments to the Trade Union Act and the Factory Act. Roads and schools had been built, health services updated, water facilities improved. Two years later, a cabinet system of government was introduced. The road toward egalitarianism, however, was still riddled with ancient potholes. 'Though the political ascendancy of the whites had been destroyed,' wrote Sir Alexander Hoyos in *Barbados: A History From The Amerindians to Independence*, 'considerations of class still appeared to weigh heavily in the Barbadian society.'

The American influence, meanwhile, was growing, as it was all over the Caribbean: in 1962, US investments in the region amounted to more than US$1.5 billion, more than half as much again as that of Britain and Canada, the other two chief investors in the English-speaking Caribbean. 'The general colonial dependence on the United Kingdom', observed Michael Manley, the former Jamaican prime minister, 'was being replaced by a new economic dependence on the USA.' Barbados, aka 'Little England', found the transition more painful than most. 'More perhaps than any other former British territory, we have accepted Britain as the Mother Country.' Conrad Hunte, that steadfast opener-turned-bastion of Moral Rearmament, may have been referring to the Caribbean as a whole, but he might just as well have been isolating his fellow Bajans.

Thus it was that Desi grew up against a backcloth of social upheaval, much of it of a positive hue. The Barbados he entered nonetheless echoed its garrison past. The local museum, with its Arawak tools, its fine pottery and its Barbados Yeomanry uniforms, was once a military prison; the pink clock tower of the Savannah Club was formerly the site of a guardroom; the Barbados Electricity Supply Corporation HQ was the erstwhile Army Commissariat, the Royal Barbados Yacht Club the ex-residence of the Chief Engineer; the cluster of red dwellings on the southern tip of the Savannah, then used to house members of the British Council, had at one time been officers' messes.

The queen of the Haynes hive was Desi's maternal grandmother, Irene, who for several years worked as janitor of the St John Baptist school. As her health declined, she enlisted Desi's elbow grease, making him the butt of his classmates' pranks. Not content with teasing him, they did their damnedest to leave as much mess as possible. 'Then one day,' Desi remembers, 'the headmaster told them they should show the cleaners more respect. I never got any stick after that.' Desi spent the greater part of his boyhood in Irene's charge. 'She brought Desi up,' Arletha avers. 'He didn't really have a father. I was still at school when he came, and then I went to work in a quarry to help support him while an aunt helped me with my schooling. My job was to pick out the different types of boulders. The only other option was to be a domestic. It was very tough. Irene suffered from blood pressure and eventually had to give up work.' At the Excelsior Hotel last autumn, Desi bumped into a couple of acquaintances from the batmakers Gray-Nicholls. 'How's your grandmother?' asked one of them. 'You always used to talk about her.' As Desi explained that she had passed away, the wistful expression was inescapable. Her death left a void: 'I still miss her.'

Idrina Richards was the other woman in Desi's early life. The Richardses resided a few doors away and Idrina was the neighbourhood matriarch, a kindly embodiment of a staunchly Protestant matriarchal society. A seamstress, she made clothes for the local families, taught the young girls needlework and, best of all, sold sweets, and Desi was just one of her tribe of godchildren. To her elder son, Hartley, now Desi's solicitor, the frail, housebound figure now deprived of her legs through diabetes is still 'an institution in Holders Hill'. To Desi, whom she 'pushed, like so many others, into confirmation class', she was 'very loving'. In time, Desi acquired two brothers, Mark, who now works in computers, and Ricardo, currently a security guard at the Colony Club in nearby St James. By the time Arletha took a husband she was thirty, and the marriage didn't last. 'Ricky, my youngest, was six then, but this man was very selfish. He didn't want kids around. No way. He had to go first.'

According to Arletha, Desi, whose first pitch was the narrow strip of land running between Chez Haynes and its right-hand neighbour, was alone among the members of the family circle in his affinity for cricket. This was surprising. Cricket, after all, occupies the same pedestal in the collective Bajan psyche as football does in Brazil, rugby union in New Zealand, bullfighting in Spain. How many other provincial or regional sides have been able to field as many as nine representatives from one international team? Yorkshire in 1962, Middlesex in 1980 and New South Wales in 1981 spring most readily to mind, but none had the gall of the Sobers-era Barbados. To mark independence in March 1967, shortly after Errol Barrow had taken Barbados to its pew at the UN, the Kensington Oval hosted a five-day match between the locals and a Rest of the World XI. Celebration it may have been, but Bajans clung to their principles throughout. Invitations sent out to Colin Bland and the Pollock brethren were withdrawn as the apartheid situation grew more polarized, the South African Minister of the Interior having recently implied that the inclusion in the 1968–9 MCC touring party of Basil D'Oliveira, Worcestershire's Cape Coloured all-rounder, would not be acceptable. In a gesture of solidarity, D'Oliveira batted at number six for the Rest of the World.

The first recorded reference to cricket in the Caribbean dates back to a meeting of St Anne's CC in Barbados on 12 May 1806, though this was apparently not the club's first gathering. In any case, did Charles Dickens not refer to Mr Jingle's single-wicket match in *Pickwick Papers*? The venue, one deduced, was Jamaica. 'We must take it for granted that cricket was played in the West Indies long before this [1806],' reasoned Rowland Bowen in the 1969 edition of *Wisden*, 'and not improbably as early as the mid-seventeenth century in Barbados.'

The history of this Bajan infatuation is a glittering one, the firsts and bests gushing like water from a perforated hydrant. By the 1830s the enthusiasm of the military had transformed the game into an increasingly prominent part of the national fabric. The message spread through the efforts of civilian clubs and private schools, one of which, Harrison College, would later boast Sir Pelham Warner as its most illustrious former pupil. Wanderers CC, the oldest surviving club on the island, was founded in 1877, Pickwick CC, occupants of the Oval, five years later. In 1891 the first inter-colonial tournament, between Barbados, Trinidad and Guyana, was played at the Kensington Oval, the hosts emerging victorious. The following summer H. C. Clarke of Harrisonians took 10 for 30 against Codrington College, believed to be the first time the feat had been achieved in the Caribbean. Standards were such that A. W. F. Somerset, captain of two MCC tours to the Caribbean after the turn of the century, found the Barbados XI a more difficult proposition than the territorial model.

To Barbados fell the honour of posting the first Caribbean score in excess of 500, and the first in excess of 600. It was a Bajan, P. H. Tarilton, who fashioned the first first-class double-century on the islands. Nineteen twenty-eight saw a Bajan, George Challenor, become the first member of a representative West Indian team to face a ball in an official Test match, and another, George Nathaniel Francis, become the first to deliver a ball. In 1942, Barbados dismissed Trinidad for 16, the best performance by a West Indian fielding side in the first-class fray. In 1946, during a game between the same protagonists, Clyde Walcott and Worrell collected 574 for the fourth wicket without being parted, still the highest stand in the first-class annals. Barbados won seven of the twelve inter-colonial tournaments staged before 1914, although Trinidad had pipped them by 11 wins to 10 when the competition was suspended in 1939. Revived under a different format for the 1964 season, it was revamped the following year as the Shell Shield, Sobers leading Barbados to innings victories over both the holders, British Guiana (as was), and Trinidad, to secure the overall honours, then taking eight of his colleagues on tour to England. In the twenty-five succeeding chapters of Red Stripe Cup/Shell Shield confrontation up to 1992, Barbados remained pre-eminent, coming top of the heap on a dozen more occasions.

Barbados is the spiritual home of West Indian cricket, Redvers Dundonald 'King' Dyall, its bewitching, besuited, bereft apostle, even if he does always lend his support to England. With his endless array of fedoras and Day-Glo bow ties, pristine pink (or peach) gloves and regal sharkbone cane, this ever-dapper, decidedly under-nourished octogenarian (at the very least) remains cricket's most celebrated addict. Told by his mother that he was 'a special child who came into this world from overseas in a golden box', his court is humble, a run-down chattel house within an envious stone's throw of the upmarket duty-free outlets of Broad Street in the centre of Bridgetown. Some, particularly the belligerent, basketball-bouncing dudes in their late teens, ridicule him, but to outsiders he radiates a unique affection for the game and its upwardly mobile possibilities. Notwithstanding this characteristic gaiety, however, Bajans can also be positively Yorkist. Palms may sway and rum punches overflow, yet beneath that undulating, lyrical drawl, intertwined with that mélange of dialects whose overtone, noted Alan Ross, is 'now of the Welsh valleys, now of Ireland or the west country', there bristles a stern parochialism. Gordon Greenidge may have been born in St Peter, but he grew up in Reading and was never completely allowed to conquer the antipathy that was the legacy of his supposed treachery. When Worrell, a Bridgetown bairn, decided to emigrate to Jamaica in 1947, many of his former compatriots refused to forgive him. 'When will they ever learn?' wondered the late Lord (Learie) Constantine.

During Desi's formative years, those responsible for the structure of the club game on the island had even more to learn. Power rested with the Barbados Cricket Association, long-time nursery for the national XI. In 1958, Charlie Griffith, a strapping nineteen-year-old fast bowler from St Lucy, attempted to join one of the BCA clubs but encountered a wall of exclusivity. 'The first division of the BCA', he later wrote, 'catered for the whites, the middle-class blacks, the police and the secondary schools. Clubs like Wanderers and Pickwick were exclusively white and others like YMPC and Carlton were white or near white and it was futile seeking membership in them since black Barbadians as such had never been members of them.' The two black clubs, Spartan and Empire, were tainted, Griffith claimed, by 'class prejudice'. Spartan was for 'the middle-class blacks, professional men and ex-schoolboys who had "breeding", brain, or cricketing ability but who, because of colour, were denied membership of the white teams'. Griffith ended up joining Empire, Worrell's club, which, though intrinsically of a similar persuasion, 'had tended to be more liberal and was more ready to accept poor boys who had shown outstanding ability in the Barbados Cricket League'. Excluding the police and the schools, 'What was left was the white and the semi-white group into which there could be no or little black mobility, and a black group of middle-class types.'

The colonials had maintained an air of élitism from the outset, keeping the natives on a tight leash and prompting C. L. R. James to refer to this segregationist policy as 'puritanism incarnate'. Recognizing that rearing and pigmentation were of greater import than mere ability, Mitchie Hewitt formed the Barbados Cricket League in 1937 to afford opportunities for the less privileged. The leading lights of the BCL came together once a season to test their wits against a BCA representative XI, and a notable performance in that match might offer an entrée to a BCA club, sometimes to the island team and occasionally, just occasionally, the Test side. As products of middle-class families, Clyde Walcott and Frank Worrell had the distinct advantage of attending Combermere School, a fertile spring of talent for the BCA, but their contemporary, Everton Weekes, soon to be the third member of cricket's ultimate alliterative triumvirate, was of poorer stock and so progressed the hard way, via the BCL. Subsequent graduates included Hunte (the first BCL batsman to reach three figures against the BCA), Seymour Nurse and Mister Pickwick himself, Garfield Sobers. Others dazzled more briefly. Cyril Clairemonte Depeiza, a wicketkeeper from St James, made his début against Ian Johnson's Australians at Georgetown in 1955. In his second Test two weeks later, at the Kensington Oval, fittingly enough, Depeiza took 122 off the combined wiles of Lindwall, Miller and Benaud, aiding his captain, Denis Atkinson, in a seventh wicket stand of 348, still the first-class record. Not that this presaged a lengthy international career: Depeiza gained just three further caps.

Hastened by the advent of independence, the gradual lowering of class and colour barriers, naturally enough, proved a boon in cricketing terms. By the time Desi was old enough to stake his claim, a team of BCL representatives had been accepted as a fully fledged member of the BCA league competition. The quest for personal recognition would not be quite as arduous.

3

Pennies from Heaven

My Lord calls me,
He calls me by the thunder,
The trumpet sounds it in my soul.

Verse from a Negro spiritual, or Sorrow Song

You could barely swing a rat – let alone a cat – in those pinched passages between the houses in Holders Hill. The gap, however, was just about wide enough to accommodate a fledgling off-drive, provided it was played with a die-straight blade. Wide enough for the six-year-old Desi to savour his first taste of Test cricket. 'I played Test matches with Glenville Haynes, my mother's sister's son, who was two years older than me. England v. West Indies, Australia v. West Indies and so on. I would always be West Indies because I already knew what I wanted to do with my life.' Weapons varied. Sometimes it would be a piece of bark and a scrunched-up ball of paper swathed in rubber bands. Idrina Richards might concoct an adequate projectile from her work basket or else the fur would be burned off a tennis ball, enabling it to be shined up. Evaporated milk tins came in handy too. 'Anything', according to Idrina's younger son, Keith, 'that would go the distance.'

Eventually the Haynes kids graduated from alleyways to pasture, to the green expanse behind St John Baptist School. They soon grew familiar with the two forms of combat, 'hand-after-hand' and 'first and second'. 'If you turned up one day and you saw somebody batting when you arrived,' explains Desi, 'you would automatically bat before him next time. We would do a circuit, play for eight or nine hours at a stretch and maybe get two hands, i.e. innings, each. There were no umpires, no lbws. The aim was to bat for so long that you'd see the other guys off, make them fed up with waiting. That way the circuit would get smaller and you would get more hands. "First and second" was a format we played when twenty or thirty boys gathered on the pasture around the same time. One would say, "Right, let's play some cricket – I bat first." Then someone else would say, "Second" and so on. With twenty or more players in fielding positions, you were always batting against the odds.'

From time to time there were inopportune interruptions. 'I was my grand-mother's favourite and she didn't hide it. Neither did she hide her convictions, making sure I went to Sunday School and to church every Sunday morning and night. I remember those Sunday evenings vividly. I would be hoping to get a long bat after hanging around in the field for an hour or two, then my grandmother would walk on to the pasture and shout, "Time for Sunday School." All the boys used to laugh. Not that I really resented it. She was very protective and also very religious, which is something I have always been grateful for because she instilled in me a firm belief in God, or at least in some higher being or thing, the force that has enabled me to achieve so much. Even though I don't go to church as often as I would like – and those twelve noon starts on Sunday this summer are hardly going to boost my attendance record – I feel very religious. I can remember a one-day inter-national in Melbourne bubbling up to a climax with our lower order batsmen in possession. It was all down to them. Suddenly I found myself on my knees in the dressing room, palms down, head bowed, promising God – or whoever, whatever – that whatever transpired in this game I would always take my Bible with me whenever and wherever I played in future. One time I left it at home and had to dash back to get it. I wasn't bothered in the least about the prospect of a hefty fine for being late. I'm not saying that if every cricketer went out and bought a Bible he would be capable of scoring 500 or taking twenty wickets in a match, but it might help to read it now and again to put everything in perspective, give it all a wider meaning. I pray for guidance both in my profession and in my life as a whole, and I thank God for all the strength he has given me and the life he has given me.' Coming from most mouths, such sentiments might be deemed sanctimonious; coming from this one they ring true.

Unemployment was high in Barbados, times were tight, the reassuring warmth of the Haynes family circle a consummate lifebelt. Toys were alien to Desi. Irene and one of Arletha's sisters would prepare the meals in a pot over a fire in the backyard, serving up yams, plantain and pumpkins, cassava and eddos, flying fish and chicken. Those members of the circle fortunate enough to be in gainful (or not so gainful) employment would pool their weekly wage packets to enable the women to purchase food. 'There was a marvellous sense of unity,' exults Desi. 'Most of the time I was at home I was asleep – people lived there on a shift basis, those that worked at night slept during the day, those working by day occupied the beds at night. We had a radio but no TV. Everyone was willing to contribute. When I began caddying in my teens I used to use the money to buy school books and put some of it into the house kitty.'

Desi's first nickname was not long in arriving: Joe Louis. 'I don't know who pinned it on him,' says Hartley Richards, 'but it was mainly because of his physique, his sturdy legs. He was pretty tough. Almost everyone in the area had a nickname, people didn't really know you by your real name. I was called Brook, after Brook Benton, because I used to sing.' 'Joe' had his first and last bout on the pasture. 'One day there was this guy, Kid Slammer, on the pasture. He'd been to the Golden Gloves in the States, so he said. He challenged my friend, Windle Holmes, to a fight but Windle backed down. So I took up the challenge. I'd never heard of a mouthpiece. I certainly didn't know boxing was illegal. A ring was set up and all of a sudden there were these coppers watching us. Only after I won did they come up and have a quiet word.'

Looking every inch a useful middleweight himself, Windle Holmes now runs Holmes Bar and its adjoining mini-market, 100 yards or so up Holders Hill from what was once St John Baptist School and is now a police station. We met at the mini-market one Sunday morning in March. Out on the pavement skipped little girls in white dresses, tripping down the hill to church. Clad in a shell suit, Windle is a burly, cheery soul in his mid-thirties. Customers come and go one by one as if part of some mutually agreed rota. Windle lost his father at nineteen, and has been minding the store ever since.

He and Desi were inseparable during their schooldays, caddying at the unimaginably plush Sandy Lane golf course where Sobers would prowl the fairways; bouncing around on a scruffy makeshift basketball court; flicking marbles; watching fifty-one-year-old Ben Cartwright and his forty-seven-year-old sons protect the Ponderosa in *Bonanza* on the TV set in Holmes Bar. Pa Holmes, whom Windle describes as 'a father-figure to Desi', owned the only shop in the area; nowadays a spanking new Texaco station lurks at the bottom of the hill but since that is a good ten minutes away the Holmes emporium remains an oasis. The two boys would sit there during the holidays, listening to Reds Perreira and his fellow commentators as they related the latest derring-dos of Sobers, Hall, Kanhai and Hunte. Windle remembers that pasture punch-up vividly, Desi's determination to win most of all. 'Desi was very short, and his head was big. If he hadn't been a cricketer I'm sure he could have been a boxer. We boxed at the back of the house quite often and after Desi had picked up the challenge from this kid Slammer he trained all week. There was a fair crowd there on the day. Just before the fight his Grandma gave him a lecture. She didn't approve. "Lord have mercy," I shouted, but Desi almost killed the guy.'

Most summers brought a Test at the Kensington Oval, furnishing Desi and Windle with visual evidence of the icons whose strokes and deliveries they had only ever heard. Unusually, while the rest of the schoolboy world was turning up its collar and practising that inimitable, slightly stooped, oh-so-cool Sobers Lope, the two friends worshipped at the altar of Seymour Macdonald Nurse. A bellicose back-foot biffer from Bridgetown, Nurse was responsible for perhaps the grandest farewell in Test history, totting up 558 runs at 111.6 in his final series against New Zealand, the last post a thunderous, chanceless 258 in less than four sessions at Christchurch. Last October he re-emerged at fifty-eight as a member of Clive Lloyd's West Indies Masters team, invoking memories of his romping pomp with an immense drive on to the roof of the players' pavilion at Kensington Oval, a blow accomplished with a lightweight bat whose delicacy evoked a pistol when compared with the blunderbuss wielded by so many of his successors. 'We used to fancy Nurse,' says Desi. 'We walked like him, talked like him, imitated the way he wiggled his head. Lots of style.'

Yet if Nurse was his Apollo, Sobers was Zeus. When Desi took the fifteen-minute bus ride to the fringes of Bridgetown to watch his first Test in March 1972, the side attractions were the New Zealanders, Bevan Congdon and Glenn Turner, Bob Cunis and Bruce Taylor, unglamorous yet workmanlike and just beginning to plug into the socket of determination that had for so long propelled their rugger-bugger counterparts. Top of the bill, though, was Garfield St Aubrun Sobers, Bridgetown's favourite son, now thirty-five but still a batsman capable of carving up an attack and picking the carcass clean, all with an ease that belied the extent of the savaging. Desi perched himself on the pasture, below the Garrison Savannah. The early going was discouraging, Taylor inflicting a duck on the dapper new young god from Jamaica, Lawrence Rowe, *en route* to a haul of 7 for 74 as the West Indies were swung out for 133, their lowest score at home to New Zealand. Congdon and Brian Hastings chimed in with centuries to construct a lead of 289 and there were five down for 171 with more than a day remaining when the slender, technically sound Charlie Davis saw his captain stroll in to join him on the bridge. Needing 11 to supplant Colin Cowdrey as the heaviest scorer in Test history, Sobers knuckled down with his customary combination of sure-footed technique and supple wrist, quickly disposing of the first target then making light of the second as he and Davis piled on 254 in six hours to salvage a draw. Desi was hypnotized. 'It was the greatest thing I'd ever seen.'

This, though, was no home town bias, and Rowe soon mounted a counter-bid. Now largely forgotten outside the Caribbean, Rowe's sporting life was blighted by an eye condition that punctuated and ultimately truncated a career which fulfilled barely half its promise (how many other players have had to fly home early from three separate tours?). This affliction also persuaded the stocky Jamaican to accept Ali Bacher's pieces of eight. Lawrence George Rowe had announced himself at Test level six weeks earlier with a fanfare and a half: 214 and 100 not out in his Sabina Park backyard, a first night to end all first nights, outshining even R. E. Foster's monumental 287 on début in Sydney sixty-nine years previously. Two years later he was back in Bridgetown, opening the innings and piercing Mike Denness's field at will with his compact, elegant waves of the wand to conjure up 302 off 430 balls, so becoming the second West Indian to amass a triple century in Tests. Desi fell hook, line and sinker. 'He became our hero. He had such . . . such style.' Thus it was that the boys began to 'style', to showboat, to garnish their strokes with an extravagant flourish, to run singles with the correct degree of disdain.

St John Baptist CC provided a new outlet for Desi's Vesuvian energy. As captain, Isaac Paris, newly enrolled to study chemistry at the University of Barbados, was obliged to prepare the wicket as well as open the innings. He soon acquired a willing helper in Desi, who assisted in the rolling and the cutting. As a reward, the assistant would receive a soft drink, perhaps even $5. Sometimes he would travel with the team to away games; at others he stood as umpire. In pick-up games he would often be offered a few dollars to bat as long as possible against a field containing three mid-ons, four midwickets, a quintet patrolling the covers and a sextet ringing the deep. There were neighbourhood family matches too, the Hayneses versus the Alleynes and so on. 'I was constantly seeking advice. The older guys taught me how to bowl a googly, how to style properly. They looked at me like a child and I thank them from the bottom of my heart for all their patience and knowledge. One of them, a guy who called himself Sinbad the Sailor, used to keep me enthralled with his tales of meeting Bradman and Ponsford during the 30s and about how he would feed them on paw-paw seeds. Trusting lad that I was, I began to wolf down paw-paw seeds until they were coming out of every orifice in my body, especially my rear! One of my chief ambitions is to establish a sports complex in St James one day and so put something back, back into an area which, sadly, is now infested by drugs and crime. That said, for all the distractions and counter-attractions available today, we're still producing talented players.'

'Sometimes Desi used to captain the intermediate team and he'd bowl this deep inswinger of his to pretty good effect,' Windle Holmes remembers. 'One season he opened the bowling and batted at nine, and emerged with the most wickets in the team. I always felt he'd be a professional cricketer in some capacity or another.' To Desi, however, batting was always going to be the chosen route: 'It seemed so much easier than bowling fast, and more attractive.' Windle had no illusions about the depth of his friend's devotion. 'In one game he was given out and started to walk home. We all called him back but he just kept walking. He used to cry a lot when he was out. Away from the middle, mind you, he was very shy, not very good with girls.'

'He was quiet at times,' confirms Isaac Paris, 'very temperamental at others. Rub him up the wrong way now and he can be a very rough customer. He was a natural ball player. You would see him pick up a tennis ball, a football or a basketball and you could tell immediately. And he used that talent to go from humble beginnings to a Mercedes, from a home in which a dozen people lived by day – and at least another dozen by night – to a smart car and a smart house. That's quite a deal in Barbados. Yet he has never lost his essential simplicity.

'The problem with our team was that we were a bit of a clique and rarely made changes,' Paris adds, 'so youngsters would leave for a while, play for another club and then come back, which is why Desi and Windle went to play awhile for the Melbourne club half a mile down the road.' Holmes and Desi had an arrangement whereby one used to call on the other before a game in case either overslept. One Saturday Windle made the grave error of forgetting to perform reveille duties while Desi lay in a deep sleep brought on by the medication he was taking for a minor ailment. 'Desi forfeiting his precious innings? He was very upset, to say the least.'

Paris reminisced from a bench on the porch of Marshall's Bar, a hostelry run by a neighbourhood fast bowler (no relation) and widely referred to in

Holders Hill as the Cricketers' Pub. The St John Baptist ground lies on the opposite side of the road. Inside, the host pauses from wiping a glass to reach back to pluck another bottle of white rum from the shelf. Rock music zings and booms from the sound system, all but drowning out the more subtle nuances of Dan Quayle's fave sitcom, *Murphy Brown*, as the voice of Candice Bergen crackles valiantly from the TV mounted high in one corner of this cosy yet Spartan bar. During the ad break, Gordon Greenidge, no less, pops up on the screen to flog some health drink. The walls are swamped with photos of West Indian teams, of local luminaries such as Franklyn Stephenson, Hartley Alleyne and Desi.

Desi himself had been sitting at one of the wooden tables the previous evening, chewing the fat with Isaac and a couple of other old buddies. Attired in a natty white fedora, he had been in a highly animated mood, despite having come hotfoot from Grantley Adams Airport following the lengthy haul from Sydney. The 1992 World Cup was over, the West Indies had crept home in virtual anonymity. Recriminations abounded. Satellite and terrestrial television alike had brought the whole shebang into the island's front rooms. It had not been a pretty sight. Internal squabbles, batting collapses, defeat, unthinkably, at the hands of South Africa. At Desi's table, the debate raged on. Why he and Malcolm Marshall were treated like outcasts by the divisive manager, Deryck Murray; the insensitive senselessness of dropping Viv and Dooj while they still had a good few miles on the clock; the fallibility of the middle order. Here, at last, was Desi's chance to loosen his collar, vent some spleen, do his Peter Finch – 'I'm mad as hell and I'm not gonna take it any more.' 'For me,' insisted Isaac, 'there's been very little change in Desi. He'll finish a game, pop in to see his mum and then be somewhere in Holders Hill by ten-thirty. We heard he was coming home yesterday and I knew that, whatever time he came in, he'd be here at some stage.'

St John Baptist, like their not-so-neighbourly rivals Melbourne, were members of the Barbados Cricket League. In the late sixties, the colour and class divisions were receding but other roadblocks lingered. 'The BCL was still for the poorer classes,' emphasizes Hartley Richards. 'We had to borrow, beg, put on various fund-raising activities to raise money for kit. Facilities were poor, and playing fields were either hard to come by or else they were the size of my lawn. At one time on the St John Baptist pasture the pitch was a mound *à la* baseball. There was one field, at St Lucy I think, where the pitch was on a slope and the batsman couldn't see the fast bowler when he ran in. Someone had to call out to him, announce the bowler was coming.

Conditions were precarious but they had a way of bringing out natural talent. When the barriers started coming down in the fifties some good players had developed, such as Clairemonte Depeiza, but there was no coaching. You just picked up the game as you went on. You'd go to nets on a Wednesday evening and the captain might say, "You're hitting too hard" or, "You're hitting in the air", but otherwise you just learned as you played. It was a way of competing between villages, a fun thing. People didn't play to get to the big time as they do now.'

The switch to the Kensington Oval for the annual BCA–BCL horn-locking session constituted a rude awakening for the less well-heeled aspirants. Negotiating a field two to three times larger than they were accustomed to took some getting used to. Batsmen expecting to clear long-on without much effort would be gullible prey for the spinners; fielders had a lot more ground to cover. Small wonder many a glittering BCL reputation floundered amid the shadows cast by those distant pale green stands.

Desi began to forge his when he entered secondary school. Leaving St John Baptist after his eleven-plus, he attended the Barbados Academy at the insistence of Idrina Richards, only for the death of the headmaster-cum-owner to force the school's closure less than two years later. Granted an element of choice this time, Desi opted for Federal High, the attraction being that this would enable him to participate in the Roundtree Schools Competition, an annual event for under-fifteens involving a series of two-day games between local educational establishments. Federal had been the brainchild of Dacosta Edwards, the Barbados foreign minister, who conceived the idea of founding and subsidizing an alternative to the pre-eminent Harrison College, for boys, and Queen's College, for girls, designed for children whose parents were unable to pay fees. The eleven-plus had recently been introduced, further opening up the way for the underclass. Even so, proffers Isaac Paris, 'There were not too many options for a boy coming out of Federal bar sport.' In the year below Desi was one Malcolm Denzil Marshall, a budding all-rounder from St Michael who also sampled Test cricket for the first time at Kensington in 1972. So besotted with Sobers did 'Macca' become that, a decade later, he would still persist in turning up his collar and lapsing into his 'Sobers step'. 'Sobey,' Clive Lloyd would later shout across to him, 'c'mon, Sobey, your turn to bowl.'

During lunch breaks, Desi would race down to the public library and pore through its less than expansive cricket section, its scorecards from bygone Ashes series, its sepia-tinted photos of Lord's and Melbourne, 'getting my head round what it would be like to bat there'. As hypnotized as he was by Bradman's insatiable number-crunching, the feats of the Black Bradman, George Headley, made no less an impression. 'It was fascinating to observe the way he made his runs. He had to be a one-man team. The West Indies would make 260 and he'd get 160 of them. I don't like comparing eras, but he must have been extraordinary to score as many as he did for a bad team. I want to build a museum for the kids one day, give them a permanent reminder of his accomplishments.' As if to bear out Desi's one-man army theory, the Jamaican Jehovah not only averaged over 60 in Tests while accounting for nine of the islands' first twelve 100s at that level (he notched twice as many centuries – 10 – as fifties), he also top-scored in 15 of his 39 international innings, a heady 38.46 per cent. Based on innings in which at least five wickets were lost, only Bradman (38.36 per cent) has led the way at an average of better than three in 10 among those with more than 20 caps. Hutton, so long perceived as England's prop during the early fifties, managed to do so 24.35 per cent of the time, Hammond, his counterpart in the thirties, 28.33 per cent, Hobbs 27.27 per cent. Interestingly, while Weekes (28.57 per cent) and Richards (24.70 per cent) head the Caribbean scroll of honour in this department, Desi's 20.15 per cent mark (up to last November) exceeded those of Sobers (18.30 per cent), Walcott (17.91 per cent) and Greenidge (14.94 per cent).

The need to catch two buses to get home each day precluded practice after school hours, but Owen Springer, the kindly Federal games master, soon espied an able body, albeit by accident while ambling through the schoolyard. 'I used to bat in the yard before the bell rang,' recalls Desi, 'and aim to be not out so I could continue at lunch and perhaps even afternoon break. Then I began to try batting all week but the rules were changed to stop me.' In order to play in the Roundtree Desi had to request his staunchly protective grandmother's permission since this meant staying away for two nights. The assent was forthcoming, if a little grudgingly, and only on the proviso that he returned home immediately the game ended. Irene could see her grandson getting sidetracked from his studies, but was coming to realize that the process was irreversible.

'I was a bit cocky. Clyde Burnay, the school's fastest bowler, once threatened to knock my head off if I didn't share my lunch with him. I didn't let him worry me. There was no way I was going to be bullied into sharing my lunch with anyone. I was so short that my pads would beat me in the ribs whenever I walked or ran. My first bat was a Gunn & Moore – to whom I am still contracted – complete with protective skin on the blade so it would last. I became school captain at fourteen and Mr Springer had a word with Charlie Griffith who, along with Seymour Nurse, was one of the coaches of the Barbados Youth team. I was subsequently recommended for a trial and Mr Springer drove all the way from his home in St Andrew to our house to request my grandmother's permission. Thankfully, she said yes. I was batting in the middle order at that stage, but I knew I had no chance of selection because I was competing with guys from the under-eighteen age group, people like David Murray and Emmerson Trotman. Still, the experience was invaluable, especially since, at the bidding of Owen Springer, Griffith took me under his wing. Little did I realize then, mind, that I would carry on going to those trials until my final year at school, when, at nineteen, I finally made it. Up to then people had said I was too aggressive, that I tried to score too quickly, that I wasn't left-handed – any excuse.'

The Roundtree tourney furnished Desi with the opportunity to pit himself against Wayne Daniel, the lumbering, affable speedster who would go on to do such stout and destructive service for Middlesex over the years only for his Test career to be condensed by the presence of fellow Bajans such as Garner and Marshall (Desi, it should be added, finds it hard to avoid the suspicion that 'someone didn't like him'). To Marshall, Daniel was 'a fearsome proposition . . . far bigger than any of his contemporaries'. Indeed, the prospect of facing this gargantuan wildebeest frequently sent opposing batsmen scurrying for the sanctuary of sick note or family bereavement.

Desi was made of sterner stuff. 'We played the Roundtree matches during the school holidays on Tuesdays and Wednesdays, and it was quite an event for us ambitious ones. The newspapers would cover the games and if you got into double figures or took two wickets you could see your name in print the next day. Even at fourteen Wayne was a strapping guy, son of a St Philip farmer. He had such an imposing physique that he had appeared in an ad for a local lumber company, demonstrating the various strengths of some pieces of wood – by snapping them in two. People used to say he lived off the milk from his father's cows. I don't know whether this was intended to scare us but just seeing him could frighten a few. Like Thelston Payne, who went on to captain Barbados, he attended Princess Margaret's and whenever we played them their umpire, Rocky, would always make decisions in their favour. An early lesson in international cricketing realities, methinks. Wayne was quick, but I can remember taking four fours off him in one over – then getting out to the bloke at the other end. Still, I had my claim to fame: the boy who smashed Wayne Daniel all over the park. There were a lot of fairly good fast bowlers among my age group, testimony, one assumes, to the success of Hall and Griffith when we were all first smitten by cricket.'

The first time Isaac Paris detected any special fruits sprouting from Desi's love affair came during a game between Melbourne and a team from St Lucy. 'St Lucy had this pretty quick bowler called Phillips and the wicket was definitely not perfect. The ball was lifting, but Desi was hitting him back over his head. You would have thought he was playing spin.' Desi eventually left Melbourne in something of a huff, objecting to the captain's attempts to pick the side on a unilateral basis. If this was an indication of inner belief then there was a wealth of encouragement to draw from. He had finally earned selection for that Barbados Youth team, batting in the middle order, keeping wicket when the regular stumper suffered from swollen palms and serving as vice-captain under his good friend Calvin Hope, now ensconced in London as a member of the Barbados Tourist Board. Daniel was also in that side, Marshall twelfth man. 'I always knew I'd play for the West Indies, even then, but I said it a little loud at one stage and was accused of being a braggart.'

Returning to the St John Baptist intermediate XI – Paris's clique remained in unshakeable occupation – he would often espy his father preening from the boundary edge. By now the BCL representative team had been incorporated into the BCA League as a regular entity, playing its home games in St Michael, but a dispute between the BCL and its secretary, Charlie Griffith, over the dispersal of monies subsequently led to the latter resigning his commission and pulling on an umpire's coat. The upshot was that the nucleus of the BCL split, compelling its leading lights to link up with hitherto out-of-bounds BCA clubs such as Pickwick and Carlton, Desi joining the latter in 1975 at the behest of its white founder, the late Reynold St Clair Hutchinson. A Queen's Counsel and partner in the law firm of Hutchinson and Banfield, Hutchinson was a former Barbados soccer international and long-standing member of the BCA board of management who spent much of his leisure time administering youth cricket in Barbados, serving as selector while assisting Desi and other likely lads with equipment they and their families would otherwise have been unable to afford. The benefactor died in 1987, but not before he could revel in the full bloom of one of his favourite shoots.

During the Barbados Youth trials of 1975 Desi's time at Federal ran out. He duly applied to do his O levels, hoping to be one of those fortunate students permitted to attend lessons between 4 p.m. and 6 p.m. and thus play cricket to their heart's content. The application was rebuffed, however, so Desi began to seek employment while carrying on caddying at Sandy Lane for $10 a round – 'enough for some nice pants and a shirt' – together with his chums David Gibson and Davison Marshall, of subsequent Marshall's Bar fame. A couple of sets of tennis with Derwin Green, the food and beverage manager at the Miramar Beach Hotel in St James (now the Royal Pavilion), yielded a position as a waiter. The Miramar, of course, had its own cricket team. 'We played against other hotels and it was very competitive. The hotel used to act as sponsor and the guests would come along to watch us play. Sometimes the games took place at the Bristol ground in St Peter, sometimes at Texaco, Malcolm Marshall's first club, and sometimes at St John Baptist. People at the hotel were very supportive. When I made my début for Barbados I was given a $200 bonus as well as a number of gifts, not to mention a great packed lunch from the cooks. The owner's wife, Mrs Young, an American lady, didn't like cricket but she ran a boutique and two of her assistants brought in a radio to hear the commentary. When it was explained to her what was going on she brought in a more powerful radio the next day and asked to meet me when I returned.'

The Carlton club was a postwar institution in Barbados, running junior and senior teams in netball, hockey, tennis and football as well as cricket. Although his and Desi's paths never crossed there, Gordon Greenidge ranks among its most illustrious old boys – even though his appearances were as a 'guest' and he never became a member – alongside lesser luminaries such as Vanburn Holder, Ricardo Ellcock and Tony Cozier, the voice of West Indian cricket. The funds needed to erect the club's first pavilion ($45, according to the fiftieth anniversary brochure of 1990) were raised from the proceeds of a play starring Daphne, future wife of Reynold Hutchinson. All the beams employed to construct the roof and dance-floor below, together with the hardwood, were recovered from the *Nina*, one of three sailing boats built at Holetown during the mid-forties as replica ships for use in a film about Columbus's Atlantic crossing.

It was at Carlton that Desi first opened an innings, volunteering to do the nightwatchman's stint one evening and adapting with such assurance that he gained instant promotion. Kenny Hutchinson, the managing director of Bryden's, an import/export company based in Bridgetown dealing in everything from potatoes to pharmaceuticals, remembers how his elder brother sought to contain the young Desi's over-exuberance. A prominent figure at Carlton himself, his son, William, was one of Desi's Barbados Youth colleagues. 'Desi certainly showed his disappointment when he received a bad decision,' recalls Hutchinson senior, 'and at times he was inclined to react in a violent way. That was one aspect of his personality that Reynold worked at, trying to stop him from becoming over-zealous. Reynold was very influential: Desi was his protégé.' Reynold's concept of equal opportunity sat well with boys of Desi's social standing. 'When Reynold set the club up the social structure here was completely different. There were élite white clubs and élite black clubs such as Spartan, Malcolm Marshall's club. He made it open to all, starting with around twenty or so members and expanding to the stage where there are now more than 300, a lot of those schoolboys and -girls. We're no longer exclusively male. In those early days we were mixed to an extent but the majority of members were white, whereas now very few whites play cricket. Social backgrounds have changed, living standards for the blacks have improved.'

One of the earliest coloured members was 'Foffy' Williams, the current Carlton president, a brisk leg-spinner who dismissed Jack Ikin and David Sheppard during the Ramadhin–Valentine jaunt of 1950 but failed to become the first Carlton man to win a Test cap. That honour was reserved for Desi. 'He is a real club man, a real Carlton man,' asserts Kenny Hutchinson, 'a rare breed now because, unlike the old days, players today switch between clubs all the time. Players play for themselves because there's money in it. He captained the first team in the early eighties and even now he turns out for us on the odd occasion and comes to nets. A grand fellow. Half a dozen years ago he came back to us for a few games and scored next to nothing. He took a lot of ragging for the next couple of seasons for that and the next time he went in for us you've never seen anyone take such pains to make a hundred. And he did, of course.'

In 1990 Carlton held a function in Desi's honour at which he was presented with a special tie, an award he treasures dearly. That, though, was some distance off in that summer of 1975 when he was named as the BCA's Most Improved Youth Player of the year at the end of his first season at Carlton. The following year he was chosen as one of the BCA's Five Cricketers of the Year after totting up a club-leading 592 runs. Senior national honours were now but a sniff away. As one of the BCA's thirty-five best players he was summoned to the Barbados trials towards the end of the 1976 season along with other aspirants like David Murray and Gregory Armstrong, another sprightly paceman who later played for Glamorgan. David Holford was the captain and Daniel, already a Test player, was on hand as well. During a series of four- and one-day matches at the Kensington Oval Desi composed a mature 80 in his most assertive knock but the nod did not come for another twelve months. The experience was, nonetheless, a revealing one. 'The success Barbados cricket has enjoyed over the years is attributable to its structure and also to the emphasis placed on discipline and behaviour. One year a guy didn't make the team because he was seen eating a *rôti* on his way to trials. I also learned how careful you had to be with whom you associated with. It was a country-yokel-comes-to-big-city situation. When the selectors assessed you they were not simply looking at your skills.'

7 January 1977 was the red-letter day. Barbados were opening the Shell Shield season with a game against Jamaica in Montego Bay, Sabina Park being unavailable due to the impending visit of Mushtaq Mohammad's Pakistanis. Desi found himself in brassy company, jazzing it up with the Test sextet of Greenidge, Holford, Garner, Vanburn Holder, Collis King and Albert Padmore. Happily, Michael Holding was handicapped by a shoulder injury and managed only a handful of overs, enabling the visitors to reach an imposing 447 that owed much to a second-wicket stand of 190 between Greenidge and David Murray, Desi having come and gone in virtual silence, trapped leg-before for nine while Holding was still able to cope with the pain. 'Gordon told me not to worry about playing with big-name players, and I must say that, walking to the wicket with him, I felt I'd arrived. Unfortunately, Holding had just enough in his tank to get me.'

Thrust aside by Garner and Holder for 154 first time round after passing 400 the previous year against essentially the same attack, the hosts made a slightly better show in their second dig, Basil 'Shotgun' Williams slugging 68 and Holding an unconquered 33 before Holford's leggies ensured victory by an innings and 68 runs. Thus was the destination of the 1976–7 Shell Shield all but settled. Desi, however, was destined for a speedy return to the ranks. 'They were nine down, the game was almost over and I hadn't done much when Holding drove Padmore towards me on the long-on boundary. Right, I thought, I really want this catch. I circled it for an age – then spilled it. A couple of balls later the exact same thing happened. I came off looking like a lost aunt.' 'My initial impression of Desi was of a batsman who went for his shots,' reflects Holding, 'albeit almost exclusively off the front foot. He was also a very ordinary fielder.' Worse was to come for the butterfingered one. 'Then I was hauled before the disciplinary committee and told that my attitude was wrong, that I wasn't keen enough – and that the selectors were dropping me. I didn't think that was fair. I'd tried my bollocks off. I was so disappointed. Having said that, it did teach me that there are times when you don't see yourself as others do, that you must always look interested out there, be seen to be buzzing.'

Although he continued to practise with the squad, all was set for anti-climax until an injury to Greenidge let Desi in as an eleventh hour substitute for Barbados' tilt against Pakistan in mid-February. Windle Holmes fielded the late-night summons. 'The call came through to our house because there was no phone in the Haynes household. At first Desi thought I was kidding him on.' The opening skirmishes found Desi granting the dashing Haroon Rashid two of his four lives: 'Some of the comments aimed at me by the crowd were, how shall I put it, very distasteful.' Haroon took due advantage and motored to three figures on a bountiful batting track, Asif Iqbal spicing the fare with an exquisite 89 before Imran Khan and Intikhab Alam conspired for a freewheeling eighth-wicket liaison worth 94 in just over the hour. On the first evening Desi was back on his beat at the Miramar, purveying room service to the gentry. Lugging a heavy tray between assignments he passed through the bar and spotted Sobers and Mushtaq. 'Mushtaq glanced at me. By the looks of it he thought he'd seen me before somewhere but couldn't quite place the face.'

By stumps the next day he could. Uncowed by the swift loss of partner Alvin Greenidge for a single, Desi was the mainspring in a second-wicket stand of 195 with David Murray, clattering 20 boundaries in a vivacious 136 spanning just four hours. The attack was not to be sniffed at either, welding the pace and swing of Imran and Salim Altaf to the artful wrist spin of Intikhab and Mushtaq and the maturing slow left-arm of Iqbal Qasim. These were the strokes of a young man bent on self-affirmation, with the zest and feigned arrogance of youth tempered by the calm of self-belief and an adult's seriousness of intent. This was the way out, the way up. By the time Holford declared at 419 for 7, the Pakistan lead was a piffling 24. The watching Clive Lloyd was suitably taken. 'It was customary for the West Indies captain to watch the game involving the host nation before it staged a Test and David Holford had told me that he had this precocious young guy in his side with a lot of ability and that I should have a look at him. Roy Fredericks was making noises about retirement and there was no obvious replacement – until I saw Desi. I liked everything about him. The style was excellent and he certainly looked to be a good bet for the future. He was very compact, very correct, a hard worker and clearly very ambitious. From that day I knew it was only a matter of time before he played for the West Indies.'

Desi was limbering up to pole vault the moon. 'I can remember a lot of pulls, and picking up the short balls very early. There were bags of shots and, to their credit, the same people who had baited me on the first day because of those drops now changed their tune and really got behind me. I felt I sent a few messages around the Caribbean but I had to be realistic because of Greenidge and Fredericks. I knew I had to be patient. They were the ideal partnership, rightie and leftie, Freddo so gifted, playing shots all round the wicket and a fine gully to boot, Gordon the complete batsman, as adept against spin as he was against pace.' On the final day, Desi turned twenty-one. With scant sense of occasion the tourists opted for batting practice – admittedly, the first Test was just seventy-two hours away – but Desi had time enough to embellish his initial effort, rustling up a quickfire 25 before being run out.

Desi's principal contribution to that Shield triumph – he made 75 runs in five innings all told – was rather more modest, coming as it did in the last match, at Bridgetown yet again, where his 37 paced the Barbados march to 511 against Andy Roberts and his fellow Windwardians and Leewardians, then operating under the banner of the Combined Islands. Viv Richards rollicked along to 124 out of his side's 235 but was unable to dispel the threat of the follow-on, Collis King's four wickets ultimately setting up Barbados for a comfortable six-wicket win.

That shaft of light between the wooden habitats in Holders Hill was fast evolving into a spotlight. In the less than stately Haynes home Desi had been part of a team, one link in a chain of mutually supportive, mutually dependent human beings. Now he was part of a winning team.

4

The Packer Pack

One day we'll look back on this
And it will all seem funny. Ha, ha, ha.

Rosalita, Bruce Springsteen

If Desi found that his rampaging arrival on the international stage drew only muted applause, the commotion in the wings explained all. The twelve months between May 1977 and April 1978 were the most fraught and divisive in cricket history, a period during which the entire fabric of the game was unravelled and rewoven; long-standing friends became bitter philosophical adversaries. For someone whose own expertise with bat and ball was confined to horses and chukkas, it says much for the impact of the man who caused all the hubbub that we now refer to this period as the start of the Packer Era.

To some, Kerry Francis Bullmore Packer is best characterized by his skittish response to being compared with Genghis Khan. 'He wasn't very lovable,' conceded the mallet-flailing media magnate, 'but he was bloody efficient.' The words, wittingly or not, were well chosen. Packer set out to extend his empire by getting his mitts on the exclusive TV rights to cover first-class cricket in Australia, and duly achieved this with ruthless efficiency. In so doing, he bloodied the noses of the pink-ginned plutocrats good and proper, cured them – temporarily – of their addiction to navel-contemplation and, inadvertently perhaps, secured the immediate commercial future of their beloved plaything.

That Fluck and Law's spitting image of this hulking, eighteen-stone tee-

totaller should have been a grinning clone of one of history's most proficient mass murderers illustrates to a T the histrionic over-reaction that greeted the forty-three-year-old Sydneysider's coup. At the time, to teenage buffs such as myself, and multitudes more besides, the advent of Kerry Packer was the ultimate betrayal. Ironic, then, that the *agent provocateur* should have been a meek child of the Australian establishment. The second son of Sir Frank Packer, an astute, unscrupulous Sydney newspaper tycoon, Kerry did not enjoy the most pastoral of upbringings. Dad had been the New South Wales heavyweight boxing champion and regularly brought his macho side to bear when disciplining his offspring, summoning rebellious Clyde and malleable Kerry to the drawing room in their cavernous Bellevue Hill home, gloves mandatory. When Kerry came home from Geelong Grammar at the end of term one winter having left his tennis racket at the Melbourne boarding school, he was sent straight back to retrieve it. After another 1200-mile train hike, he allegedly dispatched the following cable to Chez Packer: ARRIVED MELBOURNE SAFELY STOP NO LOVE KERRY

In 1977, however, no one gave a monkey's for the blighter's pukka English roots, his staunch royalist antecedents, the Packer family crest that adorned the windows of University College, Oxford, or even the succession of Berkshire Packers who attended the Royal College of Music. The polo-loving entrepreneur with the gammy hip, legacy of a car crash in Cleveland that killed the other three passengers, was depicted as a cross between knave, bounder and absolute cad, the very Devil Incarnate. How *dare* he press-gang our heroes and force them to fly flags of economic convenience instead of defending the realm? How *dare* he tart them up in those naff Day-Glo pyjamas and daub their names on the back just so the great unwashed could identify them? How *dare* he organize games at night and thus bring them within the reach of those foolish enough to work for a living during normal opening hours and unlucky enough to have run out of ailing aunts? The even-tempered foamed, the self-righteous imploded. Cricket, like its country of origin, was happy plodding along, impervious to criticism, resisting change to the last, an institution in thrall to the past, disdainful of the present, slap-happy about the future. All of a sudden, the End of Civilization As We Knew It was nigh. Buffeted by the winds of social change, one of the most gnarled branches of the entertainment business was about to snap.

If Packer had had any misgivings they had been washed away after his swoop to cover the 1977 Ashes series. 'We were subjected to high-pressure salesmanship,' whimpered Doug Insole, the chairman of the Test and County

Cricket Board as he related to ACB officials the dreadful tale of how their Pommie counterparts had been mercilessly wined and viciously dined into accepting a $150,000 bid. The ACB retaliated by telling Insole and his colleagues that from now on it would handle all negotiations for Tests involving Australia. As one door slammed in Packer's face, he kicked down another. If the seeds for the Supertest had not been firmly embedded already they certainly were now. Of the thirty-five names reported to be on his books on 9 May 1977, eighteen were Australian, five South African, four Pakistani, four English and another quartet – Lloyd, Holding, Richards and Roberts – West Indian. Two days later, Gordon Greenidge admitted that he, too, had joined up. By mid-June, Alvin Kallicharran, Collis King and Bernard Julien were known to be on board. Other prominent Caribbean players were rumoured to have signed as well, enough for a complete team.

Understandably wary of his government's trenchant opposition to any form of contact between Jamaicans and South Africans, Holding took the precaution of inserting an 'escape clause' that would allow him to withdraw from his contract in the event of it not being granted official approval. He needn't have worried. Unlike its tut-tutting opposite numbers in England, Australia, Pakistan and South Africa, the financially strapped West Indian Cricket Board of Control all but got down on its knees and begged for a piece of the action. In fact, on 22 May one board member made it known that a guarantee in the region of A$2.5 million to stage a Supertest series in the Caribbean would do very nicely.

True, England's last Caribbean tour three years previously had produced a modest profit of 62,000 Eastern Caribbean dollars (approximately £15,000) and a sponsor – Guinness – had been found for the islands' inaugural one-day international that March. On the other hand, there were no wad-waving TV networks – as recently as 1981, the Barbados Cricket Association received a paltry £30 an hour for letting the cameras capture Botham, Boycott and Gower in action during the Bridgetown Test – and no brimming crowds. Based in areas where disposable income was at a premium, three of the four Test venues, Bridgetown, Georgetown and Sabina Park, held no more than 14,000 spectators apiece. The vast distances between the islands and the costly tourist hotels, meanwhile, meant that expenses were prohibitively high. Profits from home series were thus negligible at best. The punters, furthermore, were unwilling to accept second-rate goods: the official Australian tour of 1978 incurred losses exceeding EC$200,000. Contrast this with the 'surpluses' made by the TCCB in 1977 (£1.5 million) and 1978 (£1.2 million). When

Packer brought his circus to town in early 1979, daily Shell Shield attendances were struggling to reach four figures; on the final day of the Trinidad–Guyana match at the 28,000-capacity Queen's Park Oval, fifty-one fanatics poured through the turnstiles. The West Indies board was nigh-on $100,000 in the red that year. It had been striving for some time to persuade the ICC that its hosts should cover overheads and hand over a decent chunk of the profits generated by tours of Australia and England (foreign exchange problems on the sub-continent prevented India and Pakistan from entering the equation). The ICC, though, prevaricated time and again, averring that this was a matter for the individual boards. As time wore on, it became increasingly difficult to resist making a connection between this unhelpful posture and the resentment felt by the other members of the ICC at the disinclination of the West Indies board to outlaw its rebel factions.

This was understandable. More than any of their brethren within the ICC constellation, the Caribbean stars were driven by nationalist fervour rather than visions of a swish lifestyle. Only by touting their wares in England – fourteen West Indian Test stars were due to tramp the county circuit that summer – could they make cricket a livelihood. A dozen lesser lights would traipse to the leagues and shires. Here were the game's arch freelancers, reliant for decades on stamina as much as ability, servant to many, beholden to none.

For Lloyd, the temptations were too great. 'There were no bonuses after our victory in the 1975 World Cup. In fact, we received nothing extra for winning the 1979 tournament either. Bar a walking stick, a gold medal and a gold chain that my wife now wears with pride, we got our fee and that was it. The board never said, "Let's give these guys something to remember these marvellous occasions by." I had to fight to get the fee up in 1979. The board were about to pay us £100 again but I kicked up a fuss. So did Mike Brearley and eventually we got £200. People don't understand how bad it was in county cricket, either. When I first went to Lancashire in 1968 I got £2500 for five months. Money was never a factor with me but then you start to see sports people doing various things for themselves in a financial sense and you want *your* kids to be in a better position. So we decided to better our situation, not just for ourselves but also for the young players coming through. Look at it now. Today's players are gaining from it and good luck to them. Because of Packer we got a minimum wage in county cricket. That's how it should be. Kerry Packer was the greatest thing that happened to all sportsmen, not just cricketers.'

When the first World Series Cricket itinerary was pasted on to the

Melbourne sports pages, it emerged that none of the dates would clash with that winter's official Australian tour of the Caribbean. The air, moreover, was thick with conciliatory noises. The West Indies Board of Control was acutely aware of the players' predicament. 'We didn't think of ourselves as rebels,' Holding emphasizes. 'We were still going to be playing for the West Indies, even if it was under unsanctioned conditions.' In August, the board agreed to adhere to the decree made by the ICC on 26 July to ban from Test consideration any member of the Packer pack, yet conviction was in short supply. When the board's delegates, Allan Rae and Harold Burnett, attended the ICC confab at Lord's they had expressed considerable doubt that a ban was the best course of action. At the same time, they examined the list of personnel and warned Lloyd, the West Indies captain, that, since the Caribbean nations were at the forefront of sanctions against South Africa and helping to draw up the Gleneagles Agreement, there might be trouble for him and his WSC compatriots back home, were they to occupy a greensward in the Republic alongside Graeme Pollock or Denys Hobson.

Urged on by the other delegates over lunch and a bottle or two of wine in one of St John's Wood's finer eateries, Rae and Burnett finally bowed to 'the need for unanimity'. Rae nevertheless succeeded in having the following statement recorded in the minutes: 'We feel that it is morally unfair to players who are free to enter these contracts when they did to retroactively virtually declare these contracts illegal as far as cricket is concerned and to find that by entering into these contracts freely they have found themselves barred from Test-match cricket. Feeling as we do that the Resolution is morally wrong, we feel that we are giving Mr Packer a weapon with which to fight this Conference. If it is morally wrong, which we believe it is, Mr Packer's publicity people will see to it that this aspect of the matter is properly ventilated and not a court action necessarily. Mr Packer is offering players a lot of money and most countries are henceforth going to try to ensure that players will earn more money. This is a plus factor for Mr Packer (as he is shown to have improved the circumstances). Mr Packer will also be able to say that they were free to enter contracts when they did and retroactively they have been penalized. Who is considered to be fair, Mr Packer or the ICC?'

In England, there was no question about it. Right lay with the ill-focused might of the top brass. The Australian public, less inclined to doff its cap to authority and tradition, echoed Rae's sentiments. An opinion poll published in the *Sydney Morning Herald* and the *Age* found that 78 per cent of the respondents were convinced that the players were within their rights to have a foot in both camps. As a barometer of the times, there was even greater significance in the 55 per cent share who believed WSC would improve cricket as a spectacle, as against the 29 per cent who felt it would damage it and the 16 per cent don't knows. No wonder a Packer PR bod later confessed that his organization was not catering for cricket fans *per se* but for 'the new fans, the new Australians, our audience of tomorrow'. Sell 'em the one-day bastardized son, went the rationale, 'and they might even go along to the Tests'.

Within weeks Rae was revealing plans (ultimately fruitless) to buy out the contracts of Packer's fifteen (and counting) Caribbean acquisitions by paying them the difference between their prospective WSC salary and the extant level of Test remuneration. In the meantime, Kallicharran had dispensed with his cutlass and eyepatch on the advice of his Australian agent, David Lord. In most quarters, little Kalli was hailed as a hero, a pillar of principle, a man above the lure of grubby lucre, a patriot. It should be noted that he had also struck a deal to play for Queensland with 4IP, the Brisbane radio station that had stumped up the readies to ensure that Jeff Thomson remained untarnished. The Test and County Cricket Board now went into reverse too, announcing that WSC players would, after all, be barred from county cricket. Packer promptly sought a High Court injunction and damages against Lord and the ICC. The agent was temporarily restrained pending the outcome and Justice Slade eventually ruled the latter guilty of unreasonable restraint of trade at the end of a five-and-a-half-hour, 221-page judgement. At Test and domestic level, the blanket bans were inoperable. Obliged to cough up around £200,000 in court costs, the ICC demanded, of course, that its reluctant Caribbean allies assist with the reparations.

Despite Rae's reiteration on 1 October that his board would implement the Test ban, the desire for compromise was self-evident. Had not Stollmeyer repeatedly claimed that the board was prepared to 'bend over backwards' to find a way of keeping the WSC stars happy? With such a small pool of talent to fish from, the loss of such box office attractions would almost certainly cripple the game on the islands. On 26 November, Julian Hunte, the president of the Windward Island Board, proposed a meeting between the various parties to enable WSC and the Establishments 'to go hand in hand'. Hunte, it transpired, had met Packer in secret during the summer and maintained cable contact ever since. Packer had been denied use of the Australian Test grounds but the show went on regardless. In the Victorian backwater of

Moorabbin on 16 November, I. M. Chappell's XI defeated R. D. Robinson's XI by two runs to get World Series Cricket underway. Ten days later, Andy Roberts bowled the West Indies WSC XI to a three-day win over a WSC World XI at the VFL Football Stadium, Melbourne. And still the West Indies board declined to enforce the ban. At the turn of 1978, therefore, Lloyd and his fellow travellers, fresh from victory over Chappell's Australian A team in the Supertest series, seemed likely to have their cake and eat it at their leisure. Led by a captain, Bobby Simpson, who had not experienced Test warfare for a decade, and with Thomson the sole ace in an inexperienced pack, the comparatively feeble-looking Australian B party due to begin island-hopping in February looked set to be the icing on that cake.

This, then, was the tumultuous background to Desi's breakthrough season, one that began in earnest on 19 January 1978 amid the idyllic environs of Victoria Park in Castries, St Lucia. Opening the Barbados first innings with Alvin Greenidge (whose namesake was among the half-dozen Bajans missing from action due to a more lucrative prior engagement), he was second top-scorer with 79 against a Combined Islands side featuring Derick Parry, an all-rounder on the verge of national recognition who had persuaded Desi to disrupt his own wicket in the corresponding fixture a year earlier. The off-spinner from Charlestown, Nevis, garnered 7 for 100 as Barbados totalled 315, and with Garner absent Parry was able to collect 96 against a depleted attack and so hold the deficit to 21. One of the few batsmen not to succumb to Parry first time round – he fell instead to another Charlestown boy, the exotically christened Elquemedo Tonito Willett, a slow left-armer who in 1973 had become the first Leeward Islander to represent the West Indies – Desi departed leg-before for 2 to Essex's wiry Norbert Phillip before rain scotched any chance of a conclusive finish.

Barbados' next engagement at Rosehall, Berbice, found the murderous Colin Croft on the menu. Desi was caught behind for 16, setting the gangling Guyanan on his way to a haul of 6 for 77 in an unimpressive score of 260. Again, the elements prevailed, Guyana mooring at 111 for 4. Back at the Kensington Oval, Desi raised 116 against Trinidad in cahoots with Alvin Greenidge, his first three-figure opening stand at this level. Inshan Ali's leg-breaks outwitted him on 66, and the pair later galloped to a target of 58 in 12 overs to seal a 10-wicket win engineered by Sylvester Clarke's match bag of 10–125. The Holding-shorn Jamaica were next to hit town and a first-innings lead was sufficient to earn Barbados the Shell Shield as Desi (79) and Alvin posted 145, the latter proceeding to 164 after his partner had yielded

once more to spin, this time the off-breaks of veteran Maurice Foster. Another
51 second time up celebrated the fact that Desi, having made a persuasive
case for advancement with 310 runs at 51.67 in his first full Shield campaign,
was about to fly to Antigua to play in the Guinness Trophy one-day international.

In the quest to fill the void created by the impending retirement of Roy
Fredericks – who had subsequently popped up again with Packer – the selectors were running the rule over a slew of likely lads and opted on this occasion
to rope in four untried openers. Two would be drawn from this quartet and
Desi was by no means certain of getting the nod. 'I really wasn't sure whether
I would be selected and when the final eleven was read out at the end of the
team meeting that morning I simply couldn't believe it. The wicket was
green but it looked worse than it played.' Guyana's Faoud Bacchus was
accommodated at No. 5 while Desi and his Jamaican roommate Richard
Austin were left with the task of confronting Thomson at his javelin-hurling
jolliest. At first it was nothing more than a phoney war, Thomson being
no-balled half a dozen times in his opening over to Austin, but Desi soon
felt the backlash. 'In the first over I faced from him, Thommo pitched one
short. I was wearing one of those baggy Australian caps and when I ducked
without first looking to see how high it would bounce, the ball flicked the
peak. When Austin nicked Wayne Clark to Simpson Viv came in and immediately strode down the wicket to have a word. "You mustn't bat like that,"
he told me. "You gotta have a peek first." No pun intended, I'm sure. Anyway,
I decided to take up the challenge. This guy Thomson simply had to go.'

And go he did. To the audible disappointment of his local admirers,
Richards paused but briefly before hoisting a catch off Ian Callen. Visibly
charged, Desi made amends with a flurry of meaty hooks off Thomson. 'Eyes
now turned to Haynes,' reported that estimable Trinidadian sportswriter,
Brunell Jones, 'who was carrying a bat of naked aggression. He swept, cover-
drove and scattered the field with just about every shot in the book, while
one after another of his partners came and went.' With the innings quaking
at 121 for 5, enter Deryck Murray, captain for the day while Lloyd tended
his sick wife. The pair added a priceless 126, Desi scorching on to 148 from
136 deliveries with sixteen fours and a brace of sixes. 'At one point I was
actually batting for the short one. At another stage when Simpson was bowling his leg-breaks I declined a second run and he had a bit of a dig, remarking
that I had stayed put because I couldn't play spin. "Right," I thought to
myself, "I'll show him." Then I called down the wicket: "I'm gonna give you

a stiff neck today." Then I hit him out of the ground.' Thomson eventually
wrought his revenge by bowling Desi, improving his analysis to a quixotic
4–67 (had no-balls been included in the bowler's analysis back then his return
would have been positively surreal). The new hero of Holders Hill scampered
off to the pavilion, happier than a sandboy. On his way there, one of the
13,444 appreciative folk on the premises offered some loose change. Straining
to make themselves heard amid the claustrophobic swell at Holmes Bar in
Holders Hill, Isaac Paris and Windle Holmes charged their glasses with
another tot of rum and proposed a toast. 'One guy bet everyone Desi would
score a hundred,' recalls Paris. 'Boy, did he clean up.' So did the West Indies.
Backed by a virtually irresistible total of 313 for 9 from their allotted 50 overs,
of which Desi and his wicketkeeping accomplice were responsible for nearly
two-thirds, the homeboys cruised in, Garner and Croft claiming three victims
apiece and the Aussies hopelessly out of contention at 181 for 7 from 36
overs when bad light foreshortened proceedings.

Apart from Bacchus and Austin, Desi's other rivals included Basil 'Shotgun'
Williams, Lockhart Sebastien and Alvin Greenidge but there was no dispute
now over which of them would make his Test début at the top of the order
in Port-of-Spain. Austin dropped down to No. 6 for his maiden Test, Bacchus
and Irving Shillingford made way for Lloyd and Greenidge (C.G.), and Parry's
stealth usurped Wayne Daniel's speed. 'We had three days' practice beforehand so I had time to take it all in. People all over Barbados were talking
about coming over and wishing me luck. Things were going well in financial
terms too. I'd just got a job in a sports equipment store in Bridgetown and
Slazenger had given me £100 to use their gear that season. With bats running
at $100 a throw that was quite a help. I thought I was a somebody.' Overnight
rain supplemented by a further downpour on the first morning delayed the
start until five minutes before lunch, by which time the ground staff had had
little scope to complete preparations, leaving the pitch an erratic batting trap.
Lloyd called correctly, invited Simpson to pad his men up and then stood
back as Roberts, Croft and Garner blasted out their quarry in 35.1 overs. In
the process, Peter Toohey, the latest new Bradman according to his advance
billing, was struck on the forehead by Roberts and escorted from the fray
with blood seeping from a horrid wound.

With a piffling score of 90 on the board Desi's nerves were less taut than
they might have been. 'I had no real contact with Gordon on a one-to-one
level. We'd opened together in a couple of Shield games and one game at
Carlton, but not that often, so I can't say there was any rapport. I was

probably a bit in awe of him, and I let him go through the gate first as a measure of my respect. There was just over an hour to go and he suggested we took it easy and try to hang on until the next morning. When he wished me good luck while I was padding up, Lloydy had told me the same thing. Because of his pace, we'd discussed Thommo more than anyone else at the team meeting, convinced that he was the main threat. Trier though he was, Wayne Clark was no Lillee.' Take it easy? Hang on? We should be grateful that wilful youth rarely obeys such incitements to moderation. Desi, reported *Wisden*, 'captivated' the 25,000-strong Queen's Park gallery by carting Thomson for 20 in an over, six of them with one of those whiplash hooks. At the close, he and Greenidge had plundered 79 in 14 overs, 53 to the junior partner. No one could remember the last time a newcomer had made such an exhilarating entrance. David Gower's pirouette and pull off Liaqat Ali at Edgbaston was still some four months distant, but even that exquisite moment was more elegy than overture.

Desi readily admits that the onslaught had its frantic overtones. 'It was a typical Trinidad wicket, neither hard nor bouncy. Obviously the adrenalin was flowing and I resolved to play more shots than ever before. At that age I didn't really know much about the game. I'd only played in a handful of first-class matches and as far as I was concerned, if I saw a ball to hit, I hit it. Now I know how to pace myself, but that day I just wanted to score as many runs as possible. I felt as if Lloydy was looking to see if I was ready. He'd missed me in Antigua and now he probably decided that this was the way I always played. I also think he thought it was good to see a young player not being overawed by the occasion.' The next morning, Desi added another eight runs before underlining his susceptibility to spin, snicking Jim Higgs's leg-break to keeper Steve Rixon. Kallicharran and Lloyd ransacked 170 in as many minutes for the fourth wicket to drive their side to 405, whereupon Roberts, Garner and Parry swept away the resistance, the last six Australians subsiding for 15 after tea on day three. Victors by an innings and 106 runs, the West Indies had also won $20,000, a bonus offered by Neal and Massy Holdings (Trinidad) in answer to the board's request for 'incentives'. Neal and Massy had also pledged another $20,000 for the fourth Test on the same ground.

The prospect of making Simmo, Thommo and the rest of the Australian 2nd XI boyos pay for past humiliations was a mouthwatering one. Yet doubt persisted over whether Lloyd and his WSC comrades would be released to participate in the official tour to India and Sri Lanka that coming October.

On 10 March, shortly before the start of Barbados' encounter with the tourists, Brunell Jones enquired whether board secretary Burnett could appraise him of the current 'situation'. 'What situation?' queried Burnett. 'I do not know of any situation.' Lloyd had already indicated to Jones that he had informed Packer of the conflicting dates and that the ringmaster was indeed willing to discuss granting permission for his acrobats to play in the traditional ring. Sticking fast to that unconvincing 'unanimity' shtick its delegates had practised at Lord's, the board, as it happened, had cabled back a wire informing Packer that on no account would it deal with him on a unilateral basis. Secretary Burnett continued to play dumb, directing Jones to take up the matter with the selectors.

The selectors, for their part, were already attracting a fusillade of flak for the decision during the first Test to relieve Deryck Murray, the secretary of the West Indies Players' Association, of the vice-captain's mantle, and hand it on to Richards. Lloyd was not consulted.

> No reason [scribbled one infuriated Bajan journalist, Don Norville]
> was given for the change which came twelve days after Murray had led
> the team successfully in the One-Day International against Australia
> at Antigua. However, it is known that two days before the Test, Murray
> was in a delegation seeking better terms and conditions from the Board
> for the professionals in the West Indies team.

Norville's suspicions were underscored by murmurs that, during the Antiguan one-dayer, Murray had intimated to the board – unofficially, of course – that the WSC players would not be available for the subcontinental trek.

Desi contributed knocks of 24, bowled by the all-rounder, Trevor Laughlin, and 40, pinned in front by Clark, as Barbados struggled to avoid an innings loss to their Australian guests, Albert Padmore's career-best 79 at No. 9 saving the day. On the eve of the Test came an odd twist in the ongoing Packer saga. Brunell Jones received a series of cables from Johannesburg advising him that the South African authorities had confirmed receipt of an invitation from the West Indies board for a party of 'merit-selected' players to tour the Caribbean. Little more proof emerged than this and, indeed, the alleged venture never got off the ground: the Caribbean peoples' mistrust of anything to do with the tools of apartheid would have clipped its wings from the outset. Yet if discussions were conducted, this underscored the confused state of the board's thinking. It also betrayed a hint of panic.

Three days after Padmore's last-ditch heroics, Desi was back on that familiar Kensington expanse for the second instalment of a series fast deteriorating into a massacre, Croft and Garner sharing eight wickets to dismantle the Aussies for 250 after Lloyd had again elected to field. Presumably chastened by Toohey's mishap in Trinidad, Graham Yallop made a revolutionary fashion statement by strutting his stuff in a helmet, a natty little white number with a visor that transmogrified the lean left-hander into an elongated Giacomo Agostini. To Desi the sight was decidedly strange. 'I was at bat-pad when Toohey got hit, and that made me think briefly about a helmet, but I couldn't afford one even if the stores had stocked them. In any case, I didn't see the need for one because I didn't have any fear. Then again, I wasn't thinking long-term. Now I've got a wife and kids and I realize that a cricketer's life is a short one, so you need to lengthen it by protecting yourself. Viv and Richie don't feel the need for a helmet but I don't think that's a macho thing. I just think it's sensible to wear one.'

In the seventy-five minutes left for play, Desi had cause to wonder whether Yallop had been the sensible one as Thomson let rip. Torsos tattooed by deliveries that rose steeply at a ferocious velocity, Greenidge was gobbled up at slip off the glove, Richards top-edged to long leg and Kallicharran parried to backward short leg, again off the glove. Desi looked on from the other end, grimacing but unbowed. 'The wicket was a lot quicker than the one in Trinidad and Thommo was very, very sharp. He was putting so much into it that his perspiration was splashing over me when I was the non-striker. He had no support from the other end. Although it was the quickest bowling I'd ever seen, he used the bouncer sparingly because it tended to soar straight over your head. He just concentrated on the ball that was fractionally short of a good length. You'd be looking to hit it off the back foot and it would whizz past your chin.'

Desi survived, adding 40 with Richards, the Antiguan accounting for 19 of these with an imperious barrage of hooks in one Thomson over. But when the new vice-captain was hoist by his own petard and Kalli fell soon after at 71, counter-attack gave way to consolidation. It was therefore with relief that the West Indies learned that Thomson had a strained leg muscle and could send down only three overs the next morning before going off for treatment. The temperature dipped, Desi and Lloyd put on 83 in 93 minutes for the fourth wicket and visions of a handy first-innings advantage improved substantially. Desi penetrated the boundary eleven times before finally going for 66 at 154 for 4, again nicking Higgs to Rixon, 'aiming to cut and trying to hit the ball too hard'. Clark instigated a slide to 198 for 6 but an alliance of 65 between Murray and Parry steered the hosts into the lead before Thomson rumbled back, finishing with 6 for 77, the most productive analysis by an Australian in a Kensington Test. Trailing by 38, Australia lost their front line in the final session of the second day and entered the third an effective 58 for 5.

The next morning, a Sunday, Brunell Jones blinked in disbelief as he scanned the scene outside the ground. Never before had he witnessed ticket touts lined up along Kensington Gap. Never before had he cast his eyes down the queue of would-be punters and seen it stretch all the way from 'Jason Jones's business place on Fontabelle Road'. 'The bloodthirsty fans', Jones observed, 'wanted the thing to be over and finished with on this day.' It was. By lunch Australia had been blown away for 178, Garner swelling his match collection to 8–121. Desi and Greenidge returned to sign off with a flourish as the requisite 141 runs were obtained at a hectic four an over. Between them, the openers racked up 16 fours and a triumvirate of sixes, Desi making 55 before falling to Higgs once more with 10 to get, the flypaper paws of the spidery Bruce Yardley accepting the catch on this occasion. Another comprehensive victory.

Amid the intoxicating brew of achievement swirled more sobering matters. While Desi was preparing to scintillate his compatriots, the West Indies board dispatched a batch of missives to all the WSC players under its jurisdiction, asking them if they would be available for the trip to India and requesting an answer by 23 March. Lloyd and Packer had already discussed the matter without arriving at a resolution, although there had been talk of the boss demanding compensation in the event of his boys trotting off to the sub-continent while the second WSC season was in progress. Packer, furthermore, was adamant that Stollmeyer and his chums should seek permission from him, not vice versa. There was more chance of spotting a winged sow flapping over Bridgetown. In the midst of all this Lloyd and his comrades had been pushing, much to the board's dismay, for a 100 per cent rise in match fees, currently EC$200. On 16 March, Lloyd stated that the WSC West Indians were ready to give up their places in the last three Tests in order to honour their Packer obligations, this in the wake of Stollmeyer's denial that they would be banned for those games. Twenty-four hours later the West Indies board confirmed that availability letters had been sent out, stirring up a host of rumours that those who declined would indeed be ditched for the last three Tests.

On 18 March – the second day of the second Test – Austin Robertson, Packer's casting agent, had flown into Bridgetown with a lawyer, Malcolm Turnbull, who also happened to write a legal column for the *Bulletin*, a Packer journal. Their purpose, said Robertson, was simply to take in a bit of cricket. Few were taken in. Robertson was seen having dinner with Lloyd that night and the two were also spied together at the players' hotel, the Caribee. The headhunter then picked out his prey and headed for Desi, having prepared the way by making phone contact after the first Test. 'When I first got into the side there was not that much talk of Packer but I knew that if I did well I might be in the frame for a place in the next WSC series. After the Trinidad Test there was talk that some people from the Packer regime were coming to watch me as a potential acquisition, and I thought Lloydy was watching me with the same thing in mind.'

Described after his Port-of-Spain pyrotechnics by one visiting Australian reporter as 'just about the most beautiful piece of batting merchandise not signed by Packer', Desi had few reservations when Austin Robertson came up with the offer he could not afford to refuse: US$20,000 for two years, plus prize money, of which Lloyd and company had split A$75,000 during that first season. 'Here was an opportunity to make more money without breaking any rules, or so I thought. It was a big decision but I spoke to Lloydy about it and he said it would be a great thing for me to do. And although I would be competing against South Africans like Procter and Pollock I would not be put in a compromising situation because we had it written into our contracts that on no account would we be going to South Africa. I also thought that, as a young man, I would have a good chance of getting back in the side if a ban ensued. I didn't realize that the English players were being treated as traitors. In any event, my mother had recently been diagnosed as having cervical cancer. I wanted to look after her. I'd always planned that the first thing I would do if I played for the West Indies would be to buy a house for my mum, then look to do everything I could to improve my grandmother's home, improve the lot of the family. The first thing newly capped players would usually do was splash out on a car, but I didn't buy one until 1980. When Austin Robertson first called me he got Packer on the phone and he assured me I'd have no problems. I talked to the other members of the team, to Hartley Richards, courted the views of many people I respected, people who I knew wouldn't lead me astray. All the same, I wanted to feel that if I was making a mistake then I would be the only one to blame.'

Hartley Richards, recently returned from Canada and now a qualified lawyer, approved heartily. 'I felt he should do it, that it was the thing to do. There was a very positive reaction to it in Barbados. Before Packer our Test cricketers had been treated very shabbily. The honour of playing for the West Indies was all. Money was secondary. Only with Packer were players paid an income commensurate with what they were putting out. Packer marketed the game and made it earn money. Yet even now, the Caribbean has yet to cotton on to the fact that cricket is a commercial activity instead of a social event, a tea party.'

Desi concurs. 'We have a marketing team now but it needs to be a paid team run by professional marketing people, working on commission. We have too many unpaid people working for the board. Everyone on a county staff is paid, so you can fire them. Here you have to wait for a board meeting and a vote. We've never really made any money from cricket in the Caribbean because of the problems inherent in having so many different dollars. I would like to see a day when all the Caribbean nations put in x amount of dollars, host the Tests and give each home board – which would be responsible for generating sponsorship – a guarantee. That way the West Indies board would not have to worry about how much money they were going to make, say, in Antigua. We should look at cricket in a businesslike manner. The board doesn't want to be losing money every time there is a series in the Caribbean. It's getting to the stage where the other Test nations are going to say, "Sorry, you're asking us for guarantees when you come to us but when we come to you we can't have one." Over the years, as I understand it, our board has been subsidized, especially by England. We don't expect to be given a break.'

During the Barbados Test Desi had had a series of meetings with the West Indies board. Unbeknown to him, the walls had ears. 'They wanted to know what was going on. I didn't let them know I was thinking of signing because I regarded it as a personal matter. I wasn't contracted to the board. In any case, the relationship between the board and the players had been a distant one over the years. If there had been a more personal touch it might have been different. Anyway, I was told that someone from the telephone company had overheard a conversation in which I said I was signing for Packer. "You can't have the best of both worlds," said Lloydy. Yet the people in Barbados supported me. I felt good about going to Packer. But I never thought for a second that I would be left out for the next Test. It was only a few days away, and some of the players were in Georgetown already.'

Arletha Haynes emphasizes that her eldest was not thinking selfishly when he accepted Robertson's invite. 'He went to Packer to help us. It was real hard. We was real poor, moving from rent house to rent house. I was worn out from looking after his brothers. But he looked after me. He was all I had to depend on when I got the sack. He helped all the members of the family circle. I took sick, got told it was cancer, so he bought me a home when the new development went up in Denny Road, furnished it too. "You don't worry, Mum," he used to say. "The first thing I'm gonna do is buy you a nice home." And he did. Then he put me in the shop. He pays for my light, electricity, water. Every month I get a $400 cheque. He tells me to send my bills to Hartley Richards. He doesn't need to do that. It's been like that since he came back from Packer. But what Desi went through, what he had to put up with, all those nasty words, was terrible. But all he would say was, "What you want to listen to people for, Mum? Ignore them." '

On 22 March the not entirely unexpected news broke. Three new signatories had been snapped up: Croft, Austin – and Desi. That same day, a board statement from Trinidad stipulated that all future Test players would have to put their monickers to contracts 'retaining their services for West Indies cricket for a reasonable length of time'. The statement also expressed its extreme disappointment that Desi, Croft and Austin had jumped ship 'and the apparent breach of trust implied'.

Come 23 March, with the third Test a mere week away, Stollmeyer insisted that the only communication he and his confreres had received had been a communiqué from the WSC players' representative, Deryck Murray, requesting that the deadline be deferred. The players, continued Stollmeyer, were 'vacillating and appeared to be under the domination of WSC'. It was time, he asserted, to take a stand. The next day, Lloyd presented the board with a letter signed by each of the pirates, advising of their future availability. Early on the morning of 27 March, the West Indian twelve for Georgetown crackled over the airwaves. Desi heard the announcement on Windle Holmes's car radio later in the day *en route* to a picnic: he was out, along with the out-of-form Austin and the militant Murray. 'Windle had just handed me some money to get an item or two of jewellery in Guyana for him when we heard the announcement. "Here's your money," I said when it became clear that my name wasn't there. I hadn't expected that after the way I played at Kensington.' He knew, however, that his omission had nothing to do with considerations of ability. The official explanation was that this step needed to be taken 'to expose more West Indian players to Test cricket in light of the commitments to future tours of India, Sri Lanka, Pakistan and New Zealand'.

It was well after midnight in Georgetown when Lloyd tuned into his bedside wireless. 'Do as you think fit,' an exasperated Packer had recently instructed him, and now Lloyd did just that. At 3 a.m. a furious Paddington rang Joey Carew, the chairman of selectors, and tendered his resignation as captain. 'I am not happy with the composition of the team,' Lloyd informed the drowsy Carew. 'I can understand Austin being left out on form but I cannot understand Murray and Haynes being dropped.' The board, he felt, should 'make very clear the principles underlying the selection of the present team and to take whoever is elected as captain into their confidence in terms of the criteria for selection'. Lloyd would later state that he had played his final Test.

The mutual hostility heightened when it was learned that Packer was winging his way to Guyana. On the afternoon of 29 March, the five remaining WSC players in the Test squad – Richards, Greenidge, Garner, Croft and Roberts – sent telegrams to Harold Burnett, withdrawing their labour. A new team was assembled with due haste, captained by Kallicharran. It was hard to deny that the board had been placed in a difficult, if not quite intolerable position. It owed a certain debt to the cricketing establishment, but would a mutually beneficial chat with Packer really have been such a crime? One can only assume that fear of ostracism, plus a smidgin of leftover imperialist sensibilities, lay at the heart of it all. In the circumstances, the next move, taken on the advice of Sir Lionel Lucknow, the Guyanan barrister and owner of the world record for acquitting accused murderers, was unavoidable. 'In view of the decision of the WSC players to withdraw from representing the West Indies in this Test,' Stollmeyer told a press conference at Georgetown's Pegasus Hotel, 'the West Indies Board, in the interests of the future of West Indies cricket, has decided that these players will take no further part in the series.' The meat mangler had done its worst.

Accompanied by his private secretary and the WSC West Indies manager, Dr Rudi Webster, Packer hopped aboard a chartered jet in Miami the next afternoon, touched down in Georgetown and checked into the Pegasus. A few lengths of the pool and he was ready to address his beloved media. He was there, he insisted, 'to meet some of the players I have never met, and to have a look at the cricket'. The ban was 'a tragedy', the whole business preventable. All the board needed to do was shift the Indian tour back a couple of weeks, he reasoned, and so keep everything hunky dory. 'But nobody wanted to discuss that. It's a bit late now to be talking about it.' He did, however, indicate that he was willing to talk over the possibility of bringing WSC to the islands. Not surprisingly, his request for a pow-wow with the board was turned down and so Packer proceeded to Barbados, dispatching planes to transport his Caribbean employees to ritzy Sandy Lane and laying on a sumptuous reunion party. Desi took to him. 'He was a big man in every sense of the word and I liked him. He seemed like someone who meant well. He wanted to make money, sure, but he also had a great feeling for the game and he knew that the players deserved to be better rewarded. He also made sure you realized that it was serious cricket you'd signed up for, not some knockabout affair.' Desi would soon discover how serious.

Support for the players among press and public was wholehearted. The Jamaica *Daily News* charged the administrators with 'bungling, slitting their own throats, being guilty of asinine statements and lacking the courage of their own convictions'. On 4 April, the Pan African Secretariat, a radical Jamaican group, claimed to have mobilized 100,000 people to boycott the fifth Test at Sabina Park while calling for the removal of 'autocratic, oligarchic planter-class representatives' from the board. A week later, the Committee in Defence of West Indies Cricket was launched in Trinidad, resolving, among other things, that 'the West Indies Cricket Board of Control has acted in a high-handed and arrogant manner with no regard for the interest of the Cricketers and cricket-loving people of the West Indies' and, 'acting as lords and barons, have continued to administer West Indies Cricket in their [the Board's] selfish interest, adopting at all times a Massa [ownership] policy in dealing with the West Indies cricketers'. The CIDWIC called on Packer to bring his pack to the Caribbean, on Trinidadians to boycott the fourth Test (due to start in Port-of-Spain four days hence) and on the board to resign *en masse*.

Not the least fascinating element of the politicking was the refusal of the Australians, in stark contrast to their English counterparts, to whinge about playing ball with the WSC brigade. The inquisition panel no longer populated by a horde of Torquemadas, Simpson and his embattled team took the third Test by three wickets, lost the fourth (the Trinidadians staying home in droves) and drew the fifth when one wicket short of victory, a riot sparked by Vanburn Holder's reluctance to leave the crease upon being given out bringing a turbulent series to an abrupt and not inappropriately bitter end.

And so, almost as soon as it had begun, Desi's Test career appeared to be over. A hefty dose of compromise, a word not readily associated with these Montagues and Capulets, would be needed to revive it, although most of the WSC brotherhood were confident that the war would be over, if not by Christmas, then certainly not long after. World Series Cricket, after all, had lost an estimated A$3.7 million in its first year of operation, and attendances for the *bona fide* product – the Australia–India series – were double the 127,000 who turned out for the Supertests. The loss of the best players, however, could only be absorbed while the tide of righteous indignation was in.

'The problem from the outset,' Ian Wooldridge would later maintain in the *Daily Mail*, 'was that Establishment cricket was blinded by outrage. Its English administrators, most of whom cast their votes for private enterprise at the last election, panicked badly when actually confronted by it.'

Gordon Greenidge casts a rational eye back on those acrimonious months. 'There was a need to make the Establishment aware that all your efforts were not properly rewarded. It was not a matter of getting back at them but showing them that your job was not an easy one, not one to be sniffed at. We didn't jump at it for the sake of it. It was something that had to be done. We needed that recognition, and we deserved it.'

Whatever direction the plot took from here, one development was inevitable: cricket would never return to the cosy, sepia-tinted days of yore. Technicolor and Sensurround, come on down.

5

Dancing with Mr D

It makes me laugh when I hear the anti-Packer lobby telling me
how to spend my winters. When I was a teenager, the same sort
of people did not give a damn what I did between September
and April.

Gordon Greenidge, 1980

If Desi, by his own admission, had no inkling of how his fellow circus acts
were being treated in England, a lull during the game between Kent and
Leicestershire in the summer of 1978 would have sufficed as evidence. Jack
Birkenshaw, the former Test off-spinner and current Leicestershire manager,
quipped to Kent's vaunted WSC trapeze artist Derek Underwood that the
latter might do well to pin a handkerchief to his back so as to ward off the
press hounds. The wording on the handkerchief, he proposed, should be
direct, pithy and preferably in capital letters: 'UNCLEAN'. True, Wayne Prior, the
South Australian fast bowler, had lost his job as a driver when he signed for
Packer, but the victimization in England was more insidious. (Nottinghamshire
compromised by ditching Clive Rice as captain and keeping him on the staff.)

Back in the Caribbean, further signs of appeasement. The Aussies had
gone but the dilemma had not. The Barbados Cricket Association and its
Jamaican counterpart were coming under intense public pressure to use their
influence at board level to reopen negotiations with Packer. On 22 May,
Stollmeyer, Rae, Short and the rest closed their AGM by jointly stating that
they were willing to initiate dialogue between Packer and the ICC. Within

six months the back-tracking board had obtained what it had always seemed
to crave: a WSC tour, naughty but nice.

The board sanctioned the enterprise, the BCA gave its 'blessing and encouragement'. Neal and Massy, as eager to support Test cricket as the WSC
model, undertook to underwrite the Supertest series – scheduled for the
following spring – to the tune of £50,000. Ovaltine would chip in with the
Man of the Series award (worth US$2000). The prize money per Test would
be US$7200, per one-dayer US$1000, Man of the Match US$200 per game.
Agreements were reached to site the major matches at the Test grounds (only
Kensington Oval is not club-owned so it was alone in having to grant approval
as opposed to bartering with Packer on an individual basis) while WSC offered
a goodwill grant of around £30,000. Neither the amenities nor the economic
wherewithal to install them were up to staging night games, but Hall, Gibbs
and Sobers – whose name, incidentally, had been inscribed on the trophy
competed for by Chappell's side and Lloyd's – would be at hand to conduct
coaching sessions. Organizing committees were established in each of the
venues, comprising WSC reps and local officials. These committees were
guaranteed an *ex gratia* payment on top of either a 15 per cent share of the
gate receipts or a set sum agreed in advance. Although admission prices were
raised to £3, the fans, thirsty for a top-class product, were not to be dissuaded,
and the 15 per cent turned out to be by far the more profitable alternative.
When Ben Hoyos, for twenty-seven years the secretary of the BCA, joined
the Barbados organizing committee, this was interpreted in some quarters as
a conflict of interests. Why? reasoned Hoyos. It was no different from acting
on behalf of the procession of visiting clubs from England.

Gordon Greenidge has mixed memories of his first WSC campaign. 'We
had a tough time because we were still expected to win, even though not all
the regular members of the team were there. It felt very different. It almost
felt, at least in terms of our country, as if we were forgotten men. That said,
the competitiveness was there and, for the first time, we were training properly, harder than ever. Dennis Waight had been attached to us and that, in
many ways, was the start of a new era. If the West Indies board still have
any animosity towards the players, West Indian cricket certainly benefited
from the advent of Waight.' Desi reinforces this view. 'I used to work out
on the beach a bit back home, do a bit of karate, some jogging. Dennis taught
us how to stretch, do sit-ups, do laps, get fit, fit to compete as Lloydy would
say.' Not for another decade would England follow suit.

Come the second campaign, the West Indies, loins girded and resolve strengthened, were knitting together as a close, committed unit. Desi, however, endured a ruder awakening than he had anticipated. 'I expected it to be tough, but not that tough. It was the toughest cricket I've ever known. Although the pre-prepared wickets were OK, the pitches generally favoured the bowlers and you had to be perpetually on your guard, more wary about throwing the bat. The experience bonded us, no doubt about that. The sense of playing for the West Indies was no different and there was certainly a little bit of needle, although that was mostly triggered by the hype. People were offended by the marketing, the huge billboards, the TV ads, the McDonald's connection, the never-ending strains of, 'C'mon Aussie, c'mon', but most of them are now doing the very same thing to sell their product. Off the field we mixed well. Meeting guys like Sobers and Ian Chappell was a great experience for me: I probably bored them silly with my endless chatter at post-game functions. In terms of my own form I didn't do as well as expected. I suppose I simply lacked the requisite knowledge and experience.' The experience afforded an invaluable lesson. Full sobriety would take a while, but the dervish days were over.

In Australia and New Zealand finger injuries proved problematic. Opportunities were limited and rarely grasped. Included at an unaccustomed No. 5 in the order for the first Supertest against Asif Iqbal's bejewelled World XI, Desi reached 14 before driving Garth Le Roux to Javed Miandad, then went three better before being run out when the West Indies followed on, to lose by an innings. Desi's 43 at Cairns in a two-day defeat by the scratch Cavaliers side was his most significant contribution before the Caribbean leg. To put these struggles into perspective, it should be noted that only Rowe and Lloyd among the West Indians averaged over 30 in the five-day fixtures, Hookes and Kepler Wessels keeping up a similar mean for the Australians. Notwithstanding the bumps and bruises to body and ego, Desi, an early riser, found resetting the body clock to fit in with all those twilight battles as tough a task as any. 'Wake up, you lazy lot,' barked Mushtaq Mohammad to his drowsy World XI colleagues en route to a rare morning start. 'You've got to get used to this daytime cricket.'

Normality of sorts returned when the troupers moved on to the Caribbean, although, not for the first time, there were bottle-throwing spectaculars in Barbados and Trinidad and, most grievously of all, a full-scale riot in Georgetown. In the first Supertest at Kingston, Desi was restored to the top of the order to partner Richard Austin, but fell short of double figures in both innings, run out for 9 and caught off Lillee for 8. No matter. Lloyd's 197 and a defiant 89 from Andy Roberts, augmented by some incisive bowling from Holding and Croft, sped the hosts to a thumping 369-run victory, a highly satisfactory outcome to a contest marred by Rowe's failure to pick up the flight of a cruel short-pitcher from Thomson against the lower section of the newly constructed George Headley stand. 'If they were diving, he got up their shirts,' said Greg Chappell of Lloyd's galvanizing presence at the helm. 'He hated losing. I think behind the scenes he would be standing a few up in the corner and asking them to take a look in the mirror.' Greenidge supplies confirmation. 'There were moments when he got upset, bitterly angry, particularly when things didn't happen as he wanted, when you didn't look him straight in the eye. But he's only human. Everyone looked up to him.'

The electric atmosphere at Sabina, bordering at times on the riotous according to the visitors, was offset by the general bonhomie. 'Hey, Kent, you been to South Africa?' boomed a voice from behind the chicken-wire fencing while Martin Kent, who had indeed played in the Republic three years earlier, was fielding on the boundary. The slimline strokeplayer stepped four paces forward for safety's sake, then turned and nodded. 'Are you going again?' persisted the enquirer. 'No, no, not me,' Kent sensibly avowed, triggering a spontaneous round of cheers.

Bridgetown was more combustible. Opening this time with Greenidge after leading the line with 59 in a one-day fixture, Desi managed four first time up, taken at slip off Thomson by Hookes as the West Indies stumbled to 239 all out in reply to Australia's 311. Chasing 367 more in hope than expectation, the West Indies were stuttering on 133 for 4, Desi having been caught behind off Lillee for 9, when Austin was adjudged caught at the wicket off the lively Lennie Pascoe. Austin left the gallery in little doubt as to his interpretation of the ruling and the bottles began raining down in sympathy, enough to cause an abandonment. Desi was dropped for the next Supertest at Port-of-Spain, where the plucky Bruce Laird's 122 on a dicey pitch was the only score over 50 in the sides' respective first innings, Australia proceeding to squeeze home by 24 runs in a coruscating climax. Trevor Chappell, the youngest member of the flannelled filial triumvirate, was stationed at fine leg when the first glass missile somersaulted into the outfield. 'Right,' said Trev, disdaining big brother Ian's suggestion that he come to the sanctuary of the middle and turning instead to face his purported assailants, 'if you throw them at me they're coming back at you.' Again, umpiring decisions were regarded as the flashpoints.

And so to Guyana. Desi remained out of favour, blocked as much by the fact that Roy Fredericks had tapped a rich vein of form as by his own inadequacies, and he looked on from the perimeter as Collis King (110) and Deryck Murray (82) constructed a commanding total of 476 and an equally auspicious lead of 135. The Australians, with three men gone, had yet to clear their arrears when the third day ended. Overnight rain saturated the ground but the island's lone Sunday paper contained a premature quote from a WSC official assuring the public that play would commence on time provided it stayed dry. The disciples began to file in at 7 a.m., against the wishes of the Australians, who had pleaded for the gates to be shut until it was reasonably certain that play would restart. By the time the teams arrived at ten, 13,000 were jammed into the ground, a goodly number intoxicated on rum and beer. The pitch was fit for action but the surrounds patently were not. The inspections came and went. Not until forty minutes after the 2 p.m. recce did the PA announcer inform the throng that battle would recommence – at 3.30.

That tore it. One spectator grabbed a microphone and barked: 'There's nothing wrong with the pitch. I've just inspected it, play should start immediately.' At 3.10 the first bottle sailed over the boundary and straight through the clock on the main stand, stopping it with a symbolic finality. An angry mob burst through the wire fences, ransacked the pavilion and rampaged on, wrecking the bar and administrative office dividing the two dressing rooms. Enter the riot police, cue tear gas. An armed guard closed the french windows leading on to the Australian players' balcony then promptly saw them destroyed by a hail of rocks. When the initial eruption had been defused, the players were escorted to their respective coaches by armed guards. By now the place was in a shambles. The outfield was strewn with benches, chairs and broken glass. Two of the West Indians reported cuts. The club would subsequently seek a £30,000 advance from WSC to help repair the damage.

Desi reruns the mental video. 'It was a very frightening experience, the scariest moment of my life. We saw this guy run on to the field and roll around on the pitch to indicate to the rest of the crowd that it was dry. The crowd had been sitting patiently for hours and by now they were soaked in alcohol. It must have appeared as if we had no respect for them. I'd have loved to have gone on and stopped what ensued. Then I spotted somebody making off with the cash register and all hell broke loose, so we barricaded ourselves in our respective dressing rooms. A lot of the players stuck their helmets on, wrapped towels around their arms and grabbed bats for self-defence. I was cowering in the bathroom and suddenly there was this policeman beside me doing likewise. That's when I knew it was serious.' The match, needless to say, was abandoned.

To lay the blame solely at the door of the ground authorities and organizing committee, maintained Frank Walcott, the president of the Caribbean Congress of Labour, would be short-sighted and fallacious. 'This regional explosion', he countered, 'is more than sporting discontent to be identified with an unpopular decision by an umpire or the judgement of the administration of those who control sporting events. This is a growing sign of social discontent in the area.' This reasoning could perhaps have been applied to a subsequent assault on Viv Richards in St John's. Attacked by a man wielding an iron bar, Richards sustained a jaw injury and a broken little finger, causing him to miss the first two months of the county season. The same rationale, however, could scarcely excuse another violent interlude around the same time as the riot, wherein the WSC PR officer in Guyana, Vic Insanally, was verbally insulted and punched in the stomach by Ian Chappell, an incident that cost the Australian captain G$150 in fines and quite a deal of face.

The final Supertest in Antigua was another stalemate, albeit a more natural one, Desi coming up short once more when trapped leg-before by Lillee for 9 in his only innings. A sparky 61 in a Port-of-Spain one-dayer was not much compensation, and when the last engagement at Basseterre was washed out, WSC shut up shop for good. At the end of April, much to the disgruntlement of the English authorities in particular, the ACB, chastened by a loss of A$445,000 on the Ashes series, consented to dance with the devil. Not unexpectedly, Packer got his exclusive TV deal, for an initial period of three years. Less forgivably, to English eyes at least, the board positively dived into bed with the enemy a month later, granting PBL Pty Ltd, a subsidiary of Packer's Consolidated Press, sole rights to promote Australian cricket for the next ten years. In exchange, World Series Cricket, whose burgeoning threat to the established game had been underlined by aggregate gates of 730,000 for the eighty-five days of alternative cricket played Down Under that winter, would cease operations. Acknowledging the success of some of the WSC inventions, the ACB agreed to 'consider favourably' the introduction of fielding circles, day/night games and coloured clothing.

Desi's delight at this armistice was tempered by regret. Greater exposure to the school of hard knocks, he felt, would have been beneficial: 'I was glad to be back in the fold but I wouldn't have minded two more years.' He returned to Shell Shield duty, the competition having been postponed for two months to accommodate the WSC show. Any fears about missing the World Cup were assuaged by a striking 107 against Guyana to set up a crushing innings victory that sealed Barbados' third Shield on the trot. Fredericks had gone for good; now it was Desi's turn.

So Packer was right. The dictators (Justice Slade's choice of word) did have a little of the whore in them. Before the next decade was out, they had become proficient enough to draw an approving wink from Myra Breckenridge. Rupert Murdoch would be permitted to purchase exclusive rights to cover the 1989–90 West Indies–England series on behalf of his upstart satellite TV tentacle, Sky; the Oval would be rechristened the Foster's Oval (the Boddington's Oval would at least have been more patriotic); sponsors' logos would be emblazoned in lime across outfields from Edgbaston to Eden Gardens. Heaven forbid, in 1992, the MCC would give the thumbs-up to multi-coloured garb. Is nothing sacred? Test cricket, maybe. Without these concessions to social change, first demanded by Packer, the state of the art would no longer be cost-effective. In some places it isn't. India, who replaced a Test with a brace of one-dayers in 1987, did not stage a home series between 1988 and 1993. The age of innocence was over, for Desi as well as the rest of cricket.

6

A New World

England is not ruined because sinewy brown men from a distant
colony sometimes hit a ball further and oftener than we do.

J. B. Priestley

By contrast to their winter labours, the summer of 1979, with its promise of
World Cup overflow, was not far short of light relief for Desi and his CARI-
COM cohorts. Bonded together in adversity, they were now a unit of rare
balance (excepting spin, of course), welding aggressive batsmanship with
potent pace and a vigorous, collective purpose.

They were also on a hiding to nothing. That swaggering triumph in 1975
had singled them out as the Fast Eddie Felsons of the one-day hustle and
nothing had happened in the interim to alter that perception. Indeed, with
Holding, Croft and Garner displacing Keith Boyce, Julien and Holder, the
attack was immeasurably stronger, while Lloyd, Richards, Greenidge and
Kallicharran (the only non-WSC player to find a place in the post-Packer XI)
remained as forceful a batting nucleus as the medium had thrown up. That
Australia and England – though not Pakistan – had elected to sally forth
without their Packer players served merely to gild the lily. Even with the
opposition at full strength, Lloyd and his flock would still have been too
powerful, sheepish English pitches or no. As for Desi, this was an opportunity
to plant his feet under the table. Despite his WSC tribulations, Lloyd and
the selectors believed he warranted a chance amid the easier going. The mood
during the build-up, Desi asserts, was appropriately self-assured. 'We did feel
a certain pressure to win the cup again but, thanks to all the exposure to

one-day cricket we'd had through Packer, there was plenty of confidence. We knew we were the best side by far.'

India were unable to contradict this assertion when the tournament opened on a perfect surface at Edgbaston on 9 June, Roberts and Holding extracting the most from the early morning moisture to reduce a more than useful batting line-up to 119 for 7, and although the dapper Gundappa Viswanath battled his way to a game 75, the holders seemed unlikely to be stretched by a target of 191. Nor were they, Desi playing a sturdy second violin to Greenidge in an extended prelude worth 138 before being pinned in front by Kapil Dev for 47. Victors by nine wickets, the West Indies proceeded to the Oval only to endure three days of thumb-twiddling as rain sank their contest with Sri Lanka. New Zealand put up a gritty struggle at Trent Bridge, Desi leg before to the hostile Richard Hadlee for 12 out of a so-so total of 244 for 7 from 60 overs, whereupon the pace quartet restricted Mark Burgess's gritty conglomerate to 212 for 9.

The semi-final against Pakistan at the Oval was riveting. Spared on 32 when Imran downed a hook at long leg off Mudassar Nazar, Desi drove sweetly to contribute 65 to a belligerent opening alliance of 132 that propelled the West Indies towards the highest score of the tournament thus far, 293 for 6. At 176 for 1 with Majid and Zaheer in excelsis, Pakistan were in with a shout, but Croft uprooted both in quick succession and the last six batsmen were felled for 47 to leave the favourites victorious by 43 runs. And so to Lord's, where the hosts, narrow conquerors of New Zealand, lay in wait.

Desi was rooming with Richards. 'On the day of the final Viv got up, and before he went to the bathroom, before he'd even said good morning, he stretched and said, "There's going to be a lot of people at Lord's today. It would be a good time to really turn it on." You could see it was on his mind. Millions watching on TV, big crowd, major occasion.' Irrepressible showman that he was, Richards duly turned it on – and how – though not before some early hiccups. Inserted by Mike Brearley, the West Indies soon lost Greenidge, run out by the live-wire Derek Randall from midwicket after calling Desi for a short single. Joined by his roommate, Desi himself reached 20 before bowing to Chris Old. 'I had a few early nerves as usual, but they soon went and I was feeling confident, confident enough to go through with my drives until I edged one low to Mike Hendrick at slip.' Hendrick followed up by nudging Kallicharran's leg stump and when Old reacted instinctively to intercept Lloyd's return drive one-handed, the West Indies were labouring at 99 for 4. 'That', Desi acknowledges, 'was the one time we felt we might lose.'

The feeling was soon dispelled. Aided by England's defensive selection of six specialist batsmen in addition to Ian Botham, which left Brearley with the thankless task of dividing 12 overs between Boycott, Graham Gooch and Wayne Larkins, Richards now added lustre to the occasion in cahoots with Collis King, the fifth-wicket duo lashing 139 in 77 minutes. Enjoying his finest hour, King, the West Indies' nearest approximation to an all-rounder, crashed 86 of these while Richards swept on to a magisterial undefeated 138 out of a towering 286 for 9, composing a stirring coda by stepping far outside off stump to deposit Hendrick into the Mound Stand off the innings' last ball. The composite fifth bowler went for 86 in 12 overs. Desi is proud to claim a share in the mayhem. 'Collis was wearing my half-spiked Adidas trainers. "It was my shoes, man," I informed him afterwards.' Boycott and Brearley gave their team a sound launch by adding 129, but the 38 overs they consumed in doing so passed a daunting buck. To Desi, the approach was misplaced. 'Maybe it was England's plan to keep wickets in hand but there is no way Gordon and I would have batted like that. It put too much pressure on the later batsmen.' So it proved as Garner cranked up his yorker and whisked through the frantically flailing middle order, twice taking wickets with consecutive deliveries during a spell of 5 for 4 in 11 balls, four of the victims clean bowled. The margin, 92 runs, could hardly have been more conclusive.

Potential reaffirmed, Desi returned to Australia for a three-Test tour hastily arranged by the home board to maximize the benefits of its marriage to the forces of commercialism. England were also invited, and accepted only after much humming and hawing. Objecting to the short notice and the unprecedented preponderance of Tests and one-day internationals, they declined to put up the Ashes for grabs, a decision that provoked a cynical reaction from the Australian public. For the first time since the revolution, each of the combatants would be at optimum manpower for a Test series.

Desi sped away in bullish fashion, top-scoring in both innings against Geelong and District with 64 and 59, then contributing 58 and 18 not out to the nine-wicket win over South Australia. As a dart out of the stalls it was deceptive. Dismissed for 22 and 14 in the 260-run waltz over a Tasmanian Invitation XI, he began the Benson and Hedges World Series Cup with 29 against Australia – one of four scalps for a sometime slow left-armer named Allan Border – and 4 against England, both games, to general astonishment, ending in defeat. He and Greenidge gave West Indies a fine start in response to Australia's 268 in the first Test at Brisbane, adding 68 before Desi thinedged his old mucker Thomson into the gloves of Rod Marsh, but with nothing to play for bar pride after Greg Chappell and Kim Hughes had saved the match with contrasting centuries, he fell leg before to the fiery Rodney Hogg for 4 on the final day.

A surefooted 80 out of a 205-run stand for the second wicket with the rumbustious Richards engineered a comfortable victory over Australia in the next one-day jaunt at Melbourne. This was succeeded by a fluent 74 against a Victorian Country XI then countered by a Lillee-inflicted duck in another limited-overs foray. Conspiring with Greenidge for an opening worth 109 he made 41 in the second joust with Brearley's Englishmen then embarked on a disturbing, if not quite headlong, descent. Aside from a 60 against Western Australia (in what was essentially no more than a beer match) and 50 against an Australian Capital Territory and District combine, Desi failed to reach 30 for the remainder of the tour.

If substance was lacking, there was no shortage of style. The basic fault remained overt aggression, handsome hell-for-leatherings repeatedly cut short by impetuosity. In the second Test at Melbourne, he greeted Hogg with a torrent of shots, extracting three boundaries and 16 all told from the asthmatic bowler's first over, only to nick a Lillee outswinger to second slip on 29. Undefeated with 9 as he and Greenidge tied up a 10-wicket victory before tea on day four, the happiest of New Year's Days, Desi had the decided consolation of assisting in the West Indies' inaugural success at the MCG after seven defeats in as many attempts. Having seen off England in two games to take the best-of-three World Series Cup finals (they even nicked the name), the now rampant tourists took a giant stride at Adelaide, chalking up the sixth widest Test victory in terms of runs – 408 – to win their first series Down Under. Desi managed 28 and 27, a wild swing off the wily off-spinner Ashley Mallett finding Lillee waiting at backward square leg to end an alliance of 104 with Richards in the first dig, a more composed knock in the second terminated by an unanswerable leg-cutter from Pascoe.

In Lloyd's view, the crux of Desi's inability to capitalize on his flying starts lay in matter rather than mind. Desi is less sure. 'I was still learning my trade, but Clive suggested the reason I was getting out in the twenties was because I wasn't fit enough to concentrate for long periods. I didn't agree. In fact, I thought it was a bit harsh, and I remind him of that to this day. The upshot was that I spent the lunch intervals running up and down the steps of the main stand and doing exercises with Dennis Waight, sometimes with Garner in tow.' Not that this could detract from Desi's pride in being part of an historic expedition. 'We were more settled than we were during the WSC days, more of a unit. Kalli had returned, the fast men were irresistible and Viv was unstoppable.'

On an individual level, Desi took stock and prospered, but corporate anti-climax beckoned. Enthusiasm sapped after fulfilling their main objective, Lloyd and crew (minus the injured Richards) flew reluctantly on to New Zealand and straight into the arms of controversy. Desi and Greenidge put on 81 on a lively track at Christchurch in the one-day international, but the first cracks in the edifice became evident as the fielding buckled during New Zealand's successful chase.

In the first Test at Dunedin two days later, the fissures began to widen. Lloyd, reckoning, perhaps, that it could only get worse, elected to bat on a surface offering occasionally subterranean bounce and prodigious movement off the seam, a vastly more watchful Desi being alone in having the nous to combat these idiosyncrasies by ploughing on to the front foot. Three and a half hours of restraint brought him 55 out of a pallid 140, more than double that of any other contributor. Holding, Croft and Garner then committed the cardinal sin of pitching short, 50s from Bruce Edgar and Hadlee ensuring a deficit of 109 before the elements restricted the third day to seventy minutes, long enough, nevertheless, for Hadlee to dispose of Greenidge. It was Desi versus Hadlee on the next, the former constructing his maiden 100 at this level out of the semi-ruins of 29 for 4, the latter dislodging six of his colleagues and leaving his side only 104 for victory. Headingley '81, it seems pertinent to point out, was more than a year away. Notwithstanding this parlous predicament, Desi's fortitude had earned him a unique distinction. Last out on each occasion, never in Test cricket's previous 872 chapters had anyone batted throughout both innings of a match.

Tempers frayed, however, amid the general frustration. When John Parker survived a convincing appeal for caught behind off Holding twenty minutes before lunch on the final day, the infuriated bowler, in an atypical display of petulance brought on by the latest in a series of hotly disputed adjudications, took careful aim with his right boot and divorced the batsman's stumps from their moorings. At 44 for 6, then 73 for 8, a remarkable fightback was in the offing, but Hadlee and Lance Cairns held fast until tea, at which point nine more runs were required. Holding caressed Cairns' off stump one run later only for the bails to defy most of gravity's regulations, then had Cairns caught behind as soon as the 100 came up. Enter Stephen Boock, capable left-arm spinner, incompetent bat. Boock somehow repelled Holding's next five deliveries, and handed the reins over to Gary Troup. Anxious not to reclaim the strike, Boock was all but run out trying to turn one bye into two from Garner's first ball, had a close call for lbw from the next, contrived to steer two runs behind point off the fifth to bring the scores level, then scampered a leg-bye from the last as the ball rebounded off his pads behind square leg, Derick Parry throwing to the non-striker's end and missing the target with something to spare. For only the sixth time in Test history, victory had been achieved with one wicket standing, but the tourists were in no mood to shake hands. The most telling statistic to emerge from a truculent set-to was the number of lbws, an unprecedented 12, seven of them to Hadlee.

As the series progressed, or, rather, regressed, Desi fiddled merrily while his buddies grew increasingly hot under the collar. Snared at slip off Hadlee for a duck on the first morning at Christchurch, he subsequently led a resourceful rearguard action with a strident 122, adding 225 with Greenidge – just 14 shy of the national record – to all but erase the first innings arrears. Stalemate also ensued at Auckland, where rain robbed the West Indies of any chance of an equalizing win and Desi confirmed his new-found adhesiveness. In the first innings he expended seventy minutes breaking his duck before falling to Cairns for 9, then contributed 48 to an opening stand of 86 by way of prefacing a futile declaration.

The drama, distressingly, revolved around the histrionics. Driven to distraction in Christchurch after Fred Goodall had turned down an appeal against the home captain, Geoff Howarth, and the authorities had rejected their plea for the offending umpire to be replaced, the West Indies lingered in the dressing room long after the end of tea on the third afternoon, seething with discontent and ready to pack their bags. When they eventually re-emerged after twelve minutes, a mild form of work-to-rule was imposed as fielders frequently ignored the ball when it was hit in their direction. Only after prolonged negotiations on the rest day with the New Zealand Board of Control were the aggrieved party dissuaded from returning home. The following morning, Goodall gave Hadlee the benefit of the doubt when Croft was convinced he had done enough to warrant a leg before, whereupon the irate bowler, having previously flicked off a bail in response to being no-balled, barged into the burly umpire in the process of sending down the next delivery. 'It was the height of discourtesy,' noted Dick Brittenden in *Wisden*, 'when Goodall, wishing on two occasions to speak to Lloyd about Croft's behaviour, had to walk all the way to the West Indian captain, standing deep in the slips. Lloyd took not a step to meet him.' The West Indies manager, Willie Rodriguez, accused the umpires of incompetence rather than bias, even though both he and Lloyd had advocated neutral officials. On his return to the Caribbean, however, Rodriguez asserted that the tourists had been 'set up'. There was, he argued, 'no way we could win a Test' because, in his opinion, the bowlers had to dismiss each batsman at least ten times in order to gain an affirmative ruling. With the home country celebrating its fiftieth anniversary as a member of the Test fraternity, he alleged, 'they were determined to do something about it'.

Eminently satisfied with his own performance in leading the specialist batsmen with 339 runs at 56.50, disturbed by the accompanying acrimony, Desi admits to conflicting sentiments towards one of cricket's most depressing episodes. 'We were a bit tired mentally and we simply did not adapt to the conditions as well as we should have, coming as we had from wickets where the ball was being fired past your chest to exceedingly slow ones. Had we gone there before Australia I don't think any of it would have happened. As it was, everyone struggled, leading to a sense of frustration that bubbled over with regard to the umpiring. Make no mistake, the umpiring was bad. There were some ridiculous decisions. The New Zealanders were a very quiet lot and extremely apologetic about it. Just before Holding kicked down the stumps Parker was taking his gloves off as if ready to walk to the dressing room. Michael [Holding] was very frustrated but people couldn't understand it in him.'

The miscreant himself feels his anger was justified. 'It pains me to talk about it, but there were too many examples of bad umpiring, and all against one team. I don't call that fair.'

'I didn't like Croft's barge at all,' Desi continues, 'but the media blew it all up. Some photographers went into one of the dressing rooms at Auckland, took a picture of a cardboard wall with a hole in it and the press later made out as if we had kicked it in. The whole thing was so distasteful. People were surprised when they met us that we were actually quite nice!

'Normally, it all boils down to the captain in that situation. Lloydy should have taken matters into his own hands, but it was difficult for him to maintain control and keep us motivated. It was also difficult for me because I was having a good time! When we discussed going home at Christchurch and I was asked for my views, I said: "I'm a young man, I'm scoring runs and I'm happy, so there's no reason for me to go home." Everyone accepted that. It was a ridiculous situation. It seemed as if we were never going to get a favourable decision, yet I wanted to get out there again. When we did get back on the field a couple of balls went down to fine leg and people didn't bother running after them. The bowlers were going through the motions. They weren't bothered. But you should always go on. Funnily enough, the spirit between the sides was good. The New Zealanders were cool guys.'

Lloyd looks back in genuine anguish. 'That was one of the periods in my life that I wish I could wipe off. It was regrettable, a stain. But one series like that in eleven years is not too bad. It was down to provocation and incompetence, the umpires in other words. We just felt Goodall was not a very good umpire, and nor were quite a lot of the others. One day we were off for four hours because of rain, then went out to play for ten minutes and lost a wicket. Ten fucking minutes. Competent umpires wouldn't do that. I think the New Zealand players were aware of it too, although from then on their cricket took a decided turn for the better. For us it was one tour too many.'

Not for Desi. Any uncertainty over his temperament and technique being up to scratch at the highest level was confounded at Dunedin, as Holding confirms. 'It was overcast, the wicket was green and the ball was moving around, but Desi is a fighter. He sensibly restricted his range of shots, pushed his left foot down the wicket and put doubt in the umpire's mind. In fact, I can't remember him ever going on to the back foot. He'd developed his game in the incredible intensity that was World Series Cricket. He was no longer "Hammer" Haynes.'

The ex-Hammer, naturally enough, was delighted with that maiden 100. 'It was freezing. We put towels under our doors in the hotel to keep out the draught. The crowd was small and the atmosphere totally different to Australia, the pitch was very slow, we were losing wickets regularly and Hadlee was bowling very well. I had a lot of respect for him. If the wicket had a bit in it he could do all sorts of things with the ball, but whatever the conditions, he was always so straight. All in all, I was happy with the way I adjusted. I'd been getting good starts in Australia without going on, so I was determined to make amends.'

Having done so, Desi returned home in March to help Barbados land the Shell Shield for the fifth successive year, a feat embellished by four outright victories, the first time this had been accomplished. Averaging 51.20 with half-centuries against Guyana, Trinidad and the Combined Islands, he set off for England determined to put one over the sceptics who believed the conditions would find him out. 'I was wary of the moving ball, aware that I had to adjust. There were a lot of negative vibes from people in the Caribbean. They felt I wouldn't be able to cope, so I wanted to prove them wrong.'

On the early evidence at least, this appeared an unlikely proposition. In the opening first-class fixture at Worcester, Desi's fellow Bajan, Hartley Alleyne, pinned him leg-before for a duck, and although there was consolation in the knock of 41 that guided his side to a seven-wicket victory, his next outing at Milton Keynes against Northamptonshire produced meagre returns of 4 and 5, Jim Griffiths' workmanlike fast-medium undoing him on both occasions. An unbeaten 52 in a one-day cruise against Middlesex succeeded by a top score of 46 in a limited-overs defeat by Essex hinted at better things, and the revival was underlined when he and Richards walloped 230 in 38 overs in the second one-day bash at Chelmsford to send Desi into the Pruden-tial Trophy series in good heart. Dismissed for 19 by Chris Old in the first encounter at Leeds, he scored the only half-century in the West Indies' 235 for 9 at Lord's as England levelled matters only to lose out overall on run-rate. The logic of a two-match series was hard to comprehend.

Another 50, this time an undefeated effort against Kent, was instrumental in the tourists extending their 100 per cent sequence in first-class games to five, ideal preparation for the first Test at Trent Bridge. This enthralling contest, as it transpired, was to provide the only decisive result of the rubber, and Desi played his part to the hilt. Caught at cover for 12 in Bob Willis's fifth over, after a useful English batting order had struggled to 263 on a Ron Allsopp creation that bestowed its ample favours on seam and swing alike, he watched Deryck Murray secure a lead of 45 before Garner and Roberts dismantled England a second time. Requiring 208 in a shade over eight hours, the West Indies struck an early reef when Willis had Greenidge caught behind at 11. Desi and Richards repaired the hull in a stand of 58 in 56 minutes, the Vivacious One accounting for 48 with a blistering assault only to depart just before stumps, leg-before to Botham, who was enjoying an auspicious if deluding first Test at the helm. Four wickets then ebbed away while 60 more were added, but despite a chance to slip when he had made 23, Desi's resol-ution never faltered. When Gower dropped an awful swirling steepler off Roberts with 13 needed and three wickets remaining, the game was effectively won and lost. Sadly, after 305 minutes' of rigorous application and with just three runs to get, Desi, on 62, was sent back by Roberts and failed to regain his ground as Peter Willey hit the bullseye. He broke down in tears on his way to the dressing room. Roberts lifted Botham over long-on to settle the issue two balls later with almost two sessions in hand, the two-wicket margin the closest in Tests between the participants. 'I so wanted to guide the team to victory,' recalls Desi. 'When I came off crying people thought it was because I was unhappy with the decision, but it was because I had given it away.'

He made sure there would be no repeat at Lord's. On the Friday, after Gooch's maiden Test century had led England to 269 and Botham had Greenidge playing across the line on 25, Desi was joined by Richards, a Richards who was not in the slightest bit interested in caressing the ball or even making love to it. He wanted to moider da bum. In 52 overs, the pair piled on 223, of which Richards made 145 off 159 balls, 25 fours and a six punctuating a speech from the leading batting demagogue of the day. Resuming in front of another capacity gaggle on the Saturday, 93 not out off 68 overs, Desi moved out of the sidecar. Just as Richards had done, he came close to going on 99, a miscued on-drive only just failing to locate mid-on. 'Otherwise,' reported Robin Marlar in the *Sunday Times*, 'he had demonstrated patience and a basic correctness.' The hundred arrived in just under four and a half hours, a nudge off Underwood through midwicket's grasp speedily followed by a leap worthy of a winner down the Westway at Loftus Road. An on-driven six off Willey brought up the 300. He rode his luck well, being beaten four times in one Willis over when on 144, and when he finally relented, hooking at a short one from Botham that kept low and nailed him in front, he had made 184 in an eight-and-a-quarter-hour tour of duty studded with a six and 27 fours, bypassing tour manager Clyde Walcott's 168 in the Ramadhin–Valentine extravaganza of 1950 as the highest score by a West Indian in a Test at HQ. Walcott, to his great discredit, was disparaging. Desi, sensibly, ignored the slight.

For a twenty-two-year-old Englishman drinking in all that on-side splendour and rigid concentration from the Mound Stand, it had been a rare, not to say confusing experience. Wallowing in the regality of Richards, the grandeur of Greenidge, was OK, but this blighter was different. Compact, certain and crisp, his strokeplay was the genuine article, but it was underpinned by restraint, by a pleasure in defence. What lingered longest was that infectious smile that creased his face from ear to ear throughout. While proclaiming a man at one with his craft, this smile, Desi reveals, was also a psychological ploy. 'When you smile you give the impression either that you are taking the mickey or that nothing the bowler can do will bother you. When you smile you never look under pressure. Underneath you might be nervous as hell but no one will ever know.'

There were few or no nerves on this occasion. 'It was a very good wicket, a beauty. I'd dreamed about playing at Lord's since I was a child and now here I was, driving Underwood through the covers, working balls off my legs. The crowd was appreciative too. They seemed to support cricket more then than they do now, what with all the xenophobia that has infected the game in recent times. Funnily enough, Gordon was not in form, which was unusual for him in England. In fact, we only managed one fifty stand in the whole series, and that came in the final Test at Leeds.' By then, the weather had done its meddling, popping six full days into a premature grave and masking the gulf between the sides. Desi was unable to maintain his momentum, making 1, 7 and 42 in the last three Tests to finish the series with 308 runs at 51.33, second only to Richards, his summer's exploits yielding 874 at 46 in all.

Pakistan was something completely different. After the briefest of deep breaths, the West Indies flew to the sub-continent in early November and ran into a characteristic slew of grassless, lifeless tracks. Holding (shoulder) and Greenidge (slipped disc) were injured early on and missed the entire four-match Test rubber, while Roberts skipped the tour altogether. Far from bursting the Caribbean bubble, however, the upshot was the West Indies' first series win in Pakistan and a clean sweep of the three one-day internationals. Far from drawing their sting, the comatose wickets merely underlined the ability of the pace arsenal to coax life from the most unpropitious conditions, Clarke, Croft, Marshall and Garner claiming 54 of the 66 Pakistani batsmen to fall in the Tests while their opposite numbers struck no more than a dozen times.

The touring bats, conversely, were considerably less authoritative, Richards delivering the sole three-figure innings. Desi played in all nine first-class fixtures and topped the individual run aggregates with 485 at 34.64, including three half-centuries, but was continually tantalized by the spin of Iqbal Qasim, Abdul Qadir and Nazir Junior in the Tests, where his 104 runs came at 17.33. Again, the umpiring provided a partial alibi. 'I learned on that tour that you cannot expect to get the 60–40 decisions in your favour out there. I was very disappointed with the umpiring at times. Sylvester Clarke bowled the first ball of the series to Taslim Arif, who played back and edged it to David Murray. Everyone went up – not out. That set the tone. I can remember doing the splits and being adjudged lbw, Qasim turning the new ball a mile and somehow winning another leg-before decision. After being stumped at Multan I walked up the steps to the pavilion with tears in my eyes. At the end of the series Imran came up to me and sympathized. "Desi boy," he agreed, "you had a rough time."'

The decisive Test was the second instalment at Faisalabad, the only one not bedevilled by rain. In an intriguing tussle between speed – Clarke, Croft and Marshall shared 15 wickets – and spin – Qasim, Qadir and Nazir split 20 – only Richards (72 and 67) passed 50 as the West Indies won a low-scoring game by 156 runs, thus inflicting on the hosts their first home defeat in twenty starts. Clarke, whose four wickets and equally bullish batting earned him the Man of the Match award, broke some more china on the second day of the final Test at Multan when he inadvertently laid out the president of one of the students' unions. This instigated a mini-riot that ended after twenty-five minutes with Kallicharran down on bended knees in supplication. Hardly the most appropriate way for Lloyd to celebrate his record forty-second Test as captain, still less for Multan to announce itself as the fifty-second Test venue.

It was a rum series all round. At Karachi, play began a day and a half late and then only by dint of the electric heaters that were pressed into service to dry the pitch. There was another delay at the start of the fourth day when one of the umpires, the then little-known Shakoor Rana, left his kit behind at the hotel. 'The crowds were big, very excitable,' remembers Desi. 'They appreciated good play but they also threw things at you whether they liked you or not. To them it was part of the game. At Multan they were pelting Clarke with oranges and eventually he got frustrated, picked up one of the boundary markers and, without aiming at anyone, hurled it into the crowd. Then, all of a sudden, he looked back and this guy was coming out on to the field with blood streaming down his face. Clarke apologized, of course, Jackie Hendriks, our manager, conveyed his regrets and a group of us went to the poor kid's bedside in hospital. He was OK.'

Less than a fortnight later Desi was totting up his highest score yet for Barbados, 160 against Guyana at the Kensington Oval as the Shell Shield champions opened the defence of their title in style, swamping Timur Mohamed's men by an innings and 260 runs. As it happened, this proved a false dawn, the Combined Islands wresting the crown for the first time despite a heavy defeat by Barbados in their final game. This, though, was no more than an appetizer for the main course of the winter, namely the debate for the Wisden Trophy. The preliminaries were unexpectedly even, the West Indies stealing a two-run win in the first one-day international in St Vincent to an accompaniment of incoming and outgoing aircraft at the adjacent airport. Desi reeled off eight fours in his 34 at the titchy Arnos Vale ground yet only he and the gaunt young Jamaican débutant, Everton Mattis (64), reached double figures as the West Indies were whipped out for 127, Croft roaring back with 6 for 15 to nullify Cap'n Botham's beefy 60.

The exclusion of the local favourite, Deryck Murray, from the first Test squad incurred the wrath of certain vandals at Port-of-Spain, where wet patches and inadequate covers delayed the onset of hostilities by more than three hours. Unperturbed, Desi and Greenidge took over for the rest of the day, adding 144 by the close. The following morning John Emburey's nagging off-breaks elicited a return catch from Desi when he was four short of his 100, but further half-centuries from Lloyd and Roberts, who drilled a record 24 from the first five balls of one Botham over, made sure that such estimable groundwork was not frittered away. Wrecked by Croft on their first voyage, keelhauled by Roberts and Holding on their second, England, unable to reach 180 in either innings and consigned to following on for the first time in forty-nine Tests, sank by an innings and 79 runs, their first defeat of that magnitude against the West Indies for forty-six years.

Politics complicated the equation in Guyana, where the arrival of the Surrey fast bowler, Robin Jackman, as a replacement for the injured Bob Willis, galled Forbes Burnham's stringent anti-apartheid government. A Jamaican radio commentator revealed to his listeners that Jackman (in common with quite a few other members of the touring party) had played in South Africa. All hell broke loose. The British Minister for Sport, Hector Munro, pointed out that the Gleneagles Agreement did not embrace actions by individuals – which many believed it should have done – but Jackman's permit was revoked all the same, two days before the second Test. This the Guyanan government was entitled to do, since the concordat did not seek to prevent individual states from following their consciences and acting unilaterally. Amid all the hubbub, Desi's 48, the highest individual score of an uneventful match at Berbice, went largely unnoticed as he marshalled a six-wicket win for West Indies in the second one-day international. After consulting with Lord's, Alan Smith, the England manager, announced that his players would not proceed with the Test 'as it is no longer possible for the Test team to be chosen without restrictions being imposed'. Indeed, it seemed at one juncture as if the expedition would end there and then, but the rest of the Caribbean, recognizing the legal implications and eager for the tour to continue, came out in sympathy and the party moved on to Barbados. While caring little for the whole sorry business, Desi accepted Guyana's right to do as it saw fit. 'I wasn't interested in politics but we had a lot of respect for Guyana. They had made a stand and you had to admire their consistency. After all, they had barred Sobers after he had been to Rhodesia.'

Jackman made an immediate impact at Bridgetown, sending back Greenidge with his fifth ball in Test cricket and later having Desi caught behind, but there was to be no respite for the beleaguered visitors. Ken Barrington, their stout-hearted coach and assistant manager, the devoted sarn't major from Surrey whom Wally Grout accused of having a Union Jack fluttering from his hip pocket, collapsed and died of a heart attack on the second evening. Holding plucked out Boycott's middle stump at the end of one of the finest, most non-negotiable overs the game had ever thrown up, Richards and Lloyd smote centuries and the West Indies won by 298 runs, Desi making 25 in each innings. As a side issue, the début of the genial Roland Butcher, a sometime purveyor of gorgeous shots and omnipresent in covers and bar, filled a goodly few paragraphs. Born fourteen miles from Kensington, he was the first black player to represent England at cricket, four months after Nottingham Forest's Viv Anderson had broken the barrier in soccer. Butcher and Desi had played together during their formative years and the latter, as was his gentlemanly wont, whispered the new boy luck when he came to the wicket. Desi had no quarrel with this apparent defection. 'If you live in a country and go to school there, you are entitled to play for that country. I don't want to get into the pros and cons of Graeme Hick's qualification but if you are legally permitted to play for England there's nothing wrong with that. If the law allows it and you are good enough, so be it. We played against Kepler Wessels, after all.'

The remainder of the series was less one-sided, spirited resistance from Boycott, Gooch and Willey saving England in Antigua's inaugural Test, the last two and Gower manning the burning deck to staunch effect in Trinidad. In both games the West Indies passed 440 in their only innings, Desi being caught behind off Botham for 4 at St John's then atoning with 84 at Queen's Park, where he and Greenidge posted their second three-figure stand of the rubber and Gower's unconquered 154 demonstrated that he possessed the grit to complement his aesthetic appeal. Desi needed no convincing. 'We always had respect for Gower. People say he has a weakness outside off stump, but there's no such thing as the perfect batsman. We would never have dropped him.'

In hindsight, it seems odd that the most formidable assassination bureau ever to kick off from a sightscreen should have ended the winter by beating a fruitless tattoo on the hitherto porous English blades. All credit to Botham's braves for reclaiming their dignity, yet the West Indies' inability to translate palpable superiority into tangible reward was excusable. In the two years since the end of World Series Cricket, Desi and his comrades had been constantly on the go, immersed in cricket's brave new whirl. He himself had participated in all nineteen Tests and twenty-one one-day internationals during that period, skipping from England to Australia to New Zealand, back to England, on to Pakistan and eventually back home. He had booked a berth on the game's pre-eminent ship, seaworthiness now indisputable.

There was a certain queasiness, though, when he returned to Australia the following winter. Subdued by a modest tour of Zimbabwe as vice-captain of the West Indies Under-26 side – averaging under 34 in the first-class fixtures – Desi finally acquired his first three-figure score in Van Diemen's Land with a knock of 139 against New South Wales, only to reacquaint himself with statistical mediocrity when the three-match Test series began, a series whose undulating course set it apart as one of the most evocative examples of the genre. Three-Test rubbers are a bit like three-set tennis matches: insubstantial and annoying, however tasty – like nouvelle cuisine. The possibilities are fewer. If one team wins the first game they tend to think smaller the rest of the way, settling for consolidation and setting the tone for a war of attrition. Not on this occasion.

Although roundly thrashed by an innings in the third and final Test, Australia had just muscled their way to a 2–1 victory over Pakistan, abrasiveness encapsulated in a highly unsavoury fracas at Perth wherein Lillee obstructed Miandad as he went for a single then kicked the rear end of the protesting batsman, no innocent himself, who retorted by raising his bat and threatening to decapitate the provocative bowler. So disenchanted were the cricket-sated Australian public with the five-day format that less than 90,000 of them attended the fifteen days of the series, but there was immeasurably more interest when the unofficial world champions stepped into the ring. Watched by 136,464, the first round on what was merely the latest in a string of indifferent Melbourne pitches – the authorities subsequently announced, and not before time, that the square would be relaid over the next three years – evolved into a toe-to-toe classic.

Recovering from 59 for 5, the hosts scratched together 198 on the opening day almost solely by virtue of an heroic undefeated 100 from Kim Hughes. Lillee and Terry Alderman then deleted four West Indians for 10 before the close, Desi among them as he sliced Lillee to second slip where Border clasped a splendid catch above his head. The slight Jamaican, Jeffrey Dujon, an

Above Street drive: in an era before Super Mario, Michael Jordan and the Simpsons, Desi acquired his embryonic skills on the lean streets of Holders Hill. Today's tarmac enthusiasts spend more time dodging cars than bouncers.

Right Buckling down: Desi pads up for net practice before his Test début, Port-of-Spain, 1978.

Smiling Phases (1): the new boy squeezes in between Derick Parry and Clive Lloyd as another Australian wicket tumbles in Trinidad. Bruce Yardley's expression (far left) previews more than a decade of worldwide impotence.

The first cut is the deepest: Desi looks back in angst as Steve Rixon and Bobby Simpson form a two-headed monster. The Australian wicketkeeper had just caught Desi off Jim Higgs to end an auspicious maiden Test innings at 61.

End of the beginning: the West Indies XI that trounced Australia by nine
wickets in the second Test, 1978, Desi's first in Barbados. The Packer exile
followed, the reign resuming two years later. Back row: Greenidge, Haynes,
Croft, Garner, Austin, Parry; front: Murray, Kallicharran, Lloyd, Davis
(manager), Richards, Roberts.

Contemporary culture: Malcolm Marshall, school colleague and Chandler's
Ford neighbour; Wayne Daniel, school rival and Middlesex predecessor;
Lawrence Rowe, stylish hero, genius dimmed by poor eyesight, deflated by the
rand.

Slice of luck: Alan Knott gasps, Bob Woolmer prays – fruitlessly – as Desi cuts uppishly during his 184 against England, Lord's, 1980.

Low five, high point: Alvin Kallicharran congratulates Desi on his first century against England, Lord's, 1980. Vests were mandatory in that vile summer.

Words with a wordsmith: John Arlott presents Desi with a commemorative medal after the West Indies had won the 1980 Wisden Trophy rubber at Headingley. The bashful youngster put down roots in Arlott's beloved Hampshire four years later.

Beach party for the ages: Trevor Bailey, ugly sister to the accompanying bevy of English batting beauties, shows Desi how he got to the ball, Tamarind Cove, 1981. From left: Fred Rumsey, Calvin Hope, Desi, Bailey, Don Wilson, Colin Milburn, Brian Close, Reg Simpson and Denis Compton.

Land of plenty: Desi and Gordon stand shoulder-to-shoulder once more as fourteen of Barbados' finest congregate for a game against the Rest of the World, Kennington Oval, 1982. Back row: Greenidge, Haynes, Marshall, King, Garner, Clarke, Padmore, Hope; front: Holder, Hall, Sobers, Griffith and Nurse.

Left Lamb before the slaughter: a rare misunderstanding sees Desi run out by Allan Lamb at Lord's, 1984. Greenidge went on to inspire an astonishing win with his finest innings. Derek Pringle appeals as Paul Downton takes off the bails.

Facing page Smiling Phases (2): with Mum in the crowd and 100 on the board, the Kennington Oval conjures up its Kensington counterpart, fifth Test, 1984. Note plasters covering manufacturer's logo at base of pads.

The joys of poise: a dab through point off Phil Edmonds startles David Gower; Ian Botham and Paul Downton admire the brushwork, second Test, Port-of-Spain, 1986.

Laid back: back problems cast aside, Desi springs from silly mid-off to snaffle Phillip DeFreitas off Roger Harper. Dujon, Marshall and Logie hail the floor show, Graham Gooch does his famous shoulder-droop, Kennington Oval, 1988.

impressive, stylish débutant in the middle order, then helped the assiduous, bubble-permed left-hander Larry Gomes eke out a lead of three, the latter committing treason when he edged to slip to allow Lillee to overhaul Lance Gibbs's record bag of 309 Test wickets. At 184 for 3 in their second dig, Greg Chappell's puggish battlers could contemplate setting an imposing target, whereupon Holding rode roughshod through the middle order to emerge with 11 for 107, the best by a West Indian against Australia, and so trim the requirement to 220. Bacchus (opening in place of Greenidge, laid low by a knee ligament complaint) and Richards now failed to exercise the scorers, and although Desi and Dujon mounted some resistance, Bruce Yardley's off-spin accounted for both and the quest finished 59 runs short. So ended the West Indies' record run of fifteen Tests without defeat.

Greenidge, still limping but quashing talk of an early return home, returned at Sydney, where the West Indies were denied, partly by the bad light that limited the final session to half an hour, partly by the relative lack of thrust shown by the quickstep quartet. Australia, all but out for the count at 169 for 4 chasing an uncatchable 373, thus wriggled free. Desi went leg-before to Thomson for 15 when the West Indies set off with 384, then fashioned his first half-century in the Worrell Trophy before succumbing in identical manner to Lillee as the holders trebled their lead of 117.

Dujon pulled on the gauntlets for the first time at this level in Adelaide and once more sparkled with easeful elegance at the crease as his side levelled the series in another resonant contest, one that served to ridicule the doubts expressed by Lynton Taylor, managing director of PBL Ltd, the Packer-owned company responsible for marketing Australian cricket, that Test cricket had a place in the modern world. After an unbeaten 126 from the dependable Gomes had ushered the West Indies to a 151-run first innings advantage, Border, Hughes and Laird resisted the heraldic Holding so successfully that Australia reached 362 for 4 before caving in to Garner, surrendering their last six wickets for 24 and leaving the tourists 236 to pursue in 195 minutes plus the mandatory 20 overs, the rate around four an over. Desi, driving recklessly and caught behind in each innings off Thomson for 26 and 4, was unable to make a material contribution, but Greenidge, Richards and Lloyd, who struck the winning runs with seventeen balls to spare, assuredly did. The captain, whose last Test in Australia this was expected to be, was chaired from the field by Croft, Garner and Holding.

Exposed by the imperfect pitches, Desi limped from low to low. Even the World Series Cup failed to inject its customary lift. He twice passed 80 in the preliminary tilts with Pakistan and compiled a fluent 52 on another substandard pitch at Melbourne in the second of the best-of-five finals – he himself had been one of the square's most vocal critics – but 125 runs from his other eleven visits to the middle bespoke an under-achiever. Neither would there be any upturn in his fortunes when he returned home for the Shell Shield. The success of the Combined Islands in 1981 had persuaded the West Indies board to divide the constituents, the prognostications being that the Windwards, without a Test representative, would be a doormat for the rest whereas the Leewards, with Richards, Roberts and Parry, might conceivably press the established islands. Barbados duly regained their title yet it was the Windwards who ran them closest, finishing no more than five points in arrears. Desi, overdrawn at the run bank, failed to reach 50 in any of his seven innings, cobbling together 164 runs at 23.43.

Not that Desi struggled alone. Head turned by his own apparent immortality, Richards had managed just one 50 (and only just at that) in six Test innings, the fading Croft's seven Australian wickets cost 51.57 apiece and, the peerless Holding apart, the inability of the pace battery to turn the screw with its habitual ruthlessness enabled Chappell's chaps to square a series that the respective merits of the protagonists had rendered them odds-on to lose. The cumulative effect of so much pressurized cricket was beginning to tell. The prospect of a year-long furlough – India were due in the Caribbean the following February – was profoundly welcome. One can't very well hit the ball further and oftener when one's body, no matter how sinewy, says no.

7

The Randy Rand

We talk real funny down here
We drink too much and we talk too loud
We're too drunk to make it in no northern town
And we're keepin' the Niggers down.

Rednecks, Randy Newman

While Desi was experiencing growing pains in Australia, the stunted South African behemoth barged back on to the scene like some gatecrasher indignant at being repeatedly left off the invitation list. Fearful of the interloper ruining the party (as opposed to any moral concerns), the bouncers guarding the inner sanctum of the ICC left the gatecrasher with but one option – to draw up his own guest list and hold his own bash. In their defence, and unlike their golfing and tennis-playing counterparts, cricketers are not so well rewarded that they can easily afford to put political principles before a fast buck. That said, few, apparently, were sufficiently incensed by the inhumane apartheid regime to put up much of a struggle when the invites plopped on to their doormats.

Thus it was, in March 1982, that the multiracial South African Cricket Union, rightly angered at being refused readmission to the ICC after fulfilling the prerequisites and emboldened by the bottomless resources of sponsors such as South African Breweries, was able to tempt a coterie of Englishmen to cock a snook at the spirit, if not the letter, of the Gleneagles Agreement. 'I want to go back,' wrote Matthew Engel, who sensibly refused to be deluded by Gooch, Boycott and their fellow sanction-busters, 'but, please, for a proper tour in a country run so that a proper tour is possible, not for this nonsense.' While the apolitical business world continued to wheel and deal without a pang of guilt – the volume of trade between Australia and South Africa in 1981–2 amounted to A\$236 million – the sporting authorities had taken an admirably resolute stand against injustice. Granted, sport had long been deployed as a tourniquet for society's self-inflicted wounds. Hadn't Tommy played football with Fritz between the trenches? Only last year a group of gallant Yorkshiremen ventured to the Austro-Slovenian border armed with tennis balls and lumps of wood, and proceeded to suffuse the oppressed Bosnians with the arts of cricket. Such deeds, however, can only stem the flow of blood. They cannot heal. In any case, ran the humanitarian argument, how can one play games with opponents selected on the basis of pigmentation, with players whose votes supported the insupportable? Quite easily, as it happened, provided the price was right.

With money no object – so much so that a £250,000 loss on the Gooch trek could be absorbed with ease – sport could be wielded brazenly as a propaganda tool, a means of showing the unreasonable world outside that things weren't really *that* bad. And what better way to prove it than by attracting tacit approval from the coloured world? In the autumn of 1982, a bunch of Sri Lankan second stringers, dazzled by sums they could only have dreamed about, swallowed the bait whole. Uncowed by another hefty deficit, SACU continued to make a beeline for the West Indians, the ultimate catch. This did not prove to be quite so easy. 'To the members of the black diaspora,' the former Jamaican prime minister, Michael Manley, explained, 'the oppression which continues in South Africa has become the symbol of more than a tyranny to be overthrown. Apartheid points like a dagger at the throat of black self-worth in every corner occupied by the descendants of Africa.'

Self-worth, however, was one thing, waning careers quite another. Stricken by erratic vision and hayfever, perpetually at loggerheads with the selectors over his reluctance to open the innings, Lawrence Rowe was more susceptible than most to a quick fix. Others sprang readily to mind. Colin Croft's back problems had impaired his effectiveness. Richard Austin, David Murray, Albert Padmore and Collis King had had their opportunities and been found wanting. Their willingness to sell their souls would attract vehement criticism from those who resisted. 'These men are worse than slaves,' charged Michael Holding, who spurned an offer of some £125,000. 'If they were offered enough money, they would probably agree to wear chains.' Rowe presented the counter-argument. 'Martin Luther King was a pioneer who had a tough time early on. If we can do a fraction of the good he did, I'm prepared for that.'

Desi soon discovered how keen SACU was to help its political masters by enlisting his tacit approval for a mess of pottage. Determined to make good his Australian Achilles heel, he had returned to Melbourne at the end of the 1981–2 Caribbean domestic season, signing up to play sub-district cricket with Dandenong and taking up temporary residence at Hartley Richards's apartment. Malcolm Marshall, injured on tour but scenting a regular Test place with Croft and Roberts seemingly in decline, was also in town, so too Hartley Alleyne. 'We were supposed to get paid decent money,' says Desi, 'but we didn't. Still, I was there to further my experience of Australian conditions.'

The Caribbean had been abuzz with talk of high-priced defections and Desi's name had featured prominently on the grapevine. 'I was told Lawrence Rowe had said he needed me and that all I had to do was name my price, then while I was in Melbourne I started to get calls from the top boys. I was very nervous and confused about the whole thing. I had to look at the situation in the long run, at the prospect of securing my future. I don't think that was being mercenary. I'm not saying you should become a rich bugger or get involved in some racket in order to better your lot, but I did believe it was sensible to look at how best to improve your style of living. At the same time, my feelings were very strong. I have a lot of scruples and I knew there was a lot of injustice in the world for black people – and a lot for white people too. I felt that what was going on in South Africa was wrong but by the same token I did not believe that going there would change anything. There is so much hypocrisy in the world. Why stop me going there and not the businessman? Why stop cricketers when the rest of the world was still trading with South Africa? There should have been a total ban. The sad thing is that we couldn't look at it as a means of helping black *and* white.'

Hartley Richards, now advising his Holders Hill neighbour on his contracts and investments, was all too aware of the quandary. 'The South Africans were still trying to get a couple of big names and each time they called Desi they upped the ante. He was established in the West Indies side and so long as the board's money matched the South African money there was no need to take it. But when the rands kept on piling up he had a moral dilemma. That was the overriding factor and it would have taken a lot of dollars to get rid of that. He was concerned, and rightly so. "What will I do when I come back home?" he would ask me. "How will I mix with people? They might not understand." Even now I think the guys that went still feel tainted. Take Bert [Padmore]. He was past it, over the hill even when it came to selection for Barbados, so he went and, quite frankly, you couldn't blame him. Yet I know the whole episode has tainted him.

'That was Desi's concern and that was why he decided not to go. I'm also certain Viv was an influence. Like him we were very anti-South African in Barbados, but at the same time we were more pragmatic. The feeling was 50–50. On the one hand there were those who argued that the players were professional cricketers, so why should we get in their way? We have a more open form of politics in Barbados, we didn't just follow our leaders as they did in Guyana, say. The influence was more British than in Britain. We have a British sense of fairness, a belief in the right of the individual to make his own decision. We also felt that withholding sport was not the answer to apartheid. On the other hand, there were those who felt that the South Africans were turning our people into Judases, that it was immoral for them to even consider going. There was also a degree of hostility towards people like Franklyn Stephenson because he was denying Barbadians from seeing him play for the West Indies.'

Though 'flattered' by his offer of £50,000 for a two-year contract, Marshall was less than taken with the accompanying subterfuge. 'I got in touch with Desmond and Hartley, both of whom were staying nearby [in Melbourne]. They were close friends so I knew I could confide in them and even ask their advice on my dilemma. Then came more surprises. They too had received similar temptation from Dr Bacher. They, too, had been sworn to secrecy. Like me they had been told tickets [to Johannesburg] were ready for them. All they had to do was board the plane and sign the contract on arrival. We were all still reeling from the shock when we made an alarming discovery. We had each been made offers which differed widely from one another. This put suspicion in our already confused minds.'

The Bajan threesome also knew that their punishment would be heavy, far heavier than that imposed on Gooch and company. No puny three-year bans for them. Anti-South African feelings were running high in the Caribbean, so high that the impending tour by the English women's team would be called off when the Caribbean Women's Cricket Federation decided to ban five of the tourists for holidaying on the Veld four years earlier. While Desi was wrestling with this hot potato, the *Age* somehow gleaned that Marshall, Alleyne and he were all in Johannesburg, limbering up to join Rowe and Co. In fact, they were about to return home. The welcome at Grantley

Adams Airport was totally unexpected. Cheers rent the air as David Simmons, chairman of the National Sports Council, stepped forward to meet the boys on the tarmac. 'I am so glad you boys had the good sense to turn down the offer and to come home to your own people,' he effused. 'You will not regret this. You will be able to live with yourselves which may not be the case for some of your countrymen.'

By 'some', Simmons was referring to the nine Bajans who had traded in their birthrights for an alleged £60,000 apiece, many of them friends of Desi's: David Murray and liaison officer Gregory Armstrong, cousins Emmerson Trotman and Alvin Greenidge, tour manager Padmore and fellow St Jamesian Stephenson, boyhood pals Sylvester Clarke, Collis King and Ezra Moseley, a brotherhood embroiled. The following winter, Alleyne, career assailed by throwing charges and an inability to hang on to a steady job, had a change of heart. That Barbados contributed such a disproportionate number of these traitors/rebels/individuals-with-the-right-to-choose said as much for the island's moderate stance as it did for the well of talent there. The bans were as final as had been predicted, ostensibly *sine die* but eventually lifted when the De Klerk publicity machine got rolling. By then, the sports boycott, a wilful parasite gnawing away at the intestines of Afrikaner supremacy, had achieved plenty, in the cricketing sphere probably as much as it could reasonably have hoped. Sadly, as the white supremacist strains of *Die Stem* rang out before the Springboks' unhappy return to the Rugby Union club last year, the ANC withdrew its support for such tours, making it abundantly clear the sporting community had not done enough.

Desi was a trifle embarrassed by the sports minister's airport speech, having yet to go the whole hog and give his suitors the formal brush-off. Maybe it would be nice to know how high these besuited blokes were prepared to go. Later that summer Ali Bacher pursued him to England, where he had been engaged to play in the Leagues. The pair met for dinner, Desi listening politely as the ante rose, well into six figures. The issue was clear cut. Irene and Arletha could live it up for a while with dosh like that, but could he live with himself? Mikey Holding couldn't. Lloydy couldn't. It was a wonder they'd ever gone anywhere near Viv. But these were wealthy guys, at least in Caribbean terms. By now, though, Desi was just going along for the ride. His mind was made up. 'Bacher seemed a decent enough guy and it was all very amicable, but he almost fell off his chair when I turned him down. I don't think he imagined there was any way I could refuse. It just didn't feel right.'

Like Edith Piaf, he regrets *rien*. The temptation was great, no question of that. Great enough for David Murray to finance his drug habit for another couple of years, and for Franklyn Stephenson to throw away the chance of becoming the new Sobers (or, at any rate, a pretty damn fine facsimile). Big enough, even, for Colin Croft to get ideas above his station and dare to occupy a first-class compartment on a South African train. He could not have been the first visitor to the world's foremost anti-democratic republic, a state where inequality was the law of the homeland, to receive first-hand proof of the chasm between propaganda and reality.

In the empire of the Bothas, black and white together could drink in the majesty of Graeme Pollock and Barry Richards, but when stumps were drawn they couldn't pop off down the pub together. They went their separate ways, returned to their disparate lives, unable to share so much as a pint, prohibited by law from co-existing. Clive Lloyd's response to the announcement of Bacher's coup rings with the utmost clarity: 'I know that some of them are out of work and the money is very tempting, but that is not all in life.'

8

The Fabulous Bajan Boys

Everyone talks about our bowlers, but what about our batsmen?
Every successful side in history has had two good opening bowlers
and two good opening batsmen.

Clive Lloyd, Bayswater, 1992

To forestall any further South African defections, Desi and the rest of the
West Indian regulars were requested to sign contracts tying them to official
cricket for three years, in return for an annual guarantee of US$3000. As
part of the arrangement, the players would work with their local governments,
mostly in a coaching-cum-PR capacity. Jamaica kept up its end of the bargain,
but many declined, pointing out the incongruity of paying people not to do
something. Desi was bemused. 'The board said it was incumbent on our own
governments to pay us even though we had signed the contract with them.
They should have been responsible. I bought some land in St Thomas and
built a house on the basis of that contract.'

A weight off his chest after that meal with Ali 'Baba To My Enemies'
Bacher, Desi turned his attention back to Blackhall. Situated north of Hartle-
pool in County Durham, the North Yorkshire and South Durham League
club had first approached him during the West Indies tour of 1980. Here was
one offer that did not require lengthy deliberation. Hard work but an enjoyable experience in all respects, so much so that he returned for a second
season, then later spent a summer with League rivals Guiseborough on the
edge of the North Yorkshire moors. 'The experiences I had in the Leagues
taught me to accept people as you find them. There weren't many black

people in the area but I was accepted very easily and I met some lovely, decent folk. One way and another I've been very fortunate to fit into most places I've ever been to and this was no exception. In fact, at the end of that first season in 1982 I played for the Barbados Tourist Board against a Fred Rumsey XI and won a trip for two to Barbados, so I gave it to my landlord in Blackhall. He and his wife had a week at the Paradise Hotel followed by a week at my mum's place.

'There was precious little abuse to speak of, although sometimes the temperature did get a bit hot and things were said in the heat of the moment, but you've got to expect that when you're competing. I didn't have much time to myself because I would be playing up to five times a week, one day a 50-over game, the next a 20-over affair. The bowlers would scatter the fielders around the boundary and encourage you to have a swipe, which can have a damaging effect on your technique. Lloydy, I know, believes that I acquired some bad habits as a by-product of this, but I also acquired a greater sense of responsibility. Too much was expected of the professionals. You were expected to bat, bowl, be first under the skiers, do everything basically. But that persuaded me that I could do things myself, that I did not need to depend on others, that there was no need to pass the buck. The overall standard was good, but I believe the League organizers should have used the pros as coaches as well, assembled them once a season to instruct the young kids in the area. They must have felt so detached. Unlike football, there were no scouts, so in order to get a job as a cricketer you had to up sticks and move to Northampton or Somerset.' Among these aspiring teenagers were Mike Roseberry, with whom Desi would subsequently form one of the most productive opening pairings in county cricket, and Stewart Hutton, now with Durham. 'At Guiseborough one day I promised him a bat if he made a hundred, and although he fell 30 or so short, I told him that was good enough. You must encourage players when they're young otherwise they lose heart.'

Being the overseas pro meant cooking dinner, washing up *and* putting away. Against Chester-le-Street in the first round of the Aynsley Johnson Cup, Desi struck 92 out of 124 – the next highest score in an innings of 159–7 was 15 not out – then took 7 for 50 in 15 overs to clinch a 47-run win. Being the overseas pro also meant being saddled with a celebrity status in a strange land, with all the conflicting connotations that involved. On 7 March 1983, while Desi was in Trinidad preparing for the first one-day international against India, a *Northern Echo* sub-editor composed a right little belter for the top of page nine: 'Romeo Des claim stumps village' roared the headline.

It said much for the impression Desi had created in the north-east that the story underneath was wholly favourable. 'From Barbados to Blackhall,' it began, 'they won't hear a single word said against gentleman cricketer Desmond Haynes.' Villagers, the paper maintained, 'read with disbelief how the manager of a Barbados hotel has been ordered off the island, after having Des thrown out of his lobby claiming the cricket ace was flirting with his receptionist. They heard how the hotel was virtually besieged by fans of Des protesting against the manager's actions.' 'He was a single lad and while he was here he behaved like any other bachelor,' insisted the Blackhall secretary, Tommy Pollitt. 'But no one round here ever had any reason to complain about his behaviour.' 'I just can't believe Des would be to blame for anything,' chipped in Rita Davidson, the landlady to whom Desi had given those tickets to Barbados. 'He was always the perfect gentleman and everyone in the village knows it. He lived with us for three months and in all that time I never heard a word said against him. He wouldn't do anything to upset anyone.' The hotel manager, ex-naval commander Brian Gallagher, told local reporters that Desi had (gosh) chatted up the receptionist 'in full view of the guests', though the damsel in question denied the charge vehemently. When Desi was asked to vacate the premises, the Barbados prime minister himself ordered an immediate inquiry and Gallagher was swiftly on his way. Some papers referred to racism, one to a 'racial crisis' but the uproar soon subsided.

Prior to the start of that winter's Shell Shield – a compressed affair with most of the fixtures crammed into the month leading up to the first Test against India – Desi was on the receiving end of that most sought-after of bowling feats, the 'all ten'. Playing for a powerful West Indies XI in a four-day encounter with an Anglo-dominated International XI in Kingston, he top-scored with 96 as the newly capped Nottinghamshire off-spinner Eddie Hemmings took 10 for 175, the most expensive analysis of its kind, the first such accomplishment in the Caribbean and the first anywhere for thirteen years. Denuded by the absence of eight of the previous year's regulars, Barbados were always going to be hard-pressed to retain their title and duly finished third to a revitalized Guyana, led, for the first time since 1975, by Clive Lloyd. In a low-scoring match against the Leeward Islands Desi made 97, a slimline opener named Richie Richardson retorting with his maiden first-class century but unable to prevent Barbados from nosing home by 56 runs. Further half-centuries followed against Jamaica and Guyana, but in the decisive four-wicket loss to the Windward Islands, Norbert Phillip dismissed Desi in both innings for 27 and 18.

Panicked into wholesale change by a comprehensive 3–0 thwacking in Pakistan, India had jettisoned Viswanath and the artful slow left-armer Dilip Doshi, passing the captaincy from Gavaskar to Kapil Dev, but all to no avail. Aside from the gallant Mohinder Amarnath (598 runs at 66.44 in the Tests, taking him to a record aggregate in a non-English season of 2355 at 81.21), their specialist batsmen patently lacked the wherewithal to combat the twin-engined thrust of Marshall and the canny, revitalized Roberts. Even Gavaskar, forger of ten previous 100s against the West Indies, was stumped for an answer, managing only one score over 40 in nine outings. Dev, moreover, was the only bowler not to pay an extortionate price for his wickets and the consequence was a comfortable 2–0 win for the hosts in the rain-riddled, five-match rubber, a margin that did scant justice to their overwhelming command. A sweep of the three-part limited overs mini-series was a more accurate reflection.

Desi was one of seven home batsmen to reach three figures in the Tests, ending a drought stretching back 26 innings and nearly three years, but his most valuable knock was an Oscar-worthy cameo in the opening chapter at Sabina Park. A sober pitch allied to the first *bona fide* downpour in Kingston for two years appeared to have dissolved any prospect of a result when India, having spent the entirety of the penultimate day sheltering from the rain, adjourned for tea on the last afternoon leading by 165 with four wickets intact. There must have been something pretty potent in Roberts's cuppa. Back he rumbled after the resumption to blow away three men in his first over and thus leave his batsmen 26 overs in which to gather 172. Desi set about Dev and Sandhu with a bracing 34 off 21 balls to set the table for Richards to gorge himself with 61 from 36, sixes from the pint-sized débutant from Trinidad, Augustine Logie, and, with four balls remaining, Dujon, capping a hectic chase in breathless fashion.

Excitement was in short supply thereafter, not so the oddities. At Port-of-Spain, where Desi had hammered 97 to inspire victory in the preceding one-day international, Lloyd claimed the extra half-hour despite there being no earthly chance of a conclusive finish, a magnanimous gesture that allowed his opposite number to complete the double of 2000 runs and 200 wickets. What was that about hard-hearted? A studious Desi made his customary happy return to the comforting confines of Kensington, reaching 50 for the first time in eight Test innings – only to depart in the 90s for the fourth time that season. Bogged down by Shastri's insistent line and defensive leg-side field, he began to fret: 'Tried to break the shackles and pulled him to Kapil at midwicket.' The real statistical quirk was reserved for the final act of a one-sided contest, however, as the Mysore Kojak, wicketkeeper Syed Kirmani, donated a no-ball with the first delivery of the West Indian second innings to hand a ten-wicket win to the hosts and thus collect his ticket into trivia immortality for an analysis of 0-0-0-0 (not until the following autumn would overstepping offences be added to a bowler's runs against column). In the fifth Test in Antigua, Lloyd defied probability by winning his seventh consecutive toss – he would subsequently make it eight, one shy of Colin Cowdrey's extant record – then rubbished traditional practice once and for all by becoming the first Test captain to stick the opposition in four times in the same series. Didn't lose a game either.

Reaffirmation, conversely, was the keyword for the Haynes–Greenidge combo. Posting their first 50-plus stand in Tests for two years at Georgetown, they progressed from a choogle to a crescendo. Bridgetown's free-flowing run tap yielded 98, Antigua history. With the lanky, languid Dilip Vengsarkar complementing 90s from Dev and Ravi Shastri, India totalled 457 on a typically saintly St John's pitch, their best start of the tour by a good few kilometres. The series won, the most reputable firm in Barbados might easily have taken its eyes off the till when it opened up for business half an hour before closing time on Friday 30 April. Since Rea, Greenidge's two-year-old daughter, was lying critically ill in hospital with a liver disorder, it would have been even more forgivable had the senior partner taken the day off. Instead, he channelled all that sorrow and anger into his craft, turning a job into a passion. Not until the shadows were cooling the concrete outside the Recreation Ground, five minutes before stumps the following evening, did they cease trading. The accountants in the scorers' box were over the moon when they came to cash up. Shattering Stollmeyer and Rae's 236 in Madras thirty-four years earlier, the pair had added 296, record takings by a West Indian opening concern, Desi 136 of them.

Given that he had just scaled heights he had not attained since that coming-of-age Colossus at Lord's, it might appear ungrateful for Desi to insist that it should have been more. But for a freak dismissal, it would have been. 'Yashpal Sharma came on for his first over of the innings. Medium-pace something as far as I remember. Some oddball statistical type told me that he'd been playing for India for four years, and that during that period India had used eight bowlers in an innings on four occasions, yet the only time he'd been called into their attack had been a three-over spell against England. Kapil must have been desperate. So I try to hit it too hard, the ball flies off the top edge and I get caught by Shastri at fine leg. Shameful.'

Both as a team and as individuals, Desi and Greenidge needed a stand like this. At the start of the series, in truth, each had a degree of catching up to do when judged by his own highest standards. If not exactly knee-deep in debt, they were certainly behind on their credit card repayments. Trade had been even slacker for Greenidge than Desi: Hampshire were getting them by the bucketload yet not since he and Desi merged had he scored 100 for the West Indies. Between 1974 and 1978, conversely, he had registered five and logged 70 to 96 seven times. As a partnership, the cashflow situation was better, but not that much. In thirty Test liaisons, the longest-serving regular pairing in the contemporary game had put on 50 or more eight times: not bad, but nae great. After all, Hobbs and Sutcliffe did so twenty-five times in thirty-eight, breaking three figures on fifteen occasions, while Greenidge and Fredericks had duetted for ten in thirty-one. So Greenidge and Desi had collected 1334 runs in harness at an average of 44.45, an admirable pro-ductivity rate bettered by only fourteen other regular opening duos in Test history, but this wasn't exactly legend potential. Too often, one sang and the other ducked off stage halfway through his lines. On two of the three occasions Desi had scored a five-day century in his previous twenty-eight Tests, his co-worker had made 3 and 25.

All this number-crunching proves nothing, of course. Desi was averaging 38 in Test cricket, Greenidge over 40, perfectly respectable levels of perform-ance. There was a goodly number of useful opening tandems on the market that winter: Gaekwad and Gavaskar, New Zealand's Turner and Edgar, the Wettimuny lads from Sri Lanka, Fowler and Tavaré, Wessels and Dyson, and, best of all, Mohsin Khan and Mudassar Nazar. The Fabulous Bajan Boys were still the kings of the castle. Yet, as a team within a team, May Day 1983 was the day the combo jazzed it up and moved into adult-hood.

From the start of that innings until the end of the St John's Test of 1986, a sequence of thirty Tests, they would add 50 or more 16 times, on five occasions going past 100, twice reaching 250 and once, against Australia in 1984, averaging 136.80 per stand over a five-match rubber. Over 48 innings, the 2300 runs they totted up as one came at a mean of 54.76. Unremarkable, admittedly, compared with the 3249 Hobbs and Sutcliffe stacked up at 87.81, or the 1349 Rae and Stollmeyer garnered at 71 in 21 innings. Consider, though, the talismanic factor. England won twelve and lost five of the Hobbs–

Sutcliffe Tests while the West Indies won as many – four – as they lost during the short-lived Rae–Stollmeyer reign. During their time of greatest plenty Desi and Greenidge were party to twenty-one wins and a solitary defeat in what was to prove the most bountiful harvest reaped by any international side in the modern era. Such peaks could not be maintained yet there would be few troughs, their ten subsequent series as co-drivers producing a mean of 40 or more six times in addition to a fresh milestone for a West Indies opening pair with 298 against England at St John's in 1990. No other partnership can boast record marks against four separate countries. No other has presided over a 48–8 win-loss count. In all they shared a cabin for 89 Tests spanning 148 innings. The only rivals to come anywhere near them were Bobby Simpson and Bill Lawry with 34 and 62 respectively. For quality, reliability and durability, the Fabulous Bajan Boys, the Lennon and McCartney of the sward, were in a league of their own.

With Lloyd's blessing, Greenidge took no further part in that catalytic draw with India, flying back to Barbados the same Saturday evening to be at Rea's bedside. She died two days later. Desi cannot praise his partner's fortitude highly enough. 'What can I say? That's a true pro for you. You wouldn't have known there was anything wrong. There were no outward signs, no glimpses of emotion.'

Cuthbert Gordon Greenidge had long since learned how to bite his lip. Born in St Peter in 1951, a year after those Little Pals o' Mine, Ramadhin and Valentine, had weaved their spell under the gaze of Old Father Time, raised in Reading from the age of fourteen, he was the first Test player to emerge from the new generation of West Indians whose parents migrated to England during the first two decades after the Second World War, there to be branded by Enoch Powell and injected with a heavy dose of divided loyalty. How profoundly English cricket must regret Ray Illingworth's inability to persuade the twenty-one-year-old Greenidge to make himself available for his residential home in 1972. Perhaps that's why the TCCB went to such lengths to ensure Graeme Hick didn't hop off to New Zealand. Ask Greenidge about his experiences of prejudice, of the problems in having to straddle two distant stools, and he fixes you with a knowing glare. A man of few words when not in a broadcasting booth (introspection rendered him a limited captain), *he* knows that *you* know what goes on in this world, so why bother citing specific instances? He flew off the handle on occasion, but seldom misplaced his rag completely. Indeed, his most notorious squabble was the one that saw him grab an England fast bowler by the lapels at Bridgetown in 1990, the offender in question being Gladstone Small. At fifteen, Small had himself relocated from Barbados to Birmingham.

With John Arlott acting as marriage-broker, Greenidge was seventeen when wedded to Hampshire in 1968, the same summer as a dashing twenty-two-year-old blond from Durban, Barry Richards. At Oxford two years later, these two raised 201 against Leicestershire the first time they opened together at county HQ. Bent on representing the lands of his birth, Greenidge paid his own way to and from Barbados over the two winters that followed Illingworth's invitation, pausing to pound a more than useful Pakistan attack for 273 – 202 in boundaries – in four and a quarter hours on behalf of Derrick Robins's XI (described by Barry Richards as 'probably as near to a perfect innings as I have ever seen') before forcing his way into the West Indies team for the tour of India in 1974–5.

As Greenidge became more selective in his choice of which ball to assault so he evolved into as technically sound a batsman as any of his era, the transformation confirmed at Old Trafford in 1976. On a lively wicket that subsequently saw 20 of their wickets seep away for under 200, England came as close to fulfilling their captain's promise to make the West Indies grovel as they did all summer, Selvey and Hendrick taking 4 for 26 on the opening morning. Trenchant to the last, Greenidge strode to 134 in four hours ten minutes to account for nearly 64 per cent of his side's tally, second only to Charlie Bannerman's 67.3 per cent share in the very first Test all of a century before. Hitting through the V between point and midwicket with verve and velocity, maturity did not stop him cutting a rare dash, carving open opposing attacks with the twinkling footwork and deadly precision of a celluloid d'Artagnan. At 5 feet 10½ inches and 13½ stone, he was a strong, sturdy middleweight with a distinctly heavyweight reputation, a clinical murderer in the Weekes mould rather than a flamboyant serial killer like Viv Richards. At one time the record for the highest individual innings in each of the three main county one-day competitions were all his. He is also the only player ever twice to send thirteen or more sixes soaring into orbit in a first-class innings, not bad for someone whose finest stroke was an earthbound square cut of unique viciousness.

In the spring of 1983, these landmarks were all stashed away in the memory bank, yet the best was still to come. At Lord's the following July, Greenidge would set the seal on the grand old ground's centenary as a Test venue with as devastating an innings as ever won a cricket match of significance. In five hours of supreme batsmanship, he hooked, cut, drove and pulled the West

Indies from first tally-ho to last huzzah in the fifth highest successful chase the five-day form has ever launched, peppering the perimeter with 29 fours and two sixes in a gloriously unconquered 214 assembled at virtually a run a ball. A month later he had a brush with perfection, daubing a characteristically dreary Old Trafford canvas with 30 fours and seven sixes *en route* to 223, the highest by a West Indian at Manchester, a portrait of a master at his peak. Spanning four stoppages for bad light and rain, seven serious lbw appeals and not a solitary chance to hand, its authority was such that only three times in 427 deliveries did bat seek contact with ball and miss.

Sparks crackled even as the final flames flickered. Back at Bridgetown in early 1991, on the brink of 40, long since released by Hampshire, Greenidge fired off a 226-gun salute, the highest Test innings to that point by a West Indian against Australia, winning a bitter series almost single-handed. Perversely, the sight of his limp, primarily attributable to that gammy right knee, had bowlers reaching for the emergency cord. Nonetheless, when he broke down during the Texaco Trophy game at Old Trafford five weeks later 'Daffy' DeFreitas and the other duckies were relieved. A less rash group of selectors might have picked him for the 1992 World Cup, but, like Richards and Dujon, he was part of the *ancien régime* and lost his head when the selectors wheeled out the guillotine before the *sans-culottes* had even had a chance to storm the Bastille. These days he coaches schoolboys in Scotland and plays for Greenock at weekends, commuting whenever possible from his mother's terraced home in Walthamstow, East London, to be with his beloved wife and children, returning to Barbados come winter, residing in St Thomas and working for the Barbados Tourist Board.

An opener is lucky to find more than one regular partner of similar talent, let alone three. Greenidge was exceedingly fortunate. The only comparable beneficiary was John Berry Hobbs, who linked up with Sutcliffe, Rhodes and Sandham. In a harsher, more intense, far more physical age, Greenidge, arguably, had the finer co-conspirators in Barry Richards, Roy Fredericks and Desi. Choosing between them is not a task he relishes. 'Between Desi and Roy, Desi, obviously. Roy was an excellent batsman with his own way of playing, but my partnership with Desi was very fruitful, probably the best I've had for the West Indies. Richards? That was different because it was county cricket. Barry was a great player too, struck the ball handsomely. On his day he would murder most bowlers but he got a bit stale with nothing to aim for.'

Communication, Greenidge asserts, was the key to the success of the

Fabulous Bajan Boys. 'Dialogue counted for a great deal of our stability. At the beginning one of the highlights was the way we'd talk to each other. Our discussions would range from swearing to picking up themes, topics. We'd each make the other aware if he had played a shot that was inappropriate to the situation. We'd talk about how each of us felt he was playing. Was I coming out far enough? Was he going back far enough? At times you can get distracted during an innings, so it was good to have someone there to remind you of the job in hand, to get you back into line. The understanding was so good that we had no need to call for singles. There were no physical signs either, merely a more or less perfected understanding of when either of us wanted to run – and we always got in with plenty of time to spare. There were times, mind you, when we didn't pick singles off as often as we should have because our confidence was booming and we felt we could pierce the field at will.'

'Even now I can't say I know Gordon well,' admits Desi. 'He would come out for meals, drink a fair bit of wine, but he is essentially a family man. He helped me a lot, gave me a lot of support. I learned so much from the way he built an innings, and from our conversations about bowlers. He also used to pinch the strike off the last ball of an over. The better his form was, the more eager he was to get the strike, the further he backed up. "Let me get the strike, man," he would plead with me, "let me get the strike." So I played second fiddle. I fed him. He was a good cutter and puller: I've never seen anyone cut harder. He practised a lot but withdrew into himself when off-form, unlike me: I had so many slumps I got used to them.'

Greenidge declines to single out any one stand. 'I don't think you can assess something like that because of the variables. Take the 250 we made against Australia at Georgetown in 1983–4. We played well, sure, but it wasn't a pressure situation. I do know that, as an opener, you always find it comforting to know you have a competent, capable partner. Who took the initiative depended on who was playing the better at the time. I might take a bowler he was having trouble with, and vice versa. Desi, for instance, played Lillee as well as anyone. He has never lacked confidence but at the same time he is a very deep person, very conscious of what he's doing and what's going on. He has always been very conscientious, very watchful and careful. I'm very cautious and careful by nature as well. Like him, I always wanted to know that my game was still of the highest quality. We are both perfectionists, both seeking the positive despite the clinical way we appear to go about our job. Perhaps that is why he sometimes gets despondent and annoyed when he gets back to the dressing room after getting out. Even if I got out first he'd be the one who screamed, threw tantrums, just trying to release that sense of disappointment and frustration.'

One of the more remarkable facets of the Fabulous Bajan Boys' record-strewn relationship was the way an early departure for one would so often inspire the other. While one or other made a century in over 30 per cent of their Tests together, of the sixteen Desi collected when Greenidge began the innings at the other end, seven arrived after his partner had been dismissed in single figures, one after he had gone between 10 and 20, two when he managed 20 to 40, three after he had reached 50 and three after he had acquired three figures. In consort with Greenidge's fourteen 'tons' during the same period, Desi fell in single figures on six occasions, between 10 and 20 twice, 20 to 40 twice, while forging one half-century and three full Montes. In 50 per cent of Desi's centuries, therefore, Greenidge made 20 or less, while in 57.14 per cent of the latter's he made 20 or less. As a consequence of this, states Greenidge, 'I've watched some of Desi's most beautiful innings from a distance, the best of which was that 143 on a real Sydney turner in early '89. That effort at Lord's in 1980 was superb too. He was physically and mentally drained by the end of it but he'd broken Walcott's record. Afterwards, Walcott passed some unwarranted comment at him, which he smiled at at the time, but I wonder how much it hurt.' The concern is touching. 'Where do you stop? A disparaging comment like that diminishes the achievement.'

The *faux pas*, few as they were, remain vivid. 'There were four run-outs as far as I can recall,' says Greenidge, the first against Australia at Kensington in 1984. 'I thought it was my fault,' Desi told the *Nation* at the time, 'because when I pushed the ball past Border I could not really see the guy who was backing up Border and I said yes to Gordon. After that I changed my mind and said no. I find that batting with Gordon makes it easier for me and I felt really bad when he was run out so I figured that the best thing to satisfy him was if I could get a hundred.' He did.

The second mishap followed at Lord's soon after. 'Desi played the ball to square leg and we both set off, then I sent him back because the ball was going towards Allan Lamb quicker than he thought and I didn't think I'd make it. In the end, he was the one who didn't make it, Lamb hitting direct with an underarm throw. At Antigua in 1990, not long after we'd beaten our own record by putting on 298 against England, Desi played DeFreitas to long leg, a comfortable two. When Gladstone Small picked the ball up and prepared to throw there was no way I could imagine him hitting the stumps from there, so there was no point in rushing. As it happened, the throw just pipped me. Not only was I speechless but hurt too – the bails hit me in the face. Ironically, our last Test innings together saw us both run out, Desi unluckily when Merv Hughes deflected a drive of mine into the stumps while he was backing up. We could have asked for a better sign-off than that.'

To Greenidge, Holders Hill provided an ideal grounding for an aspiring cricketer. 'All the players there were very close and highly competitive at the same time, so that instilled an early edge in Desi. Opening is not a position every youngster craves or even welcomes, what with having to go in to face fresh bowlers and the new ball on a fresh wicket whose behaviour you cannot forecast. You need a will, a positive attitude. Desi not only had those qualities, he was never afraid. He only needed to be at the crease for a short while and the rhythm would arrive. He always had the drive to succeed but it took time for him to build up the technical side of his game. The mental capacity was always there, it was just a matter of bringing it out. One could not have asked for a better partner. He kept going, kept growing, not just in batting terms but also in his all-round cricketing knowledge. He should have been given a position where he could use that know-how.'

That last, flimsily veiled attack on the West Indies selectors pre-empts the subject of a later chapter. For now, let us concentrate on the batsman. Longevity in any professional sport is a considerable achievement, demanding a consistency of performance that eludes all but the foremost practitioners. In the real world, the greatest hurdle a job seeker faces lies in getting a foot in the door, yet precisely the opposite appears to hold sway on the playing fields, where sackings are ten-a-penny and tax-free redundancy cheques somewhat thin on the ground. Staying at the top is the most arduous task of all, as Greenidge affirms. 'When you reach a certain stage in your career people tend to take you for granted, yet they forget that at times the job gets harder, no matter how well you may have done it in the past. The opposition have scanned you, worked you out. They know where and how you score your runs, so you have to change, rearrange the way you score. Desi's done that. He's changed his stance, changed some of the angles. Yet he's never had the credit he deserves.'

Desi returns the compliment. 'It was a privilege to be at the other end of the pitch watching Gordon play the quick bowlers. In my formative days as a Test player when Lillee and Thomson were firing away at us, I couldn't comprehend how he could get on to the front foot with such ease against the world's fastest bowlers, then drop the ball dead at his feet. Naturally, I decided to watch closely. A couple of games later Lillee gave me a few short balls so I pulled them, but then he brought one back from off stump and had me leg-before. So I told myself I had to learn to get back and across but at the same time get forward when the ball was up to the bat. The differences in technique stemmed from our backgrounds. Gordon developed his game in England whereas I learned with a soft ball on the pasture and on the beach where one had to play back and across all the time.'

It is doubtful whether an international side has ever shifted as smoothly between opening partnerships as the West Indies managed to do in the late seventies. The join was invisible, although Clive Lloyd is in no doubt about their respective merits. 'Fredericks was an excellent player, a more attacking player than Gordon or Desi, a batsman who played spin as well as pace and did not lag far behind either of them when it came to the latter. But as partnerships go there was no comparison, although Desi and Gordon had so many good stands together that I couldn't really distinguish between them. Gordon was more of an all-round player, more correct, a complete batsman. He also had certain advantages. Growing up where he did, coming through the English coaching system then playing county cricket before he made his Test début, meant that his grounding was much better. Desi didn't have that kind of background and his inexperience obviously led to some indiscreet shots early in his Test career. On his first trip to Australia he wasn't doing too well and he was also getting quite fat, so I encouraged him to do some extra training during the Adelaide Test. Dennis Waight later told me that Desi hated me for doing that, but at the end of the season he came up and thanked me for doing him a great favour, saying that more young players should do the same.' Captain and player, it seems, have differing memories.

Lloyd, by his own admission, was watching out for Desi. 'I was looking after him personally. I didn't want to see him go to waste. Since then, apart from a bad patch around 1983 and 1984 when he went a couple of years without a century, he's been a tower of strength. The intensity of the situation has got to him at times but people must understand that when you're totally dedicated you will throw your bat around. I did it. We all have these moments. It's that dedication, the dedication that enabled him to score that 184 at Lord's, that makes him such a professional person. He believes that you have to make every day *your* day. Or, at the very least, if you put that bit extra in you'll get something out of it. I couldn't fault him in any way, other than that he's the only fielder I know who has to fall down whenever he catches the ball. It's probably because he's a bit top-heavy. His knees must be pretty weak by now.'

The crash-landings ceased with the advent of Logie, a spring-heeled jack-rabbit whose astonishing reflexes would make him the game's most prehensile presence in the perilous bat-pad position. Desi was not unhappy to vacate the role. 'The wear and tear on the knees and back, all that crouching and those sudden turns, diving on those hard surfaces then bouncing up to sprint for the ball, it all took its toll in the end. Ideally I would like to have fielded at first or second slip, but with all the inherent risks of finger injuries I was never comfortable there. I like gully, but Gordon or Joel had that cornered so I ended up flitting between mid-off, mid-on or cover – and doing all the chasing. When captaining a side I feel I can make a greater contribution to the bowler if I'm close to him, so mid-on and mid-off are the best vantage points. That way I can go back with the bowler to his mark, remind him of our plans, discuss field settings. Viv and Lloydy were our best slippers, however, so it was only right that they should captain the side from there. Same with Mike Gatting at Middlesex, although he sometimes takes himself out of the cordon in order to take a breather and also view the game from a different perspective.'

Despite their serene progress against India, the West Indies were by no means certain to retain the World Cup in England during the summer of 1983. Their fourteen-man squad numbered no fewer than six fast bowlers, an inordinate proportion that reflected concern over the capacity of some of the ageing warriors to last the pace. Roberts and Garner, after all, were both thirtysomethings, Holding in his thirtieth year. They remained firm favourites none the less, although this status took an immediate knock in their opening altercation with India at Old Trafford.

On the surface it appeared a gross mismatch. India had gained only one victory in the previous two tournaments, and that against East Africa, while the holders had never tasted defeat. Kapil Dev's team had one decided advantage, however, namely a stream of oddjob all-rounders who added depth to batting and bowling alike. The West Indies, conversely, would be forced to fiddle 12 overs from the unprepossessing dobbers of Richards and Gomes. As it happened, Gomes tempted Sandeep Patil and Kapil Dev into indiscretion and at 141 for 5 all was going swimmingly. Yashpal Sharma then restored the innings to rude health with a bold 89 from 120 balls, enough to land him the match award, although it took some heaves from two of the handymen, Roger Binny and Madan Lal, to lift India to the heights of 262 for 8. After

Desi had been run out for 24 to halt the opening stand at 49, the same pair proceeded to rip the heart out of the middle order, Richards, Bacchus, Lloyd and Dujon perishing in a blaze of inglorious shots as the pursuers plunged to 157 for 9. Roberts and Garner supplied some oxygen in adding 71, shelling Shastri as they went, but when the gangling young slow left-armer returned he had Garner stumped with his first delivery, wrapping up the greatest shock result in the competition's brief history.

Australia felt the backlash at Headingley, Gomes leading the way with 78 before the stringbean Winston Davis, a former flour mill worker from St Vincent and the youngest member of the pace phalanx at 24, swept aside a powerful batting order, taking 7 for 51 as the 1975 finalists barely managed to survive half their allotted 60 overs. Caught behind off Lawson for 13, Desi went in identical fashion at Worcester, succumbing to a Peter Rawson outswinger for 2 as the West Indies romped to an eight-wicket win over Zimbabwe. He fared better in the return bout with India at the Oval, a steady 38 as Richards's outrider in a second-wicket stand of 101 leading to a formidable score of 282 for 9, to which only Amarnath could muster much of a riposte as the giantkillers slid down the beanstalk and folded for 218. The Fabulous Bajan Boys then launched the charge after Australia's impressive 273 for 6 at Lord's, scooting along to 79 in 18 overs before Desi dragged an offering from slow left-armer Tom Hogan into his stumps. Richards brought out his threshing machine to secure the spoils with 13 balls to spare, a close-run thing by comparison with the final Group B contest at Edgbaston, wherein Desi (88 not out) and Bacchus (80 not out in place of the resting Greenidge) scampered to a 10-wicket massacre of Zimbabwe with an unbroken alliance of 172 in 45.1 overs.

As winners of their section, the West Indies swanned into the semi-final at Kennington with the bookmakers installing them as prohibitive 8–13 favourites, a show of faith that was duly rewarded with an emphatic eight-wicket triumph over a listless Pakistan. Taking the attack to Abdul Qadir with some forthright lofts over the top, Desi contributed 29 before driving over a googly. And so to Lord's, where India, surprisingly, lay in wait, having seen off England by six wickets at Old Trafford. For half the duration of that unlikely Saturday, the champions, Sonny Liston to India's nimbler Cassius Clay, lived up to their billing. Kris Srikkanth, international cricket's very own blacksmith, hooked Roberts for six into the Warner Stand *en route* to a typically effervescent 38 but the early loss of the out-of-form Gavaskar – Roberts's first victim in three finals – was never made good. No other Indian reached 30 and the West Indies could contemplate a doddle: 184 to get.

Lulled into over-confidence, they suffered a uniform lapse in concentration. 'We'd have made 270 if that had been the target,' Greenidge would observe in hindsight. Quite possibly. As it was, Greenidge himself went in the fourth over, playing no stroke to a ball from Sandhu that cut back and removed his off stump. Richards hit haughtily for a time, but Desi failed to keep up, scooping a half-volley from Madan Lal to extra cover. He returned to the fray almost at once when Lloyd, beset by thigh and groin problems, summoned a runner, but the lemmings continued to scurry over the precipice. Richards skied Lal towards the grandstand, Dev timing his 30-yard dash to perfection before hugging the catch to his chest; frustrated by Binny's constraining 5–4 legside field, Gomes nicked to slip; Lloyd drove to mid-off. At 66 for 5, the plot had not so much thickened as curdled.

Tea failed to refresh the parts that common sense had deserted, Bacchus slashing at the third ball after the resumption to be caught behind off Sandhu. Sanity resurfaced, Dujon and Marshall putting on 43 for the seventh wicket by dint of sensible application, but when the wicketkeeper played on after failing to withdraw his blade from the line of a gentle Amarnath inswinger, the right hand that pounded the turf in exasperation encapsulated the air of self-admonishment. Eloquently depicted by David Frith in *Wisden Cricket Monthly* as 'an elderly bank clerk out jogging', Amarnath bobbed in to dispatch Marshall in his next over, then applied the *coup de grâce* by trapping Holding leg-before with the last delivery of the fifty-second over. Dickie Bird's raised finger, rejoiced Frith, 'granted countless millions of Indians a joyous if short-lived reprieve from the miseries of poverty and deprivation'. Rooted to the spot in disbelief, Holding was all but trampled underfoot as the hordes spilled over the boundary, Southall and Srinagar united in celebration. There were no alibis from Lloyd, who rated Jim Fairbrother's pitch as 'near perfect'. Given that not one of the twenty batsmen on parade reached 40, this might seem an overly generous assessment, yet this was a game lost in the mind. 'We got carried away,' Lloyd confessed. 'It was an amateurish performance.'

Desi was shattered. 'I didn't think we'd knock them over easily but I did think we'd win. To be fair, Clyde Walcott warned us beforehand. "These guys have already beaten you," he said, "be careful." It was just one of those things. The wicket was good and we thought the runs would be so easy to get, so we probably relaxed a bit. When it was all over most of us went back to the hotel. Some of the guys were crying. They didn't want to show their faces. We felt that we'd let the whole Caribbean down. It was one of the worst days of my career. I try to put it out of my mind but every time I go to India somebody reminds me of it. Going there a few months later felt like a revenge mission, but although we beat them five times in a row in the one-dayers they were still the world champions.'

Windle Holmes, who has been to England for all four of Desi's tours and both his World Cup finals, was around as usual for a bit of light relief. 'I've watched every Test innings he's ever had in Barbados. I'd listen on the radio, dash down to Kensington as soon as the West Indies finished fielding, then nip back to Holders Hill when he was out and turn the radio in the bar back on. That summer I was in London with the British West Indian Airways Cavaliers team and we ended up in the same hotel. Desi was having a tough time during the tournament but I was having fun! One day I made a hundred and absolutely lorded it over him. After the final I left him alone. All he wanted to do was sleep.'

Oblivious to the incessant beat of the bhangra as the Indian contingent at the Westmoreland Hotel cavorted long into the night, rubbing in the ignominy of it all, Desi somehow managed it. He always could switch off.

9

Paddington and Vivi

The Don, it appears, had two views of bouncers – one when they
were bowled against him and the other when bowled by his side
with no fear of retaliation.

Batting from Memory, Jack Fingleton

If the passing of the reins of power can be a traumatic process, *weltschmerz*
reigned in the case of both the West Indies captaincy and the islands' pre-
eminence at Test level. Having resigned the head honcho role after the World
Cup and announced Viv Richards as his successor, Clive Lloyd was persuaded
by the West Indies board to revoke his decision. Having overheard Clyde
Walcott make it abundantly clear to Lloyd that his anticipated ascent was
far from cut and dried, Viv Richards knew full well that this *volte-face* was
attributable to the board's reluctance to appoint him. This, most certainly, was
not the yes-man required. The owner of cricket's most merciless broadsword
was a volatile character with passion stitched into his shirtsleeves, unable to
suppress emotion as Lloyd had and therefore deemed unlikely to do much to
improve international relations already strained by racial jealousy. A one-eyed
interpretation from an over-sensitive liberal? Perhaps. On the other hand,
while no other non-white team had ever exerted such command of the Test
stage, none had been so frequently castigated for tarnishing the game's
laughably pacifistic image. Coincidence? Doubtful. For all that, the Antiguan
was the only viable option.

The leadership issue, however, was shelved as humble summer gave way
to autumnal authority. Extracting full retribution for their humiliation at

Lord's, the West Indies took India by storm, winning the first, third and fifth Tests in addition to sweeping the five one-day internationals. Ironically, an Indian batsman, the incomparable Sunil Gavaskar, stole the laurels by registering his thirtieth Test century at Madras, supplanting Bradman's thirty-five-year-old landmark and ploughing on to an unbeaten 236, in the process becoming the first man to score thirteen 100s and three double-100s against the West Indies. He was no aficionado of the Caribbean Crusher. 'This was not great captaincy,' he said of Lloyd after five Indians had been unable to complete the Kingston Test of early 1976, 'it was barbarism.' Barbarism or not, Gavaskar quelled the barbers better than any of his contemporaries, correct, neat strokeplay, nimble, precise footwork and concrete defence wedded to remorseless concentration and oodles of courage to produce a serene marriage of mind and body. 'He was the best opener of my time,' Desi confirms. 'He played pace so well, a complete player.' Not complete enough, however, to prevent Holding and Marshall from sharing sixty-three victims in the six-match rubber, the latter equalling the national records of Valentine and Croft with thirty-three. The most productive bat on either side was the one wielded by the oldest player, an atypically stolid Lloyd, zing of old behind him as he struggled with a niggling back ailment, yet averaging 82.66. Such resourcefulness was sorely needed, too, since the rest of the top order was riddled with holes. Desi, gallingly, gaped the widest, trailing in behind Marshall, Holding and Roberts in the averages with 176 runs at 17.60.

Desi had limbered up for the sub-continent in ruthless fashion, ruining Greenidge's benefit match with an unconquered 121 for Barbados against the beneficiary's Anglo-West Indian XI. Indeed, he began the tour promisingly enough, scores of 45, 67 not out, 64 and 38 preceding a matchwinning 55 not out in the first one-day international at Srinagar. Timing increasingly unsettled by slothful pitches, he slithered downhill thereafter. In only one of his ten five-day knocks could he manage more than 24, and even the exception, a reviving 55 at Bombay after Greenidge had gone early and Richie Richardson had succumbed for a duck in his maiden Test innings, was tinged with degradation. Facing Kapil Dev, Desi joined Mohsin Khan, Andrew Hilditch and Russell Endean by becoming the fourth player to be given out 'handled the ball' in a Test. Seeking solace in the troubles of others has a habit of placing matters in their proper perspective and comfort could be derived from the inexorable descent of Mohinder Amarnath, the titan of the previous series between these two, whose abject failure transformed Desi's blues into purple patches by comparison. Plummeting headlong into a

bottomless trough, the World Cup final Man of the Match made five ducks
and one lonely scoring stroke – a single – in six Test innings. Fate is often
more sadistic than fickle.

Desi readily acknowledges his own deficiencies. 'I simply did not adapt to
the slowness of the wickets as well as I should have. Bedi, Chandra, Venkat
and Prasanna were no longer on the scene and the Indian spin attack was
nowhere near as mesmerizing as it had been, but the pitches were prepared
for turn regardless of the quality of spinners at their disposal. I had a few
bad decisions but you always get those overseas, so there was no point in
seeking excuses on that count. To their credit, the selectors showed a lot of
faith in me, although if we hadn't been winning or there had been someone
pressing for my place I'm sure I would have been dropped.' What, then, of
that Bombay *faux pas*? 'Viv and I were going well when Kapil bowled one
down the leg side. It deflected off my pads and I panicked and tried to knock
the ball away with my hand. I tried to plead my case to Kapil but he had a
discussion with the umpires and I was on my way. I was embarrassed, to say
the least. The rule has always seemed an odd one to me. After all, you
can kick the ball away in that situation.' Although he refused to allow his
disappointment to communicate itself to his colleagues, he was already looking ahead for a chance to atone long before the end of the series. 'I felt let
down, chastened by the sense of failure, looking forward to going home and
making amends against Australia.'

The pre-tour barometer was set fair. Stricken by the simultaneous retirements of Greg Chappell, Rod Marsh and Denis Lillee, the Porthos, Athos
and Aramis of the Ugly Australian court, and further depleted by the unavail-
ability of Graham Yallop owing to a knee complaint, the visitors were certainly
distant second favourites in the starting stalls. Rod Hogg, Carl Rackemann
and Geoff Lawson were the only bowlers likely to trouble the hosts but injury
subdued all three. Pummelled by Garner, Holding, Marshall and Daniel, the
batsmen proved even more vulnerable. Kepler Wessels returned home with
a wrenched knee, fellow openers Graeme Wood and Steve Smith suffered
broken fingers, the upshot a different first-wicket pairing in each of the five
Tests. Throw in an ongoing tiff over contracts and a number of unseemly
tantrums, notably from Lawson and his captain, Kim Hughes, and the scars
of a miserable venture were unmistakable. Overwhelmed on the field by a
team hailed by Hughes as 'the strongest, most professional and most disciplined' he had ever crossed swords with, Australia were distinctly fortunate
to keep the margin down to 3–0 in the Tests, while only the toss of a coin

in damp conditions at Port-of-Spain spared a whitewash in the four-match one-day series. Men against boys.

For Desi, the mysteries of the East were soon buried away in the farthest recesses of the memory. Outwardly unflustered but inwardly perturbed, galvanized both by the need to justify the selectors' patience and a return to pitches with a semblance of pace, he returned to form in the World Series Cup prelude, rustling up 418 runs at 52.25 as the West Indies reasserted their presence in the shorter format despite being on the wrong end of one of the more ludicrous bits of official conniving in the modern game. Even though the guests lost five wickets to the nine shed by their Australian hosts, the second act of the best-of-three finals was decreed a tie. And there were we imagining that the principal marketing ploy used to sell 'instant' cricket had been its promise of a decisive result. How naïve. After all, the extra booty from a third instalment was not to be sniffed at.

Revitalized, Desi thrived as never before when the sides adjourned to the Caribbean. In twelve Test and one-day knocks he amassed 808 runs at 134.66, rolling merrily along to five centuries all told. So sure was his touch that, in eight five-day innings, he was never caught. Topping the Test averages with 468 at 93.60, he sprinted away with 60 and 103 not out at Georgetown, where stalemate beckoned from the moment Kim Hughes led seven specialist bats into battle while the West Indies relented and brought in a full-time spinner, Roger Harper, for the first time since 1980. That said, half an hour of birthday boy Richards in full regalia on the final afternoon would surely have decided matters. But history, rather than drama, held sway. Left foot throbbing from a Lawson yorker, Desi added an undefeated 250 with Greenidge as they expunged Rae and Stollmeyer's 239 against India in 1948–9 from the record books and rewrote the entry for a West Indian opening stand in a Test.

The target was a taxing one, 323 at almost five runs an over, on a pitch that seemed to have evened out following the shooters of days three and four yet which had still permitted Winston Davis to hit Hogg on the head and Lawson on the forearm before Hughes declared half an hour before lunch. It was addressed with wavering interest yet the visitors began the final 20 overs needing 171, a plausible equation, just. The Fabulous Bajan Boys had maintained a pace of better than four an over for more than four hours – Greenidge, said Hughes, 'was mis-hitting sixes over long-off ... if any pair of openers could have done it, they were the men' – but Desi, understandably, grew hesitant as he approached his first Test ton against Australia, adding only 30 during the last 16 overs. Defensive fields and the accuracy of Lawson played their part in preventing him from stepping up a gear, but Desi was booed all the same before the ghost was surrendered with 99 still wanted from 10 overs, his unbeaten 103 incorporating 265 minutes and nine boundaries.

Typically, he saved his best for Kensington, six hours or so of strident mastery bringing nineteen fours and a six before a creeper from Hogg bowled him for 145, his highest score at this level for almost four years. Recollections, as ever, are self-effacing. 'I was pleased. What more can I say? I suppose I was having one of those spells when everything clicks. It was a good wicket for the first three days or so but then, like many of the surfaces during the series, the bounce became increasingly low and Australia made the mistake of thinking it would remain true throughout.'

This turned out to be the turning point of the series. Kept afloat by two rafts of trenchant Border-line resistance at Port-of-Spain, Australia had somehow survived the first two Tests. At the end of the second day, 429 to the good after being sent in, they had had a sniff of victory here. Instead, Richardson, retained only because of Logie's late attack of flu, followed up with his maiden Test century and the West Indies totalled 509 to lead by 80 shortly after tea on the fourth afternoon, whereupon Holding and Marshall ripped through the Australian batting, provoking a stampede to the pavilion that saw Hughes's men melt away to 97 all out, the lowest Test total yet recorded in Bridgetown. And so, just before lunch on the fifth day, Desi strolled out once more to co-author a 10-wicket win, the first in what would prove to be a record-breaking run. His signature also adorned the most remarkable feat of all: not only did he and Greenidge co-produce eight stands worth a combined 684 runs at the weighty average of 136.80, the visitors did not lose a second-innings wicket in the whole series. No international side had ever achieved such overwhelming control as this. Thus were 100 hours of labour edited down to one succinct highlight. For once, statistics imparted the truth.

A puffed-up incident in the fourth one-dayer in St Lucia showed that Desi, with a career and an improving lifestyle to protect, could be as single-minded as the next man. With 10 runs required for victory and stacks of overs in hand, Dujon straight-drove Rackemann for four. 'The shot was greeted', dramatized Peter McFarline of the Melbourne *Age*, 'by a bat-dropping display of petulance by Haynes, who was then 96 and covetous of his second century in three one-day matches. Dujon took the hint...' Emotions, of course, have no place on a cricket field. Desi's intolerant view of injustice, hitherto suppressed, surfaced during the Barbados–Australia match. Judged innocent when David Hookes claimed a bat-pad catch off Greg Matthews's off-spin, he whacked his left pad with an apparently aggrieved bat to emphasize that there had been no grounds for appeal. Later in the same over, Desi's partner, Arnold Gilkes, was pronounced not out when another ear-splitting plea rent the air as Dean Jones clung on to the ball at short leg. The non-striker turned his bat around and aimed it at various members of the fielding side as if it were a Kalashnikov. At the end of the over, Hookes playfully pushed Desi in the back. Boys will be boys.

Especially the Australians. In the final Test at Kingston, Hogg sent down twelve successive bouncers to Desi and Greenidge, his concept of Ocker vengeance for a similar gambit pursued by Garner and Marshall the previous day. Never one to waste an opportunity to intimidate umpires or express displeasure, Lawson, an optician by trade with a quick wit and a lively intelligence, performed a highly credible impression of one of those Foster's-swilling 'hoons' who polluted the Hill at Sydney. At Georgetown he showed Aqib Javed the proper way to snatch back a hat from an umpire with an expert display of yobbery that produced a £150 fine. Thanks to a diplomatic note wherein Allan Rae advised the Australian manager, Col Eagar, that such regrettable conduct might incite the crowds, there were no more ruckuses worthy of the name. 'We didn't believe in sledging as they obviously did, but at that stage the relationship between the sides was actually pretty good,' Desi asserts. 'We drank together after the game then.'

The seeds, nevertheless, had been sown. Lloyd, for instance, had missed the third one-day international at Castries because of his obligations in the libel court. In January 1982, the Melbourne *Age* had accused the West Indies of deliberately losing a limited-overs fixture, prompting Lloyd to slap in a writ to defend the honour of his homelands, the defence resting its case on the lack of any mention of a specific player. Awarded A$100,000 in damages, he subsequently saw this adjudication quashed on appeal, took the matter to the House of Lords and had the original ruling upheld. More tangible evidence of the growing Caribbean–Antipodean antipathy came after Desi and Greenidge had completed that Kingston caning. Having seen them cap their captain's hundredth Test in due style by swatting 55 in 11 overs, Lawson sidled up to Desi. 'Congratulations, old boy, best team won,' was not his chosen greeting. What he did say was more along the lines of 'See you Down Under, sunshine. Bring an extra helmet.'

Not, though, before the West Indies had dropped in on Albion for Lloyd's farewell mission there, and introduced a new word to the lexicon: blackwash. Laying claim to the unprovable title of the greatest collective in Test history, the squadron's unerring aim notched a kill in each of the five Tests. From the very first morning of the series at Edgbaston, when local boy Andy Lloyd's brand new representative career was ended by Marshall's brutal if accidental blow to the temple, a combination of seventeen homegrown players plus one apiece from Germany, South Africa, Kenya and Jamaica had no answer to the corporate desire of the Caribbean.

Even before this, a triumphant overture from Richards, the supreme soloist of this heavy metal age, had trumpeted the arrival of an extraordinary ensemble. His 189 in the inaugural Texaco Trophy international, an innings of majestic, brutal force, set the tone for an exposition of cricketing expertise the like of which Blighty had never witnessed. In the summer of 1984, coming directly after duckings in Pakistan and New Zealand, Britannia did not so much rule the waves as audition for the post of galley slave. The South African fallout, of course, had hampered Peter May and his fellow selectors, but with Botham, Gower and Gatting still in the ranks the battalion they put into the field was far from meek. Yet if a player bubbling with as much confidence as Amarnath could be so easily deflated, surely better to praise Marshall, Garner and Holding than bury their prey. In ten innings the harried home batsmen hurried from the crease as if occupation were going out of fashion, 97 English wickets going down while the moderate heights of 300 were scaled precisely once. Only just at that, Gower declaring at 300 for 9 before inviting Greenidge in for that sumptuous feast at Lord's. Other teams – Australia against England in 1920–21 and South Africa in 1931–2, England against India in 1959 and West Indies against India in 1961–2 – had achieved a similar degree of superiority; none, though, had ever swept a five-match rubber in their victim's backyard. So this was what they meant by corporate hospitality . . .

In July a letter in *Wisden Cricket Monthly* from one Norman Joughin proposed that Barbados be made an independent Test country in order to disrupt the Caribbean dictatorship. By August many English supporters were bemoaning the fact that the TCCB had agreed to prevail upon the counties not to field any players against the tourists who had been barred from Test cricket because of their South African connections. Had this not been done, the tour might never have proceeded. Yorkshire, not untypically, refused to comply, compelling the cancellation of the William Wilberforce commemorative match at Hull. Lancashire stepped in, the proceeds to go towards financing Hull University scholarships for deprived West Indians. The weather, cruelly, meant not a penny was raised.

Hosts of legendary combinations are invoked when the inevitable comparisons are drawn: the Australians of Armstrong, Bradman and Ian Chappell, Ali Bacher's 1970 South Africans, F. S. Jackson's 1902 Englishmen, even Lloyd's 1976 Caribbean conglomeration, whom he, incidentally, rates higher than this 1984 vintage. Such analyses are purely academic, of course. The constituent factors are too variable – pitches, weather, contemporary laws and practice, opposition strength – for there to be any all-embracing form of measurement. It is nevertheless hard to recall one side so thoroughly outplaying the other in every department of the game as the 1984 West Indians did to England.

Allan Lamb, Gower (even though not on form) and Botham might conceivably have squeezed into a composite twelve culled from the respective squads, but that would have meant ditching Gomes (average 80, nearly double that of the leading Englishman, Lamb), discarding the sole spinner (Roger Harper) and perhaps jettisoning one of the captains, Gower or Lloyd. The West Indies even held a handsome advantage on the subtlety front, Harper's 13 wickets retailing at 21.23 runs per head to undercut the 10 turned out by Nick Cook, Pat Pocock and Geoff Miller at nearly three times the price. Harper also happened to be far and away the best fielder in either camp. With Marshall and Garner sharing more wickets (53) than eight English seamers could muster, and Holding, Baptiste, Winston Davis and Milton Small supporting them to the hilt, the architects, of course, were the bowlers, yet the depth of the batting was such that all five of the specialists reached three figures at least once while nine men in all recorded an innings of 69 or more, three of them pacemen.

In Desi's estimation, Greenidge's finest hour came at Lord's. 'At the start we thought, let's play it as we see it. Gordon looked confident from the first over but I was run out after a full-length dive. I sat inside the dressing room for a while, feeling down, then I began to watch again and saw some truly amazing shots. So I figured, well, at least that makes up for my failure. An exceptional innings.'

While citing the 1984 team as the finest in his experience – 'a blend of disciplined and aggressive batting, a pace attack to match any, one of the best wicketkeeper-batsmen the game has known, bowlers who could bat and field in the slips' – Desi feels that England, to an extent, dug their own grave. 'No one thought about a "blackwash" in advance, I can assure you of that. The mistake the English authorities made repeatedly during the eighties was to try and leave the wickets flat so as to nullify the threat of our fast bowlers, but all they succeeded in doing was making it extremely hard for their own bowlers to bowl us out twice, which is the only way to win a Test match. At the same time, Marshall, Holding and the rest of our guys could still do a bit on dead wickets. England would have been better off with wickets that moved sideways to a greater extent, as their bowlers are accustomed to. The aim should have been to match our batters against their bowlers, rather than their batters against our bowlers, which was the tack they took. As usual, the series was played in a good spirit. It always was when we got together with England because so many of our players had been on the county circuit. And, as ever, the relationship between Beefy and Viv was a major catalyst.'

Amid this regal procession, however, Desi was little more than a footman. Aside from a two-and-a-half-hour 100 in a non-first-class fixture against the uninspiring Blues of Oxford and Cambridge, his highest score going into the first Test was the frisky 89 he made at Worcester on the opening day of the tour, his remaining three knocks yielding 20 against Somerset (caught behind off the unassuming seam of Martin Crowe), a duck against Lancashire (a one-day game), and 12 against Northants. Run out by Botham off his own bowling during the second over of Viv's Manchester masterpiece, he made 4 in the low-scoring second chapter at Trent Bridge, where England bumbled home by three wickets, then 18 in the concluding eight-wicket cruise at Lord's. His subsequent tally of 235 runs in eight completed Test innings was a disappointment, though hardly critical. He and Greenidge both fell leg-before to Willis within the space of three balls on the first evening of the rubber at Edgbaston, but Gomes (143), Richards (117), Lloyd (71), Baptiste (87 not out) and Holding (69) rollicked along at over four runs an over to post the not insignificant matter of 606. The West Indies did not get as far as 400 again – they had no need to – but Desi's overall input, or, rather, lack of it, was not missed because there were so many other capable chaps around to pick up the slack.

Only in the fourth Test at Leeds, furthermore, did the Fabulous Bajan Boys pump up the volume to its customary wattage, adding 106 *en route* to an eight-wicket victory. Yet the one time in the series that the juggernaut stalled, Desi was on hand with the jump-leads. With only 28 runs between the teams on first innings at the Oval, Desi reawoke for a defiant final rally, acquiring his third century in eight Tests with a diligent seven-hour 125 during which he featured in three separate half-century stands to provide the backbone of a matchwinning 346. 'I was going along pretty well in the county games and I was playing straighter than I had been a year earlier when I kept getting edges, but I have no idea why I was unable to put it together in the Tests. Viv stressed how we had to be careful not to give it away, that you could get an unplayable ball whether you'd made 0 or 100. Perhaps that made me a little hesitant, I don't know. I was the only one of the top five batsmen to have no county experience behind me, admittedly. But we were winning. That was all that mattered. Obviously I wanted to contribute more, but I don't think I was riddled with fear or anything like that. Being part of a winning side allows you to get away with a few failures, which is a damned good thing in my view. Why should you always be on trial? The selectors deserve credit because they were always prepared to give you a good run – and thank God for that. Then again, maybe you simply worry less when you belong to a side that is beating the opposition at will.'

All the same, Desi was given a gentle boot up the backside that Friday afternoon. 'Before the second innings started Lloydy said that the selectors were looking ahead to the Australian tour that winter and that this was therefore my last chance to state a case – and I knew it. I'd brought my mother over for the last couple of weeks of the tour, giving her her first taste of overseas travel. She must have been a lucky talisman.'

Arletha herself found it an unusual experience. 'I listen on the radio, even when he's playing at Bridgetown. I can't stand watching him because it scares me to see the ball going for his head. I can remember going to see him at Kensington in 1979 when Lillee and Thomson were in town as part of the Packer tour. "Lord have mercy," I said to myself when I saw how fast and nasty they were. "Forget about this cricket thing," I pleaded with Desi. It really frightened me. But Desi was pretty laid-back about it. He used to try and reassure me, saying things like, "They're not bowling so fast, Mum." It wasn't quite the same that summer, of course. When I arrived just before the Oval Test, I said to him, "I can't believe it. I've come all this way and you haven't made a hundred for me." So he went out and made amends. Just for me.'

Desi also did right by Alan Rogers, a twenty-year-old all-rounder from Barbados, arranging a sponsorship/scholarship package via the travel firm Caribbean Connection whereby Rogers was able to spend a summer playing for Chester Boughton Hall. *Pour encourager les enfants.*

Lloyd, it transpires, was indulging in a bit of psychological motivation. 'I felt, and still do, that Desi's problems were attributable to playing in the Leagues. He had the butcher, the baker and the candlestick-maker bowling at him. He wasn't facing top-class bowling on a regular basis so he was getting into bad habits. Just like Carl Hooper before he joined Kent. They'd make 100 in no time but neither the bowling nor the concentration would be up to standard. And whereas they might hit that century in an hour, they might spend the same time making 20 or 30 in a Test. Once you lapse in concentration you get taken because these are world-class players you're up against. Yet there was no thought of dropping Desi as far as I was concerned. I knew him inside out, knew that sooner or later he would come good again. I only invested in players whom I knew to have the requisite qualities. They knew that once I had made that investment I would stick with them. I didn't drop people willy-nilly. The same is true now. Hooper had been awarded 30-odd caps up to the end of the 1991–2 season and made three centuries, but the selectors and captains have kept faith because they know he has the ability.' Contrast this with, say, the comparatively adulterous English approach of the eighties. For a player to develop at a natural rather than forced pace, long-term investments are infinitely preferable to short-term deposits, especially when profits accrue from the remainder of your portfolio with some vestige of dependability.

Lloyd's formal adieu came in Australia that winter, ironically in defeat at the SCG, where a decidedly un-Tigerish, grey-stained leg-spinner named Bob Holland spirited the West Indies to their first reversal for three years. A mildly discordant cadenza, then, to the tenure of the most durable and successful Test captain in history: 74 games, 36 wins and 12 losses, all this despite a less than masterful display of coin-tossing that saw the opposing captain secure the first option more than half the time. More often than not, it would be his first and last victory. Just as they did against the same opposition in the fifth Test of 1965, and would later do in the fourth Test of 1988–9 and the final instalment of the 1990–91 rubber, the West Indies faltered with the series won, on this occasion having overhauled Australia's record sequence of eight consecutive victories over England in 1920 and 1921 and gone on to establish a fresh mark of 11. A draw at Melbourne – which might easily have been another notch on the bedpost had Lloyd declared fifteen minutes sooner – displaced England's 26-match unbeaten run under the canny Ray Illingworth between 1968 and 1971 in Bill Frindall's computer. Paddington could scarcely have asked for a more glowing testimony.

Now a British citizen, Lloyd is domiciled in Cheshire, where his wife, Waveney, runs a nursing home. Melissa, one of their daughters, is training for the stage. Since ending his cricketing career with a duck in the 1986 NatWest Trophy final, Papa Clive has spread his talents far and wide, working for Manchester's Piccadilly Radio, managing the West Indies on tour, serving as an ICC referee and devoting unstinting effort to an inner city housing trust based in Liverpool. A member of the Sports and Arts Foundation, he received the CBE in 1992; on that same day Gower, a more native hero, was presented with the inferior OBE.

Lloyd's decision to run for his local council as a Tory surprised some, disappointed others. Many more decried his achievements either by accusing him of doling out licences to maim or else of possessing the kind of firepower that rendered leadership and man-management irrelevant. When Kim Hughes decided to stop carrying the can for Australia's shame following the second Test of that winter's rubber, resigning his post in a reservoir of tears, Keith Fletcher's sentiments were not unusual. 'Without being unkind,' the Gnome was quoted as saying, 'a donkey could lead the West Indies at the moment. But put Clive Lloyd in charge of Australia and even he'd struggle.' Almost without exception, captains stand or fall by the quality of their crew, but Lloyd's skill lay in persuading his marvellously able seamen to mesh as one and operate on full steam for voyage after voyage. Graeme Fowler, a Lancashire colleague and international adversary, illustrated the *modus operandi* in his perceptive diary, *Fox on the Run*: 'He doesn't work by changing people in the structure. He tries to mould them, get them round to his way of thinking and put them on the right track. He believes that the best way of having a good ship is to mould the crew, not to change the shipping company.'

In my own limited dealings with him, Lloyd came across as a caring, paternalistic bear of a man imbued with the growl imperative to any member of a minority seeking to break down the established order. Aggressive when required, tough as teak at the tiller, yet anxious to uphold the values of the game he adored – where he deemed those values worth respecting – and bent on improving the self-image of his people. When cheque-brandishing ad execs pursued his team from Perth to Brisbane during that final tour, he felt it only fitting that a goodly percentage of the endorsements and personal appearance fees be donated to charity. That he was nominated for a place on the Lancashire committee (the late Roy Marshall, a 'white' Bajan, is the only black presence I can remember occupying a similar position of authority in a county boardroom) speaks similar volumes. 'That man must be a bigger ass than I thought he was,' he retorted after Mike Brearley, along with Imran Khan the only other truly inspirational captain of the heavy metal era, had lambasted his helmsmanship. Yet the differences between the two are not as vast as this may infer. The bookish, brilliant, quietly ruthless Brearley has titles like *The Divided Self* and *Human Aggression* dotted around on his book-shelves; Lloyd, a more earthy, less calculating character, prefers tomes such as *Inward Hunger.*

Described by manager Wes Hall as 'an unmitigated seeker of pleasure', Desi was honoured to have shared a dressing room with Lloyd. 'I was distinctly lucky to begin my Test career with Clive. Like Viv he was aggressive, but his aggression came out more in his batting than his captaincy. As a batsman he was particularly fond of the pull and sweep, exceedingly severe on spinners and fast bowlers who pitched consistently short. I remember only too well listening to the radio while he was crashing Bedi all over the place in India in 1974–5. It sounded as if Bedi was bowling then looking for a place to run because the ball was coming back at him at such a tremendous speed. In fact, he was playing better over the last five years of his career so I consider myself fortunate to have been around at that time. My only regret is that, great slip though he was, I never saw him at his feline best in the covers.

'The critics thought he had an easy job because he had a good team, four fast bowlers, etc., but I object to that. He was a great captain, a great leader of men. By getting us to play as a team rather than regard things purely from our own selfish perspective he did so much for West Indian cricket. Generally speaking, the better a team is the more likely its constituent parts are to play for themselves. When games are being won, the tendency may be to examine one's own contribution more closely, but that was never the case under Clive. Perhaps that's why I did not worry as much as others might have during my lean spells. Before Clive took over, the West Indies had never played together in the real sense, and we certainly did not have a professional attitude. Clive had been one of the first players signed during the English import drive of 1968 and he instilled in us the professionalism and discipline he himself had acquired. He ensured we prepared properly, keeping Dennis Waight on board after Packer and making sure we didn't mess around in the nets. There was always a youngster coming through so we had to set an example. Because there was no coach, he was responsible for organizing net practice. You'd have fifteen minutes at the crease, then help the bowlers out. One session the batsmen would have a net, the next it would be the bowlers' turn. He reasoned that if they were prepared to dish it out then they should be prepared to take it. There are times, after all, when you depend on tailenders as much as you do on your front line batsmen.'

Billed as another Conrad Hunte by admiring Aussie journos who had witnessed his prolific displays against their boys the previous year, Desi bade an unexpectedly muted *au revoir* to one of his most faithful supporters, nine completed Test innings in Australia comprising three half-centuries, 247 runs and an average of 27.44. 'I thought we let Lloydy down in Sydney. We wanted to give him a proper send-off, but he accepted it. We'd always accepted defeat graciously under him. It was history the next day.' The precocious pace of Craig McDermott, a rangy teenage redhead from Queensland who made his début in the fourth Test, accounted for Desi twice in three innings. 'He was very fast. I couldn't believe it in a nineteen-year-old. I thought he would be a world beater from the word go.' Yet again, the World Series Cup balanced the books, 514 runs at 51.40 helping his side win twelve of their thirteen games when the serious business was done. Through all the ups and downs, a sense of humour, of perspective, shone through. At one point, Marshall noted, 'He tied three knots in his tie so that it looked about three or four inches long. When we asked him why his tie had shrunk he told us it had got shorter because he was short of runs. Sounds trivial, I suppose, but as a way of destroying any anxiety it was brilliant.'

Prior to this, however, Lawson, that needler supreme, had pushed him to the brink. The West Indies were completing the last few furlongs of an eight-wicket win in the second Test in Brisbane when the world's fastest optician bowled Desi off an inside edge with five runs needed, this just two overs after Lawson had berated the batsman for an under-middled stroke. The bowler, excited beyond the context of this meaningless thrust, bounded down the wicket in a needlessly extravagant gesture of triumph, to which Desi responded by pointing to his bat, indicating that that was the only reason Lawson had defeated him. The batsman followed up with a bi-digital sign and headed for the pavilion. Lloyd seethed. 'I was disgusted,' he informed the gentlemen of the press as the latter pounced gratefully upon any semblance of a Caribbean chink. 'If this sort of thing happened again a player would be catching the next plane home. I was very disappointed in both players. It was very stupid. I didn't think Test cricket could come to this sort of thing. It was bad sportsmanship from both sides. We've always had good camaraderie with Australians.' Not for much longer.

The next day, Hall, who also chaired the tour committee, revealed that Desi had been severely reprimanded. 'That's the end of it as far as we are concerned,' he announced. 'But what is the Australian Cricket Board going to do about Lawson? We recognize that Desmond was under severe provocation, and he recognizes and understands that he should not have done what he did.' Eschewing his captain's diplomacy, Hall highlighted the growing rift between the combatants. 'We have come to Australia not only to play cricket, but to cement relationships between the teams. We don't want to be constantly provoked and abused. Some players can take it, others can't. Desmond couldn't take it any more and gave vent to his feelings. Lawson does it all the time.'

After confrontations with Richards and Greenidge in Melbourne had prompted an official protest from the tourists, Australia's sharpest pace prong belatedly received his comeuppance in the shape of a A$2000 fine. In Sydney, the vice-captain, along with Border, the new Australian captain, and the home wicketkeeper, Steve Rixon, were reported by the umpires for verbal outbursts. After being adjudged leg-before to Lawson in Melbourne, Greenidge received Border's permission to beard Lawson in his lair and duly gave the New South Welshman a substantial piece of his mind. The unrepentant Lawson, it seemed, was taking his 'new Lillee' tag rather too literally.

On reflection, Desi traces his own anger to a show of callousness in the first Test at Perth. 'Gomes was hit on the head, Dujon too, and not one Australian went to see how they were. They didn't even look at the fallen batsman. They expected us to bowl bouncers but we pitched the ball up and they kept on edging. That's where it all started. I don't go to Australia these days and expect to hear someone from the opposition wishing me good luck. I'd probably think he was taking the mickey. I expect to be called a silly so-and-so if I get out. That's the way it is, and I'm not too bothered about that. I like to compete too. I found it harder back then, however. Lawson was always chatting, saying abusive things. At Brisbane he twice trod on his own wicket and the umpire denied seeing a thing. Then, when he got me in the second innings, he came down the wicket, said something abusive and began to jeer me off. So I retaliated, I told him where to get off. I waited until he came off the field and then said a few more things. A few members of the side had to restrain me but I never grabbed him, as some suggested. I've never done that to any cricketer. If I did, I wouldn't stop there.' At the Gabba eight years later, Lawson, now working as a radio commentator, bumped into Desi at the end of practice on the eve of the first Test. 'Be good, Desi boy,' quoth the former. A term of endearment rather than a sarcastic rejoinder. Desi grinned as he returned the greeting: 'You too.' A hatchet cremated by the flames of time.

Establishment reservations shelved for the time being at least, Viv inherited Lloyd's throne for the home series against the dogged, Hadlee-driven New Zealanders starting in late March 1985. To Desi it was a natural if not entirely ruffle-free progression for the Masterblaster. 'Watching him play the swinging ball in England was an awesome experience. He would put his left foot across the wicket and hit the outswinger to all parts of the leg side. I had him down as the biggest "Lennie" in the world, a batsman with a marked preference for shots off his legs, but his offside strokes were even better. What I found amazing were those hawk-like eyes of his, eyes that seemed to enable him to tell in advance whenever the bowler was going to drop short. His approach was so aggressive that he always looked in total control. One time, we were batting on a raging turner in India and the spinners were putting on the pressure. As usual, there was a right old party going on close to the wicket when I was on strike, but as soon as the Master came in he smacked two lofted drives and the party suddenly dispersed to man the boundaries. Then as soon as I was back on strike the party started up again. Just watching him from the other end made me feel aggressive. At his peak he was a masterful batsman, a unique talent. I've never seen any cricketer who could so demoralize an attack, take a ball that Gordon or I would have left alone and hit it through midwicket for six with such ease. Shots like that made the message plain: "I'm Number One." I've never seen him scared, but in his prime he genuinely frightened the opposition. When things weren't going well he had a saying: "I guess someone's going to pay for this." No matter what form he is in he always feels that somewhere down the line he is going to dominate the bowlers again.

'He is also extremely tough. He always played hard, bent on winning, "a real soldier", as he used to put it. The first time we played golf together in England he had no idea that I'd been a caddy for so many years and, much to his surprise, I was beating him easily. So much so that at one point he decided to drop another ball from his pocket after he had driven one out of bounds. As a caddy I had been taught to watch the ball at all times but he denied having substituted the original ball. So I walked on into the woods to where the original had landed, picked it up and gave it back to him. At first he continued to insist that it wasn't his, but eventually he agreed he had cheated a little. All that does is illustrate how much he hates to lose. The only stake we were playing for was a meal that would have cost him about fifteen quid.'

While this all-consuming competitiveness was certainly no hindrance when it came to captaincy, king and dauphin were poles apart in Desi's estimation. 'Lloydy made it easier for Viv because of the success the team had enjoyed under his leadership, but his greatest strength was his ability to get the best out of people. He would appreciate your good deeds and understand the low ebbs. Viv, on the other hand, didn't understand that there was only one Viv, just as there was only one Sir Garry and only one Sir Donald Bradman. He expected high standards and real soldiers. Because of his talent he could not understand how you could drop a catch. He always loved people who were willing to give everything, willing to die on the field. He couldn't always accept the fact that someone might only *look* as if he wasn't trying. If Clive saw someone giving that impression he would try and find out why. Viv could have put himself in the other guy's shoes more often, realized that we're only human.

'Viv was always positive before a match, stressing how he would play and how he expected everyone to follow him. He would go through the opposition line-up, suggest how we would bowl to certain batsmen and how their bowlers would tackle us. If it was a one-day game, say, he would emphasize the importance of making the most of the first 15 overs when the other side were obliged to have a few fielders positioned inside the circle. There wasn't much discussion. Lloydy canvassed views to a greater extent, making a few more suggestions to individual bowlers as to what they should do if our plans went awry, whereas Viv would expect them to work things out for themselves. Lloydy was a bit more astute in a tactical sense, but he involved the whole team in that process. Viv sat back and just let people get on with the plan, putting the bowlers on auto pilot, shorter spells from those with explosive pace like Marshall and Holding, longer ones from Garner and Walsh, waiting to see if things went wrong and then trying to put them right. Lloydy, conversely, would look to make changes beforehand. Neither of them, happily, were moaners, although they both let you know in no uncertain terms if they didn't think you were doing the right thing. Lloydy would almost always maintain his cool and his control of the game but he wasn't perfect. If he was displeased with our efforts he didn't have to say anything. All we had to do was spot The Look.'

The new regime began much as the old one had thrived. New Zealand clung on for draws in the first two Tests, four vital hours being lost in Trinidad due to a leaky tarpaulin, Geoff Howarth withdrawing his close fielders but still failing to stop Desi and Richardson adding 191 in 215 minutes at Bourda, where Martin Crowe's commanding 188 almost single-handedly kept Marshall, Garner and Holding in check. Then came a resounding 10-wicket win at Sabina Park, a bruising encounter that saw Hadlee pitch five bouncers at Garner in one over and the home speedsters retaliate in kind against the Kiwi middle order on a pitch enlivened by rain. Richards simply reiterated Lloyd's assertion that his countrymen had received similarly short shrift at the hands of Lindwall and Trueman. 'This is our weapon now, so we have got to use it,' he argued. Hall delved deeper. 'Yes, for fifty-five minutes on Sunday, Marshall and Garner were persistently short. But I ask you, who started it? Who started it in Perth last year when Dujon and Gomes were flattened? I do not condone intimidatory bowling, but if Hadlee bowls five bouncers in an over to Garner, what do they expect the reaction to be? I say that if you do not wish to get burnt, if you cannot afford to be burnt, stay out of the kitchen.

'To the best of my knowledge,' Hall continued, 'not one West Indian fast bowler has been warned for intimidatory bowling in the past five years, but the press continues to condemn us. The umpires must determine what is fair and unfair play, not the press. The point is, why are they always getting at the West Indies? They are getting at the West Indies fast bowlers now, but they got to the spinners, Ramadhin and Valentine, in the 1950s and destroyed them with that front-foot leg-before rule. And they came at us again in the 1960s when they brought in the front-foot bowling [no ball] rule to cut down on Griffith and myself.'

Even if it did stem from the less than impartial viewpoint of the sixties' most thrilling fast bowler, Hall's sense of grievance was acute, leaving the usual pertinent questions hanging in the air, to be scorned and ignored. Perhaps there was a vestige of paranoia in his railing, yet the circumstantial evidence was suggestive enough, all the more so when the one-bouncer-per-over-per-batsman rule became currency. Paddington and Vivi were perceived as the Dillingers of cricket, not just Public Enemies but No. 1 With A Bullet, the price on their heads financed by the guardians of Anglo-Australian self-esteem. 'One of my greatest sources of pride,' says Desi, 'is to have been part of a side that kept on winning while the world tried to change the rules to stop us.'

10

The Battle

You have to grasp the reality of smashed faces and pain, and
understand how they can be part of something courageous, exciting
and beautiful.

Mike Jones, boxing manager

Pugilists and quarterbacks aside, the opening batsman runs a greater risk of
experiencing extreme physical discomfort than any other professional sportsman. Confronted by bowlers armed with a bouncy new doodlebug and primed
to claim the psychological high ground, he also has a 50–50 chance of entering
the target area before the whereabouts of the landmines have been ascer-
tained. When Joe DiMaggio stood in the batter's box at Yankee Stadium he
was constantly aware that the pitcher leering down at him from the mound
might buzz a rising fast ball at him as a means of asserting authority. In the
event of being hit, however, no matter how negligible the contact, Joltin' Joe
also knew he would be awarded first base, a concession that made this a
sparingly used ploy. Barring the rarely used warning for intimidation – either
umpires are too frightened of provoking hostile stares, shoulder barges and
snatched hats, or we are too sensitive – cricket, conversely, refuses to punish
bowlers for direct hits.

Although the West Indies teams of the armour-laden post-Packer age
contained more prospective GBH merchants than any of their contemporaries
or predecessors, it would be naïve to suppose that their opponents had a
monopoly on bravery. Desi has still found himself up against any number of

nasty assailants – Lillee, Thomson, Hogg, Lawson, McDermott, Pascoe, Hadlee, Dilley, Willis, Allan Donald, Devon Malcolm and Imran, to name the dirtiest dozen in the international arena. Lest it be forgotten, he has also had to withstand Roberts, Holding, Patterson, Bishop and Ambrose at domestic level. Hand-wringing has been commonplace, busted fingers an occupational hazard. A blow to the jaw delivered by Hadlee at Wellington in 1987 was his worst moment, the payback a stirring century. What the exchange lacked in beauty it more than made up for in courage and excitement. Without that element of physical risk, of challenge, cricket would have about as much spectator appeal as cribbage.

Only once, during a one-day international at Sabina Park in 1986, did that strong constitution succumb to revulsion. After losing Tim Robinson and captain Gower for 10 in a jittery initial encounter with the brooding Jamaican bruiser, Patrick Patterson, England were beginning to recover their poise when Mike Gatting, clad, a trifle foolishly perhaps, in a helmet without a visor, essayed a hook at Marshall. Halfway through the stroke he appeared to conclude that discretion was indeed the better part of valour – too late. Redirected by an involuntary edge, the ball thudded shockingly into the bridge of an unprotected nose, insult being added to serious injury as it proceeded to trickle into the stumps. When the weapon of destruction was thrown to Desi on its way back to the bowler his first response was nausea. 'I noticed that a piece of gristle had embedded itself in the ball. I tried to pull it out but couldn't, so I handed the ball to Garner. His hands are extremely hard and he duly removed it, but I was sickened. Gatting looked as if a shotgun had blasted a hole in his face. I didn't have lunch and missed my dinner at the hotel. I felt so bad about it. I kept on thinking that if I was ever hit like that I'd never play again.' There had been anger when the Australians struck down Gomes and Dujon, but this was fear.

Having profited from the riskiest stroke at an early stage, Desi rarely hooks nowadays. When either the pitch or the strength of the opposing attack dictates it, he straps on a small chest pad. His greatest concern, naturally enough, is for his hands. 'Gloves are the cause of so many finger injuries. Openers are more susceptible to them because the leather is harder and the bounce steeper when the ball is new, and we have so little rest that fractures and bruises take longer to heal than they might do ordinarily. Some ex-players say we're soft but that is grossly unfair. Gripping the bat with an injured finger can be very painful as well as restrictive in terms of your range of shots. That's why I would like to see someone design a glove with a strip of

Velcro that could be stuck over any finger you might have taped up. That would certainly make life easier.'

If no bowler has managed to shake Desi's innate self-confidence to the point of dread, he has frequently observed fear in others. 'Standing close in at bat-pad especially, I saw some very scared faces, particularly at Sabina Park during the first Test of that 1985–6 series. The wicket was up and down, to say the least, and when Patterson ran in the fear in the English batsmen's eyes was a frightening sight in itself. Then there was poor old Andy Lloyd picking the ball up late at Edgbaston in his first Test and suffering that horrible blow to the temple from Malcolm. I was about five yards away and he clearly picked it up late, but nerves must have had something to do with it. Mind you, our opponents often look fearful even before the match starts. When I watch them practise they sometimes look as if they feel they have no chance of winning, that we are too good for them. It's a great feeling, an unbelievable feeling.

'And no, I don't think it's fair to say that we wouldn't have been the same side if we had had to face our own bowlers. That's a lot of twaddle. No one worried about how the Australians would have batted had they had to face Lillee and Thomson in 1975–6. I suppose things like that will always be proposed when a team is successful and people want to isolate the reasons. We played against Holding and Marshall in the Red Stripe and Shell Shield. We adapt, we cope. By the same token, the world shouldn't mess around with the rules to curb us. They should learn to adapt too. In any case, restricting bowlers to one bouncer an over per batsman is plain silly. What if the batsman hits it for six? Before that rule was brought in a bowler who knew the guy at the other hand couldn't handle the short stuff could let him have a couple. Nothing wrong with that. It's part of the game plan. You're psyching him out. And while he's watching out for the bouncer you pitch it up and induce an edge. I like that. It's a battle of wits and bluff as well as technique, an essential part of cricket. Our guys were just better at it than anyone else.'

And how. Spanning March 1985 to March 1989, the World Test Premier League looked like this:

	Played	Won	Lost	Drawn	Tied	Points*	%†
West Indies	36	21	5	10	0	73	67.59
Pakistan	30	9	3	18	0	45	50.00
India	30	7	7	15	1	38	42.22

New Zealand	28	6	7	15	0	33	39.29
Australia	36	6	11	18	1	38	35.19
England	40	5	16	19	0	34	29.82
Sri Lanka	15	2	7	6	0	12	26.67

* 3 points for a win, 2 for a tie, 1 for draw
† Points gained divided by points available

Bear in mind, furthermore, that during this period the champions surrendered three faithful retainers to the retirement home in Garner, Gomes and Holding. In all, the West Indian selectors called on twenty-seven pairs of hands, replacing piece by piece while their English counterparts opted for panic-stricken clusters, tinkering with such zeal that they commissioned enough men over those forty-eight months to stage their very own World Cup semi-finals. Of the Caribbean conscripts, Desi, Dujon and their captain each missed one match, Greenidge and Richardson two apiece, Marshall five, Walsh seven and Logie eight. Selectorial consistency is easy enough when times are good, especially when the field of choice is so unavoidably narrow; but patience, as exemplified in the treatment of Logie, Carl Hooper, Phil Simmons and Keith Arthurton, is an admirable philosophy. Old-fashioned educationalists, motivational bods and Brian Clough may spiel on about whipping staff into shape and putting rockets under backsides, but confidence is such a fragile thing for a leading sports figure, threatened as he or she is by injury, policy changes and outside distractions, that encouragement and reasoning are almost always preferable to bollockings and droppings. In terms of instilling a sense of community spirit in a sporting team, continuity is imperative.

The first player from outside the main islands to captain the West Indies, Richards began his term in office with that 2–0 home win over New Zealand in the spring of 1985, the first time the victors had defeated the Kiwis in a series for twenty-nine years, an old fact rendered only marginally more explicable by the staging of only three rubbers in the interim. 'Hadlee gave them a lot of self-belief,' Desi avers. 'Individually they weren't that gifted but they scrapped to the death.' Desi dashed off to Guiseborough after the fourth and final Test to light up the leagues for the last time, then returned to Barbados to prepare for the arrival of Gower's Englishmen. Employed as a coach by the National Sports Council, he spent his working days passing on his expertise in the rural areas, setting up coaching programmes on the school playing fields of St Lucy and St Andrew, enjoying every minute. 'I had a chance to observe the talent there, and there was a lot of it. The conveyor belt hasn't shut down yet.'

Participation in at least two Shell Shield games was a pre-condition for selection, not that that was a particular concern. Appearing in the competition for the first time in three years – touring commitments had kept out all the Test regulars over the previous two seasons – Desi was one of just five batsmen to average over 45 in an event that had evolved into the truest test of a Caribbean batsman's worth. He collected centuries in successive matches against the Leewards and Windwards, yet, in the context of Barbados' overall triumph, his 30 and 65 against the hit squad of Patterson, Holding and Walsh, the most productive batting display against Jamaica in that season's Shield, was of infinitely greater merit. A final return of 914 first-class runs, nearly 300 more than his nearest challenger, constituted a statistical précis of what turned out to be a notable winter.

Impressive in victory against India and Australia over the preceding twelve months, England entered that Wisden Trophy series in early 1986 with grandiose expectations, the more imaginative segment of the press corps contriving to promote the venture as an unofficial play-off for the world championship. The reality resembled one of those fist charades Joe Louis indulged in when there was no challenger worthy of the title; and England's ineffectual attempts to slug it out toe to toe rekindled the wild and woolly haymakers of Tony Galento, one of those bums of the month the Brown Bomber would habitually carry for a few rounds in order to keep the promoters off welfare. Optimism evaporated with the thwack of leather on bone when Gatting, the epitome of the British bulldog, was put down in Jamaica. Had it been possible for a referee to step in and halt the contest he surely would have done just that after Patterson's seven wickets on a treacherously undulating Sabina strip had made the decisive contribution to England's 10-wicket tanning in the first Test. In eight of their 10 innings the tourists totalled 200 or less, the lightest of their five defeats a seven-wicket loss at Port-of-Spain. In 1984, Lamb had risen above the ruins; on this occasion they were all lambs to the slaughter, denied even the consolation of an individual century. Gower (37) was alone in averaging 30 or more; the twelfth name in the order, a nifty double agent referred to by the code name Ex Tras, ranked third behind Gower (370) and Gooch (276) in the aggregates with a dutiful haul of 274. Not so much a blackwash as a grey one streaked in blushing pink.

To cap it all, the selection of Gooch, whose South African dalliance had been neither forgotten nor forgiven, angered many on the islands. That unintended, unwitting endorsement of apartheid, as David Lemmon observed in the 1986 edition of *Benson and Hedges Cricket Year*, 'had consequences beyond his comprehension'. Restored to the fold six months earlier after serving a three-year ban, Gooch had compounded his felony in some eyes by picking up a hefty cheque for a ghosted confession entitled *Out of the Wilderness*, an insubstantial tome which yielded little by way of explanation, let alone justification. Cognizant of the hot reception he was bound to receive in the Caribbean, he hesitated at length before accepting his tour invitation, and only then following an extensive exercise in diplomacy by the TCCB. If there have been few more reluctant tourists, the four half-centuries Gooch concocted during a traumatic rubber bespoke a doughty professional. How he must have wished he had stayed by his Brentwood hearth with Brenda and the Goochettes. Even more than the hostility his presence aroused, the sense of victimization upset him. Why was his best pal Embers not subjected to the same treatment? Or Willey? Or Les Taylor? Because he, as captain of that misguided, mercenary trek, was perceived as the ringleader. There was a virulent anti-apartheid demonstration in Trinidad; armed guards prowled hotel corridors, the environment occasionally so oppressive that it took the persuasive tongues of Gower and Donald Carr to prevent Gooch from returning home before the fifth Test in unfriendly Antigua. As far as Desi was concerned, public reaction to Gooch was as much a protest against injustice generally as it was a gesture of solidarity with black Africa. 'People felt it was wrong to ban our own kind and let the other rebels in.'

Powered by Marshall and Garner, the West Indies, by contrast, were unruffled, relinquishing a mere five second-innings wickets *in toto*. Heading the lists with 469 runs at 78.16, Desi supplied the backbone while Greenidge stumbled along in his slipstream. 'Although I felt I was maturing with every innings, I still felt Gordon was No. 1, that I would still be the one to go should the partnership begin to falter. Even then the doubts persisted. Having said that, it was good to score runs against England because people in the Caribbean remember them. I also felt that it wasn't just the Barbados fans who appreciated me. The inter-island rivalry is always there, and the crowds can be a bit aggressive towards you if they feel their man could do a better job, but you accept that. Again, perhaps I was lucky that there was no other opener really pressing a case.'

Even if there had been, Desi's sign-off in Antigua would have been thoroughly disheartening. On the most trustworthy pitch of the series, he survived a slip chance to Botham on 2 and another offering off Emburey on 38 to run up a dogged 131, enhancing a record at St John's that, by the end of 1992, stood at 646 runs in eight innings, average 80.75. Sent in with Richardson to embellish a lead of 164 after Greenidge had injured himself in the dressing room, he was in a more frivolous mood in the second dig, twice lifting Richard Ellison for six in a robust 70 before responding slowly to Richards's call for a leg-bye and being run out. 'Sorry, tough luck,' sympathized the apologetic Richards as Desi dusted himself down, vacating centre stage for the Antiguan to strut it as only he could. This particular *tour de force* was as violent and vivid as any assault even Richards had ever mounted, his 100 coming off 56 deliveries, comfortably the swiftest Test century in terms of balls received.

Despite his soaring form, Desi was not the most prolific batsman in the Shell Shield that season. That honour fell to another Bajan, Carlisle Best, a pencil-thin banker from St Michael whose wide-mouthed method of addressing the bowler remains every bit as expansive and expressive as that of his compatriot. An astute, eloquent university graduate, an unusual background for a West Indian cricketer, Best made his Test début alongside Patterson in Kingston, yet despite a superbly crafted 164 against England at Bridgetown in 1990, an effort chock-a-block with ripping cover drives, he has been unable to secure a regular niche at international level, much to the consternation of his many admirers. Had injury not prevented him from capitalizing on that Kensington century in the final Test at St John's, who knows, although a perceived bumptiousness at the start of his international career may have thwarted him in any case. As it is, at thirty-four his controversial omission from the recent tour party to Australia suggests that his tally of caps will remain at eight, a paltry total for one so able, not least in the slip cordon. A surfeit of riches will always incur one or two grievances from the fringes, especially from outsiders willing to speak their minds.

A colleague since 1980, Best has seen Desi's metamorphosis at closer range than most. His affection and respect are all the more magnanimous when one considers not only that Desi's consistency hampered his own international aspirations to a degree but also that Desi replaced him as captain of Barbados. 'When I made my début for Barbados Desi was full of shots, an almost continuous array of them, but before long his approach became more restrained. I can remember one game against the Combined Islands when Andy Roberts was bowling. Andy was one of the smartest bowlers I've ever faced and the wicket was a bit helpful but Desi played him superbly. It was a joyful learning experience just watching him from the other end that day. His patience, judgement and concentration were marvellous. Andy gave nothing away, and there were no drives, no hooks, yet that innings taught me more about batting than any other. I have learned a great deal from his patience and judgement, the timing of his shots and the way he chooses which balls to hit. I once watched him throughout a series and did not see a single edge, and only rarely a play-and-miss. He never seemed to miss a drive: every time he launched into one it would go for four.

'I also have a lot of respect for Holders Hill, which is a unique area in Barbados as far as cricket is concerned. I reckon around 90 per cent of the best players in the country come from there. Why? Perhaps, because of the poverty there, people turn to cricket for absolution, as a way of dealing with deprivation. Cricket is an outlet, a way of dealing with social pressures. When Desi scores a century for the West Indies Reds Perreira or Tony Cozier will mention Holders Hill, but they wouldn't bring up Greenidge's home town or Garner's or Marshall's if any of them had made a notable contribution. Desi has always given his all for Barbados. People see him as a true sportsman, a man with an obvious love for the game, and he is appreciated and respected for that love, and also for his tenacity. He has never changed his corner of the dressing room at Kensington as long as I've known him.'

Best, one might imagine, is in an ideal position to compare the Fabulous Bajan Boys. In fact, the prospect of doing so embarrasses him. 'Actually, that is a fairly difficult question for me to answer because I used to call myself "Gordon Greenidge". From the time I was a little lad I believed in him. He was more classical, more copybook than most players. The contrast between him and Desi was sharp: not chalk and cheese, more bread and cheese. Desi was quiet at first but the humour soon developed and he always made a positive contribution at team meetings. Gordon is introverted, which is possibly a legacy of his English background. Most West Indians find themselves becoming more docile, more inward-looking, more reserved when they are in England. Perhaps that contrast is a necessary one. When they were playing for Barbados I would go in at three, but when they were away I would open. I always saw myself as having to live up to their standard so, rather than that being a deterrent or applying pressure, it was inspirational, a great challenge.'

Remembering less than fondly his vexations there in 1980, Desi's next challenge was the brief jaunt to Pakistan in the autumn of 1987, one undertaken without the travel insurance customarily furnished by Holding and

Garner, both of whom declined to tour. He met it head-on, topping the averages for both sides and compiling the highest individual score of a rollercoaster series, even if 149 runs at 37.25 and 88 not out do sound a mite modest. Ramiz Raja and Javed Miandad collaborated for the solitary three-figure stand by either protagonist and for only the second time since 1888, a series of three or more Tests failed to produce an individual hundred, the bowlers exerting control to such an extent that a wicket fell every 20 runs. The West Indies exceeded that rate comfortably in the second innings at Faisalabad, where Abdul Qadir (6 for 16) reeled them in for 53, the visitors' skimpiest ever total, this after they had gained a first-innings lead of 89. 'Pakistan played very well, we didn't,' is Desi's blunt appraisal of his team's third loss in 54 Tests and Richards's first as captain. 'Qadir turned it a great deal but I grew up on leg-spin so at least I had a general idea about his googly. I'd been taught to bowl it myself on the pasture after all. Gatting talked about reading him from the shoulder, others from the hand – although his whirring action made that tricky – but I found the most important thing to do was watch the ball off the wicket and delay committing yourself to a stroke for as long as possible. Pad play wasn't for me.'

With young buds like Asif Mujtaba, Ijaz Ahmed and Wasim Akram coming to the fore, Pakistan were beginning to bloom under the tutelage of Imran Khan. 'He got them together as a team,' says Desi admiringly, 'got them going in the same direction.' All the same, the direction of the tour altered abruptly a week later in Lahore, where the West Indies demonstrated hitherto undetected powers of recovery (having ruled the roost for so long, they had had little need of them). For the first time in 58 Tests and 14 series, they nominated two spinners, but the off-breaks of Guyana's Clyde Butts never received an airing while Roger Harper sent down one lonely over, Marshall, Walsh and the lofty young Trinidadian express, Tony Gray, mowing down the hosts for 131 and 77. Greenidge's 75 was the game's sole half-century, while the 49 he and Desi put on in the West Indies' only innings (of 218) was the most durable liaison of the three days. The full complement was needed for the concluding episode in Karachi, where Desi became not only the third West Indian after Worrell and Hunte to carry his bat, but also the third from anywhere to do so in a Test in Pakistan. Enduring 95.3 overs in all, he facilitated a target of 213, a daunting one on another turgid, uneven pitch and one that had long since receded from practicability by the time Pakistan adjourned nine overs early on 125 for 7, reprieved by bad light. Deprived of their eighth series victory in succession, the West Indies, having cruised home in the one-dayers by winning the first four, could nevertheless reflect on a creditable job.

Onward to Sharjah, where the subcontinental combatants renewed their rivalry in the Champions Trophy, a four-cornered affair also involving India and Sri Lanka and won easily by Richards and his battalion, Desi ushering them on to the good foot with an unbeaten 59 in the opening victory over Imran's youthful corps. The silly season began in earnest after Christmas, in Australia – where else? With eight wins out of nine in the winter's one-day labours up to this juncture, the West Indies lost two of their three fixtures in the Benson and Hedges Challenge in Perth, an event designed to make even more mileage out of the America's Cup racing off Fremantle. With Desi, their talisman, dislocating a finger against England and missing the last two qualifying games – both of which were lost – they then failed to qualify for the final stages of the annual World Series Cup.

No matter. Next on the horizon was New Zealand, for the first time since that shameful tour seven years earlier. Desi had few illusions about the diplomatic import of the visit. 'We realized we had made a mistake in 1980. A lot of people wanted to forget it, put it behind them. Happily, the series was played in a good spirit throughout.' Desi's own spirit was at the forefront in the first Test amid the blustery winds of Wellington. Coming forward prematurely in Hadlee's opening over, he was caught on the jaw when the ball kicked. One side of his face was swollen but he carried on. There was a further alarm when the leg bail was disturbed as he set off for his eighth run. Surviving the ensuing claims for hit wicket, he chugged along to 121 in a shade over five hours, interspersing lengthy bouts of surveillance with 20 fours before being bowled on the third morning offering no stroke to a John Bracewell off-break. John Wright and Martin Crowe saved New Zealand with meticulous centuries and when Garner pulled out with a chest infection to deepen the wound caused by Holding's retirement from the international fray, another stalemate beckoned at Auckland. Instead, Greenidge went on one of his inimitable solo flights, striking 213 out of a score of 418 for 9 before handing over the cane for Marshall, Walsh, Gray and Butts to administer a 10-wicket drubbing, New Zealand's first home defeat for five rubbers. The one cloud was an allegation by their team manager, David Elder, that Richards had 'taunted and abused' umpire Fred Goodall during one of the multitude of interruptions for rain and bad light that delayed the execution until the sixteenth of the final 20 overs. Motivated, almost certainly, by a desire to keep things hunky dory, the New Zealand Cricket Council turned a blind eye.

The roles were reversed at Christchurch, where nine wickets from Hadlee sent the West Indies spiralling to their first three-day loss since the fifth Test of the 1965 rubber against Australia in Trinidad. Inserted on a damp pitch after the first day had been washed out, the visitors were 67 for 6 at lunch and never recovered, Desi surrendering his off stump to Hadlee to suffer his sixth duck in 107 Test innings. Requiring a cursory 33 to square the series, the home team lost five for 30 before the task was nervily completed, providing the retiring Jeremy Coney, the captain whose resilience had so personified his country's rise to international prominence, with a fitting farewell. It is unlikely that he was unduly bothered by losing each of the three one-dayers. Mortality, meanwhile, was creeping up on the West Indies.

Desi's dislocated digit needed a rest, compelling him, on his doctor's advice, to opt out of the subsequent Shell Shield programme. Unusually, the competition adopted an abridged format of two zone games per island culminating in a grand final, this having been forced on the board by the heavy losses sustained during the previous winter's tour by England. The economic strife in the Caribbean was thrown into sharp relief by the staging in India and Pakistan seven months later of the Reliance World Cup, a shindig that the West Indies were in no position to stage themselves.

As an appetizer, Desi was invited to open the innings for the Rest of the World at Lord's against a glittering selection drawn from the multinational talents of the county circuit in a showpiece affair organized to commemorate the two hundredth birthday of the MCC. With national pride running a distant second to the air of celebratory abandon, here was a match that would have had Hugh de Selincourt and Harold Pinter duelling over the screenplay rights. Conducted in impeccable spirit and good humour, there was something to satisfy each and every one of the 80,555 spectators: centuries from Greenidge, Gatting, Gooch and, in his last five-day performance, from Sunny Gavaskar; supreme fast bowling from Marshall; Qadir's enchanting wrist spin and, best of all, Harper's clean take of a return drive and instantaneous throw at the stumps to run out Gooch and flabbergast a generation. Not even the rain that capsized the final day could taint the memory. So it had as much in common with the eye-for-an-eye mentality prevalent in the real thing as baseball's annual All-Star game bears to the World Series. It was unreal, an ideal briefly realized. One for the time capsule nevertheless, if only to fool future generations.

For the first time in a match of consequence, the Fabulous Bajan Boys limbered up in opposite corners, Desi going in with Gavaskar, his sparring partner with Chris Broad. For the first time since the schoolyard, moreover, Desi faced his old mucker Marshall. 'We all knew it wasn't a real Test, but there was plenty of individual pride at stake and Malcolm was pretty pumped up when we went in on the second afternoon. His first delivery was a no-ball to Sunny, his second must have come within a whisker of producing a leg-before instead of a leg-bye, and his third saw me edge to third slip where Gatting kindly put the catch down. We then added 46 in just under an hour before I edged Malcolm to Clive Rice, who took a superb catch at first slip. Malcolm has never let me forget that one. In the second innings I was aiming to get my own back, of course, and I told him afterwards that it was a pity for me – and lucky for him – that the rain came. We all had a good time, Australians, Indians, Pakistanis, West Indians, South Africans, Sri Lankans, New Zealanders and Englishmen all playing together and drinking together. It was good for cricket and I regret that there aren't more of those sort of matches. With all the turmoil in the game it might be nice to put a Rest of the World team together and organize a tour of exhibition matches. I believe it is important that the cricketing fraternity stays together. After all, surely we ought to be able to relate to each other when we retire. "Hi," we should be saying to each other, "we had a ball. We had some differences and so forth but we are all cricketers." You have to live a life after cricket.'

To Courtney Walsh, the silent, spindly, selfless operator who has spent so much of his career doing the donkey work into the breeze or up the slope, that last statement of Desi's sums up the man and his muse. 'He's always saying there's life after cricket, which is something I believe too. You must respect people, be good to people. Desi and I have roomed together on a number of occasions and I have always found him very easy to get on with. He is a very caring person, someone who takes his responsibilities seriously and doesn't suddenly switch off and forget about them once a game is over. I first came across him during my first full season in 1982. In fact, he was my first victim, caught behind hooking. He was very encouraging, terribly helpful. He would challenge me in the nets, firing me up by telling me I couldn't swing the ball in and so on, so I would try to land it just outside off and moving away. He is a very relaxed character until the game gets going, at which point he switches on.'

The West Indies, however, failed to tune in fully when the World Cup hove into view. With Garner stepping down from his lofty perch, Greenidge ruled out by a knee injury and Marshall taking a furlough, they were handicapped from the outset, all the more so by legislation decreeing that deliveries bouncing over shoulder height be called as wides. Those of a cynical, not to say blinkered, disposition swiftly forged a link between this and the absence of Garner and Marshall. Those prepared to acknowledge that neither bowler was a slave to the short stuff, that each possessed a guile that far outstripped mere macho posturing, later conceded that their presence could well have made all the difference. Even though spinners were *de rigueur* on the soporific surfaces that prevailed, Australia emerged victorious by placing greater reliance on seam than any of their rivals.

As it was, the tournament proved a severe disappointment for the long-time monarchs of the biff-bang game. The West Indies achieved the most rapid scoring rate in Group B but three defeats in six games sent them home early, Desi's one noteworthy innings a rugged 105 in an ultimately meaningless splurge against Sri Lanka in which Richards, coming in on a hat-trick, slugged a World Cup high of 181 off 125 balls to do his bit towards setting a new one-day international record of 360 for 4. The brickbats were reserved for Walsh. In the opening encounter with England at Gujranwala, he conceded 31 from his last two overs to allow Gatting's gunners to win by two wickets, then exacerbated this show of philanthropy at Lahore by doling out 14 in the final over to Pakistan's last pair of Abdul Qadir and Salim Jaffer and so score an even more numbing own-goal. Had Walsh been half as mean-spirited as West Indian fast bowlers were meant to be, he might have averted this humiliation, yet he resisted the legitimate temptation to run out Jaffer off the last ball when the non-striker backed up too far. Amid the cacophony of delirious yelping in the stands Walsh's chivalry, unsurprisingly, went largely unnoticed.

Desi traces his side's failure to inadequate planning. 'I don't think it's fair to say we didn't care, but our preparation was not as professional as it might have been. The one-day game was changing. It was now more of a batsman's game, which is what the public want. They don't come along to see wickets tumbling, they want to see fours and sixes and last-over dramas, and rules like the one introduced to cut back on short-pitched bowling accelerated that process, making bowlers bowl deliveries that the batsmen could hit. It was good to see the tournament staged outside England at last, giving other nations a chance to make some money. There were a few hiccups in terms of travel and gear collection in India, but none at all in Pakistan. The early morning starts caused problems because of the dew, but the wickets were good. A pity we didn't see any of them in the Tests.'

As a sign of the times, the West Indies tour of India could hardly have been more explicit. The locals flocked in, not to lap up the five-day chess as of old, but to get their kicks from the one-day Snakes and Ladders. The second Test at Nagpur was cancelled at the last moment and replaced by a couple more one-day internationals, much to the displeasure of the tourists' amiable manager, Jackie Hendriks. 'We were told that the match was cancelled because the hotel was unsatisfactory and the wicket was poor,' recalls Desi. 'We later understood that this was not the case at all.' An eighth limited overs foray was staged in Ahmedabad, billed as a one-off in aid of the Cricketers' Benevolent Fund but declared by the home board to be part of the Charminar Challenge series. Hendriks objected to this classification and got his way in the face of incessant pressure. Ravi Shastri, the Indian captain, only learned that his board had backed down while walking out to toss with Richards. The public, naturally, remained in the dark.

For the record, the West Indies won that Ahmedabad abomination and took the Charminar Challenge 6–1, Desi, for once, contributing little. Book-ended by a cyclone at Hyderabad and a mass hari-kiri in Madras, the first-class segment of the tour was rather less successful, even though Walsh, carrying the Marshall-shorn attack with 26 wickets, was restored to his usual depend-ability. On the opening day of the four-match Test series at Delhi, where generous portions of swing and bounce saw 18 wickets served up for 193, Desi stood tall as each side tumbled to its lowest total against the other, his diligent 45 being more than double the next highest individual score in either first innings. By the fifth morning there was turn aplenty for the three Indian spinners as the West Indies chased 276. Desi made 27 out of an opening stand of 62 before falling hit wicket for the first time in a Test, but Richards picked up the thread with a turbo-charged 109 not out from 102 balls to fire a five-wicket win. The loss of 156 overs to rain prevented the West Indies from going two up in Bombay, where the unlikely task of making 118 from the final 11 overs was soon given up. A run-swamped draw on a bowlers' black hole at Calcutta, where Carl Hooper, a lean, languid Guyanan, became the third youngest West Indian to score a Test century, thus left Madras as the Indians' last chance for redemption.

Drafting in a bespectacled nineteen-year-old leg-spinner, Narendra Hir-wani, for his first Test, they grasped it with a will, assisted by a capricious, wholly unworthy pitch. While seven other spinners gleaned a combined return of 7 for 154, Hirwani's flighty fizz claimed 16 for 136, narrowly outdoing Bob Massie's entrance at Lord's in 1972 for the most productive Test début yet. Writing in *Wisden*, the eminent Indian journalist, Dicky Rutnagur, castigated the surface as 'deplorably under-prepared . . . a mockery'. Desi, the only West Indian not to throw away his wicket in the second innings – Hirwani trapped him leg-before – concurs. 'It was dreadful. The ball was turning a mile. Having said that, our boys kept on charging down the wicket and getting stumped, so much so that Kiran More was able to set world records with six stumpings in the match and five in the second innings. Our spinners, on the other hand, simply didn't get the same results. I opened with Phil Simmons in that game because Gordon was injured, just as I had done during the World Cup. People asked me if it felt odd but it didn't because I felt I had come into my own.

'I also felt that, having recovered from that bad trot of 1983–4, the board should have looked towards giving me a greater amount of responsibility as a potential future captain, Malcolm too. We needed experience in the role so that we could be ready to take over if necessary. Harper had captained the West Indies youth team and then led Guyana to the Shell Shield in 1986–7, so he was obviously in the frame, but he wasn't as sure of his place in the side as we were. I did not see the sense in making, say, Holding vice-captain a couple of years earlier when it was clear that he wasn't going to carry on for much longer. Where was the forward planning in that? The board showed no confidence in us. Barbados was no different. When I took over in 1989 I was the fifth captain in eight seasons, although the fact I was away so much may have been a factor in my not getting the captaincy until then.'

Desi's misgivings about the policy over the national vice-captaincy were underlined for some, albeit not immediately, when Pakistan came over in early March. It was a fleeting visit, a blueprint for what many envisage will be the archetypal twenty-first century tour: five one-day internationals, three Tests. There were, in addition, three fixtures against scratch combinations but not so much as one against an island. The cynics had seen the future and its name was expediency. Desi stuttered through the West Indies' leisurely 5–0 trot in the one-day series. After a ducking in Kingston, he twisted his ankle in practice and missed the second game, then rebounded with a rousing unbeaten 142 off 132 balls in Trinidad, his tenth 100 in this branch of the international game coming after he had been recalled at 85, having indicated that he had got some wood on the ball when adjudged leg-before to Salim Jaffer. The ankle then played up again before the next match and he managed only 9 in the concluding debate at Georgetown.

With Richards convalescing following haemorrhoids surgery, Greenidge had been promoted, even though his renowned introversion had already suggested him to have been an unwise choice to lead Barbados. The *hors d'oeuvres* may have been sublime but the entrée left a bitter aftertaste as Pakistan underlined the advances they had made the previous summer in winning a rubber in England for the first time. The flak, more than a little unfairly, rained down in torrents on the deputy's head when Imran, seduced out of the first in a lengthy sequence of unconvincing retirements by his President, plundered 11 wickets to engineer a nine-wicket win in the first Test at Georgetown, the first home defeat by a full-strength West Indian side since Mushtaq Mohammad drove Pakistan to victory at Port-of-Spain almost exactly twelve years earlier. In one respect, Greenidge, who relegated himself to fourth in the order to accommodate Richards's replacement, Phil Simmons, deserved criticism, electing not merely to go against company policy by batting first but by taking first use of a newly relaid pitch. Imran, it should be said, was in inspirational fettle, black mane flapping against the nape of that elegant neck, slanting the ball in and darting it away with equal facility, all at a fair old lick. Only Logie and Richardson reached 50 in either innings. Their teammates' growing tendency to view the popping-crease as some sort of decorative irrelevance scarcely helped, 53 no-balls – plus 15 more that were scored from – making a man-sized donation to a new world mark of 71 extras. Our double agent was working overtime.

Desi, who experienced his worst Test yet with 1 and 5, defends Greenidge to the hilt. 'A lot of people criticized the way Gordon handled the bowlers but they did not appreciate the fact that, after some early life, the pitch became very flat, which makes life difficult for a fielding captain. Curtly Ambrose was making his début and he went for 100. And losing Malcolm before the game to a knee injury wasn't exactly propitious. Yet the bad-mouthing got to such a ridiculous stage that Gordon was blamed for those 71 extras. And no, I don't know why our guys no-ball so frequently. Maybe they are simply trying for that little bit extra, or maybe the umpires are that bit quicker off the mark because of their reputation. Personally, I feel the old back-foot law might be worth reintroducing because that would enable us batsmen to take proper advantage.'

Richards and Marshall returned for Simmons and Patterson at Port-of-Spain, where the extras count sank to 61 in the second Pakistan innings. This time, though, no one gave a hoot as fortunes swung like an over-excited pendulum. Imran won the toss, took the first over and dispatched Greenidge with his sixth delivery, he and Qadir going on to disrobe the opposition for 174 by tea as the last five wickets oozed away for 27. At 68 for 7 Pakistan were going down the pan with even greater haste, but the slammin' Salims, Yousuf and Malik, stumped up 94 to earn a lead of 20. Imran then ejected the first four in the West Indies order and at 81 for 4 with barely two days done Pakistan's first series win on Caribbean soil appeared pretty much done and dusted. Centuries from Richards and Dujon now transformed matters, the wicketkeeper's derring-do dragging 90 from the last two wickets, setting up an intriguing dénouement as Ramiz Raja and Mudassar Nazar embarked on a quest for 372 in a touch over five sessions. Winston Benjamin continued his flying start in Test cricket by shooting out Mudassar and Shoaib Moham-mad, and when the dashing, crashing Ramiz edged Marshall to slip after scoring 44 out of 67, the pendulum seemed to have run out of oomph.

At this point, preposterously, the rest day intruded with Pakistan on 107 for 3. Pause to de-addle the senses. Perfecting his streetfighter's routine, Javed rebounded from the ropes with an atypically grafting 102 and when Ambrose finally induced a mis-hit to Richards at slip, 84 more were needed from a fraction over 20 overs with three bottles standing. When Marshall knocked Wasim off at 311, there was only going to be one winner. Yousuf and Ijaz Faqih blocked stoutly, bringing their side within six balls of safety before Richards, in a last frantic roll of the dice, brought himself on for the final over – and trapped the startled Yousuf first ball. Qadir came in at 341 for 9, survived the next five deliveries – oh, that Marshall or Benjamin had been loading the slingshot – and a minor gem was over.

The third Test in Bridgetown was another belter. There were 11 scores of 40 or more, of which Richards's first innings 67 was the highest; there were no century stands; Pakistan contrived to outstrip the masters of the art on the extras front, 49 to 47 – and Desi played his slowest Test innings. In reaching 309 after being inserted, Pakistan were emboldened by their gutsy if overly voluble wicketkeeper, Salim Yousuf, who added 50 in five overs with the lusty Akram before a mis-hook off Marshall shattered his nose in two places. Undeterred, he later shared in a critical eighth wicket stand of 52 with Imran on the fourth morning. Between times, Desi expended four and three-quarter hours over his assiduous 48, negotiating the contrasting vil-lainies of Imran, Akram and Qadir with due care and attention.

Trailing by three after two innings, the West Indies set off in pursuit of 266 on the fourth afternoon courtesy of Marshall, whose inestimable value was encapsulated in a match analysis of 9 for 144. At 154 for 5 come 6 p.m., they were teetering on the brink. Ambrose and Richards were both gone within thirty-five minutes of the restart. At 207 it was *sayonara* to Marshall,

whose prowess with the ball did much to prevent his creasework from matching either his own expectations or his ability. Enter Benjamin, another fast
bowler with all-round pretensions, exit Pakistani visions of that first series
victory in the Caribbean. Benjamin and Dujon put on 61 to steal the spoils
half an hour after lunch, much as Deryck Murray and Andy Roberts had
done at Edgbaston during the inaugural World Cup. It was a victory to match
any in the Maroon Age, achieved against the only team fit to occupy the
same ring on equal terms. That the West Indies had failed to win a home
rubber for the first time since Ian Chappell's raiders stormed the islands in
1973 was immaterial. The resilience would have done credit to Leon Spinks.
Pity that some of the gloss should have been stripped away by an unfortunate
incident, doubtless triggered by the tension of the occasion, that saw Qadir
wade into the crowd and assault an abusive spectator.

Javed, the poor devil, was on the receiving end of that Roberts–Murray
resistance too. A gunslinger who took an inordinately long time to hang up
his spurs, he was Billy the Kid to Imran's Pat Garrett, humble origins placing
him a distant second to the aristocratic pin-up in the public and selectorial
pecking order alike. An audacious, at times impetuous, batsman, he also has
the dubious distinction of being the most defamed player of the past twenty-
five years. Those shards of naked aggression undoubtedly reflect the manner
in which the face of Pakistan has altered since separate statehood progressed
from a cause to a way of life. True, eliciting an lbw verdict against him in
his home town of Karachi is only marginally more feasible than persuading
Lady Thatcher to embrace socialism. On the credit ledger, though, he is right
up there alongside Richards and Greg Chappell as one of the three most
authoritative strokeplayers thrown up by the Savage Seventies.

Desi is an unabashed fan. 'Like all the best Pakistani batsmen of my time
– Zaheer, Majid, Haroon Rashid and Imran in particular – Javed has a lot of
flair. I do think he's been unfairly criticized but that is one of the problems
of judging people too quickly, which seems to be an unfortunate trait in
modern society. It all seems to depend on how people perceive you early on
in your career, because that impression tends to stick. To me he is simply a
great batsman and a great competitor who just loves to win. Despite the way
the odds were stacked against him when Pakistan were 81 for 4, he demonstrated that will to win in that second Test. Had he not gone when he did,
we might well have lost. As it was that was a terrific series. Although they
brought over a few youngsters like Aamer Malik and Naved Anjum, they
were extremely competitive. They also received a lot of support from the

Indian communities, especially in Guyana and Trinidad, which made them feel more comfortable, I'm sure. All in all, even though that 48 at Kensington was my highest score, it was a marvellous series to play in, a perfect example of Test cricket at its finest.'

After all that, a breather was in order. The West Indies got it too, skipping over to England to hand out a 4–0 drubbing to a coterie of twenty-three ill-starred locals. Increasingly constrained by a back complaint (payback time for all those years at bat-pad), Desi missed the first two Texaco Trophy games, returning for the third and final act at Lord's where, according to *Wisden*, his was one of three 'self-inflicted' run-outs in an inadequate score of 178 for 7, England prevailing by three wickets to complete a whitewash. Any fond imaginings that this might presage a modicum of success in the ensuing Tests were rudely shattered by the time the teams reconvened in NW8 less than a month later.

Gooch's 146 and the loss of four hours on the Saturday at Trent Bridge had enabled England to avoid their eleventh consecutive Caribbean crunching in the first Test. When Desi was caught at short leg off Graham Dilley, this just after glowering clouds had usurped the sunshine that had been smiling so beneficently over St John's Wood when Richards won the toss, there was a discernible note of glee in the voices of Johnners and Blowers. Dilley's swing and lift helped ferry the first five visiting batsmen back to their point of embarkation with only 54 on the board, prompting an exchange of disbeliev- ing grins among the bacon and egg ties. Logie and Dujon soon had them choking on their sausage rolls however, adding 130 for the sixth wicket. The chance had gone. As the cloud banks flitted between blue, mauve and seal grey, Marshall's 6 for 32 secured a lead of 44, Greenidge bagged his custom- ary 100, his sixth both in and against England, while Lamb, ever bullish against the kaffirs, was alone among the eventual losers to exceed 30 second time round. From then on, meaningful competition gave way to pitiful surren- der as a succession of different English chiefs – Gatting, Emburey, Chris Cowdrey and Gooch – strove to turn back the waves. At the very last, England contrived to nose ahead on first innings at the Oval – for the first time in thirteen attempts against this insistent foe – but by then the puttering vehicle that had tuned up at the Texaco station was long overdue a major service.

Exhibiting an affinity for Sussex bowlers that would endure long after that May day, Desi began with a rollicking 158 at Hove, but his subsequent output in the Cornhill exchanges was ordinary. There was a 60 at Nottingham, a steadying 54 at Leeds and an unbeaten 77 to round things off in Kennington, affording a respectable return of 235 runs at 47. Along the way he fell short of a notable slice of history, missing the Old Trafford encounter after appearing in 72 consecutive Tests, ranking him fourth behind Gavaskar's 106 (Border subsequently left that milestone well behind). 'I wasn't really conscious of the run, more worried about letting the side down. Somebody hit the ball out to the boundary at Canterbury and Viv and I both set off in pursuit, having our own little race. As ever, he got there first – and I pulled up clutching my left hamstring. It was hard, very hard, terribly frustrating, watching from the dressing room knowing I couldn't play my part. Not that I felt like an outsider. I tried to be my normal self, gee the guys up, have a few laughs, but it was an odd feeling. I listened to some tapes, soothing soul stuff like Teddy Pendegrass, Otis Redding and Al Green, and glanced at a few papers. That made a change because normally I don't like reading reports. On the one hand they can be misleading and disturb you, get under your skin if an error has created a false impression. On the other, if you hear or read too many complimentary things you put pressure on yourself, needless pressure. Sometimes people's expectations can be too high.

'I could have done better but overall I was generally satisfied with my own form. You couldn't exactly say the England selectors felt the same about their players. England were demoralized, and the ultimate sign of that was Cowdrey's original selection. I realize he was doing a fine job for Kent, who were confounding everyone's expectations by making a strong run for the County Championship, but he wasn't a proven Test player, and I'm no believer in the English philosophy of picking the captain and then the other ten. With very few exceptions – Mike Brearley in his later years, for instance – the captain should be worth his place entirely on merit, regardless of any leadership qualities. You have to pick your eleven best players. And, of course, it is also extremely difficult to generate team spirit when a side go through so many changes of personnel, particularly in terms of the captaincy. I thought Gatt was treated unfairly but they, the press, set out to get him – and when that lot are out to get you, they get you. The TCCB gave him a bonus after that Pakistan tour then sacked him for the barmaid business. Where's the logic in that? Had Rothley Court never happened he would never have gone to South Africa. He would have done a fantastic job for England just as he has done at Middlesex. Embers? Very knowledgeable, could have done an excellent job, had he been given an extended chance instead of just two Tests. How can it be fair to pitch someone in to lead a losing side and expect them to prove themselves over such a short period?'

With 35 scalps at 12.65, Marshall was far and away the series' most influential figure, scampering in with a quiverful of quicksilver leg-cutters to nail all comers. Even so, his new sidekick, Curtly Ambrose, he of the furiously wagging right wrist, was not far behind. Formerly a basketballer of considerable ability, Long Tall Curtly, a quiet Antiguan longshanks with a predisposition for clamping on the headphones and shutting out the world that many mistake for aloofness, combined steep bounce with relentless accuracy in a manner that defied credence in one with barely a year's first-class experience. On the zippier surfaces Down Under the odds were that the man they called 'Little Bird' in deference to Joel 'Big Bird' Garner, would be an even greater threat. He was. In the first three Tests that winter he clocked up 20 wickets, winning one Man of the Match award and being pipped for another while sewing up the rubber by the New Year.

Of all Ambrose's strikes, the cruellest came at Melbourne, where he bowled Border for a duck in the latter's hundredth Test. Australia – and Border – rebounded in Sydney, where their captain, as much to his own astonishment as anyone else's, spun them to a yarn of a victory on a slow turner, then gave as good as they got on an Adelaide pitch that would have lasted a fortnight without getting testy. If Border's 11 for 96 at the SCG was the most remarkable statistical feature – the best analysis ever, incidentally, by an Australian skipper – then the remainder of the home bowling averages told the most salutary tale. Border's freak show enabled him to finish top; second was Mike Whitney, recalled for the fifth Test and gaining his fourth cap in eight years; the highest wicket-taker, Merv Hughes, got 13 of his 14 in one match; the only other man to reach double figures was Steve Waugh, a batting all-rounder. Ambrose, Marshall, Walsh and Patterson, meanwhile, divvied up 72 Australians.

The man of the moment, however, was Desi, a virtually unanimous nomination as International Cricketer of the Year. There were 513 runs in eleven World Series Cup games, including two centuries against Pakistan, the second of which, his twelfth altogether, established a one-day international record. Better still, in ten Test starts he accumulated 537 cultured runs at 59.66 to head both the aggregates and averages. In Tipp-exing out Rohan Kanhai's record series tally for a West Indian against Australia he also ended a bothersome bout of travel sickness that had seen him fail to average 50 in an overseas rubber since 1980. Strangely, although five of Desi's nine Test centuries up to this point had come on alien turf, the overall disparity between home and away output detailed a different story. Of his 4523 runs up to the end of the

Right Summer of content: Desi acknowledges the applause for one of his favourite centuries, Middlesex v New Zealand, Lord's, 1990, a day when the ball 'kept missing the fielders'. Ian Smith prepares to bow in humble reverence.

Below Bajan to Bajan: Desi shapes to pull Marshall at the start of his commanding 80 at Southampton in the 1989 NatWest semi-final against Hampshire, in Mike Gatting's estimation his best innings for Middlesex.

Left Colour me beautiful: Desi models the latest line in sartorially challenged jammies, Sydney 1984. A freer spirit over the shorter course, no one can match his tally of centuries in one-day internationals.

Below Victorian value: Desi and his future wife, Dawn, enjoy some hospitality during his sojourn with the Melbourne club, Dandenong, 1983.

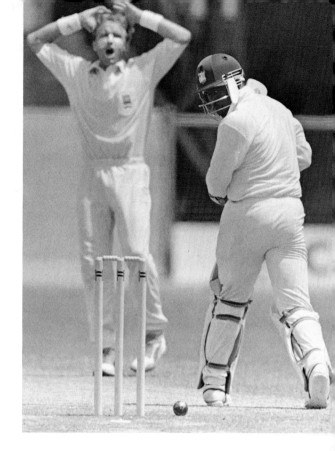

Right Donald trumped: an obedient ball comes to a halt after the South African spearhead had hit the stumps without budging a bail, Kensington Oval, 1992.

Below Lions' pride: Richie Richardson hugs David Williams, Desi tries to make it a *pas de trois* and the rest of the West Indies team celebrate their astonishing fightback against South Africa, Kensington Oval, 1992.

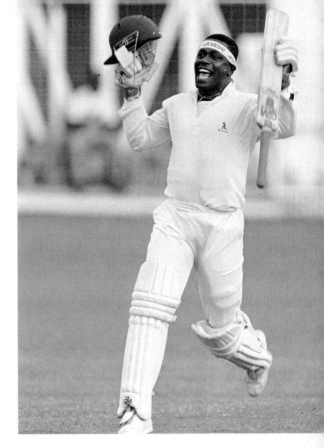

Facing page   Centurion bold: a rock comes of age as Desi off-drives during the unbeaten 57 that guided the West Indies to a series-levelling victory in the third Test against England, his own hundredth, Trent Bridge, 1991.

Right   Desi's characteristically low-key reaction to reaching three figures.

Below   Last stop before the final ascent: the Fabulous Bajan Boys take a breather, St John's, 1990.

Facing page Code of the road: Desi and the pendant that encapsulates his approach to the world within, and beyond, the boundary – live, love, laugh.

Right Ringcraft: known as 'Joe Louis' in Holders Hill, Desi performs his best craggy old pug impression in the company of that elegant grey fox, Jeff Dujon, second one-day international v England, Bridgetown, 1990.

Below Old guard, young gun: Desi listens intently to Brian Lara, whose glorious 277 against Australia in Sydney at the turn of 1993 confirmed the Trinidadian as the master craftsman among the new breed of Caribbean batsmanship.

The way we were: Desi in reflective mood during the 1992 World Cup, a tournament that saw Malcolm Marshall's international career end in acrimony and a new era begin in sombre fashion.

1988 Wisden Trophy series (average 39.67, better than Gooch, Gatting or Lamb), 2418 had been imported at 31.40 a time, compared with a healthy home produce level of 2105 at 44.79. The ratio of three to two in favour of innings overseas, a necessary by-product of the Caribbean's precarious financial position, was not to his advantage. The most conspicuous gulf, in fact, could be found in his dealings with Border and company: in Australia, his 511 runs had dribbled forth at an average of 25.55; back home, 650 had gushed from his bat at 81.25.

The turning point came early in the tour. 'I was staying with some friends in Sydney one day, just before the first Test, when I casually picked up a book on psychology and started leafing through it. It really had a dramatic effect on the way I thought. It told me how and why I got nervous, that it was better to visualize good days than thinking, shoot, I might not make any runs today, or I might lose my money. That book – it sounds terrible but I can't even remember the title now – instilled a sense of the positive, both in my cricket and in my life outside. I stopped being negative, fearing it could all end tomorrow. I learned to believe in myself more, learned more about myself. Far more productive than reading a Dick Francis or a Robert Ludlum. Through that I started reading more books on the same subject and learned how to meditate. I wasn't very good at it but at least it helped me relax. I'd never been a worrier as such, but I was always seeking to protect what I had, what I'd earned, always scared of losing it all. It was a legacy of my background, of course. Then of course there was the nervous tension that is so prominent among cricketers – all that waiting, then all that time to dwell on an innings after the fact.

'It was difficult to explain to my teammates about positional sayings and visualization. I know Gordon thought it was all a bit naff. All I know is that now, when I'm batting, I believe I'm the best batsman in the world, that the bowlers are second class, that I am in total control. If I feel negative at any point I stop the bowler and make him wait for me, just to reassert that control. Through these books I now had a greater sense of what I wanted to achieve and, for the first time in my career, I began to set goals for myself. The main one was to make a century in Australia, something I'd never previously accomplished, and in Holders Hill the general view was that if you don't score runs there you can't bat. You weren't considered the complete article. Gordon hadn't made a hundred there either, so when he broke his duck at Adelaide, in what was his last chance to do so, I was naturally delighted for him too. I know how much it meant. During practice for the second Test at Perth I walked back from the nets to the dressing room with my bat raised as if I'd just made that hundred. I visualized it, then I lived it.'

That second-innings crack at the WACA was merely a taster for Sydney, where Desi played what is generally hailed as his finest Test innings. In the first dig the Fabulous Bajan Boys opened up with 90 on a slow-motion track requiring discipline and patience from the batsmen. Desi went on to 75, adding a further 54 with Richardson, but the last nine wickets were frittered away for 80, collapsing in an ignominious heap to Border's hitherto anonymous left-arm spin (16 victims in his first 100 Tests, 10 in his next 24). David Boon, that squat, moustachioed walrus from Tasmania, eked out 149, Border ground out the slowest Test 50 by an Australian and the home side led by 177, whereupon ten West Indians aggregated 107 in the second innings on a discernibly wearing pitch. That Australia were left with anything else to do, let alone make as many as 80, was solely down to Desi's five-and-a-quarter-hour 143, a masterpiece deemed by Border and Richards to be one of the best either had ever witnessed. Stretching forward to smother the spin, enveloping the threat in an immaculate forward defensive, leaning back to whip away anything loose, cutting late and delicately, never yielding the initiative for long. Batting on another plane.

'As far as the technical side of his game went,' notes Greenidge, 'that was the best innings I have ever seen Desi play. It was turning a great deal, but everything he had learned, everything he had accumulated over the years came together in a polished innings, a beautiful innings, a *great* innings, all that in a pressurized atmosphere in which a lesser person might have folded. I don't think he was commended enough. It was one of those innings people dream about but never get close to. He just stayed there. Simple as that.' 'From both a personal and a team perspective that was Desi's finest hour,' agrees Walsh. 'A remarkable innings blending a very positive approach with a sound technique.' 'It was an excellent innings, probably his best, a tribute to his dedication and application,' emphasizes Lloyd. 'He came of age that day.'

'That was probably my most satisfying Test innings,' acknowledges Desi. 'Ball selection, placement, concentration – they were all there. I remember playing an innings like that for Middlesex against New Zealand at Lord's in 1990, when every shot went just wide of the fielder. It was one of those wonderful days. Sometimes, even when you are in form, you find yourself picking up the bad ball all right but end up hitting it straight at the fielders time and again. That day they all went to the boundary. The wicket was one of those Indian-type turners, slow and awkward, and as a team we didn't tackle it well at all. I waited until the bad ball came along while others chased it and got caught at mid-off or mid-on. There was always something we couldn't handle, seaming wickets, deliveries leaving the bat. Basically we were too good so everyone kept looking for our Achilles' heel. On this occasion, to give him his due, Border bowled well, but there was no sense in giving him the charge.'

In among all this personal and corporate delight lurked two areas of concern for cricket at large. That recurring affliction, no-ballitis, drained the West Indies in more ways than one. Decelerated by nigh-on 250 overstepping offences, their over rate, rarely more than sluggish at the best of times, cost them around £10,000 in fines – 80 per cent of their Test winnings. Lucky they won the one-dayers. Richards, though, was far from perturbed. To him and his team, he pronounced, winning meant more than mere cash. Desi regards the issue as a complicated one. 'There should be a minimum number of overs in a day because you have to give the punters value for money, and I thought the requirement of 90 set for that series was a fair number. But at the same time there should be some form of compensation for taking wickets, say, one over less for every two. How can you be fined when you beat someone in three days? What we have to be careful about is not turning Test cricket into another one-day game. The public need to be shown the intricacies involved. It's not only the bowlers. Batsmen may slow things down if, for instance, the wicket is damp.'

More disturbing was the rancour between the teams, a spillover from recent altercations. Individual incidents were few but a fiercely antagonistic mood pervaded the entire series. There were enough glares, pouts and affronted gestures to fill a whole *Serie A* season. Sensitive lip-readers – a rare breed in Australia, admittedly – were fainting in the aisles. Neither was all this seething soothed by the inexplicable choice of umpires: three of the four nominated to oversee the last two Tests boasted one such appointment between them; Tony Crafter, the official for whom the tourists had the greatest respect, stood only twice. At the end of the tour, the Australian Cricket Board, the brains behind these appointments, forwarded a scathing report from the Adelaide umpires to the West Indies board.

John Woodcock, that most esteemed of all postwar newspaper correspondents but by now far from enamoured of the direction the game was taking, chastized Clive Lloyd, the West Indies manager, for being 'more inclined to blame the incompetence of the umpiring than to admonish his players' for any 'recalcitrance by his team when they disagreed with a decision'. Woodcock was horrified by the tactical spectacle, above all at Melbourne, where the variable bounce made batting, for Australia, 'largely a matter of evasion'. Not that he apportioned the blame any more to victims than victors. 'There were clear and ugly echoes', he frowned in *Wisden*, 'of the bodyline tour of 1932–3. So deliberately intimidating was much of the bowling, not only by the West Indians, that it was as though Law 42 (8) had never been written.' For some, there was more than a hint of irony in the fact that Geoff Lawson should have been dealt the nastiest blow when he misjudged the bounce of a delivery from Ambrose at Perth and sustained a fractured jaw.

'It was an aggressive series,' Desi concurs. 'The relationship between the sides was not very good at all. There was no drinking in each other's dressing rooms at the close as used to be the case when Lillee and Marsh were around, for all their bluster on the field. Even on our last tour four years earlier we'd had a party at the end which the Aussies came to. I don't know who stopped it, but it was probably an Australian plan. They probably reckoned that if they chatted more on the pitch and less off it, they might stand a better chance, but all the sledging did was fire us up even more. Look back on all the provocative and derogatory statements that have been made towards us over the years, make 'em grovel and what have you. That just gives us more determination, more pride.'

II

Thoroughbred in the Shires

We may some day be able to answer Tolstoy's exasperated and
exasperating question: What is art? – but only when we learn to
integrate our vision of Walcott on the back foot through the
covers with the outstretched arm of the Olympic Apollo.

Beyond A Boundary, C. L. R. James

In 1991 an aficionado named Robert Henderson penned a heartfelt missive,
detailing the number of county players who were not true Brits, and popped
copies in the post to an assortment of English cricket writers. This, he argued
with much eloquence and no little jingoism, was A Very Bad Thing. Angered,
I wrote back, and we subsequently exchanged a few letters, neither of us
willing to give an inch. He wanted an England for the English, a national
team without DeFreitas, Malcolm and Lewis, let alone more blatant mercen-
aries such as Lamb and Hick. I agreed that neither the South African, who
had whistled through the qualification period in four years, nor the Zim-
babwean, whose loyalty might have enabled his country to play Test cricket
a good deal earlier, should be classified as Englishmen. My hackles, however,
rose at virtually every other sentiment his words imparted. I accused him,
harshly perhaps, of racism, then halted what had been a pointless correspon-
dence from the very start. We never met, or even spoke. No need.

To some the employment of foreigners, of whatever racial origin, is an
obstruction blocking the progress of *bona fide* Brits. To others, the development
of Lewis into an all-rounder of world renown has been as much an English
achievement as Sherpa Tenzing's, while the endless delights purveyed by

Zaheer and Richards (B. A. and I. V. A.), Bedi and Intikhab, Van der Bijl, Holding and McKenzie, have made the pavilion dwellers of Albion the most fortunate of all. Besides, in a divisive world, what better than a multinational group sharing a common culture and purpose?

Unlike the majority of his Test confreres, Desi joined the county circuit deep into his career, a mature player with little to prove. Of the XI that defeated Australia at Brisbane in 1984, for example, eight had sampled the unique bump 'n' grind of seven-day working weeks, three-sweater weather, two-dog crowds and the M25. They had attended what may facetiously be referred to as the English finishing school. Yet it would hardly be accurate to suggest Richie Richardson was a toe short of the full complement before he joined Yorkshire, or that the silky athleticism of Jeff Dujon, the foremost wicketkeeper-batsman of the post-Knott era, suffered for not being pursued by a chief executive laden with all manner of sponsorship goodies. What Dujon did miss out on was the bonhomie and badinage, the comparatively tranquil atmosphere that distinguishes county cricket from the greater mass of professional sport. Standards may not always be uniformly high, but just consider the friendships forged down the years.

The main reason Dujon never entered this hail-fellow-well-met world was that wicketkeepers were one thing the counties had in spades, and, in any case, by the time he made his mark the barriers were beginning to go up again. In 1966, two years before the import boom commenced with the glorious advent of Sobers, Kanhai, Majid, Procter, Asif Iqbal and Barry Richards, an influx that would regenerate cricket in the shires, there were thirty-seven non-residents on the counties' books. In 1968 this quota rose to fifty-one, and by 1971 had leapt to sixty-five, prompting the TCCB to instruct its registration committee to assess the effect on domestic standards.

The overriding concern, not unexpectedly, was that restricted opportunities for homespun talent would ultimately denude the national team, the upshot being that, over the next two decades, import restrictions were gradually restored, the need for an exclusion zone apparently reinforced by evidence such as that provided by the 1981 first-class averages: not one of the leading seven batsmen was eligible to represent England, and only two of the first eleven. Among the bowlers, eight of the first eleven were of overseas stock. Initially, counties were limited to two hired guns – in 1972, Warwickshire won the Championship with a little bit of help from their Caribbean chums Kallicharran, Kanhai, Deryck Murray and Gibbs, who had, admittedly, quali-fied by residence, plus the former Pakistan opener, Billy Ibadulla – then to fielding one at any one time, and finally to one registration apiece. Residential qualifications, meanwhile, were tightened up considerably, only to be loosened again when an apparent God-in-the-making from Zimbabwe started notching quadruple centuries. Fuelled by parochialism, the debate was far from clear-cut. What about the benefits to young Englishmen of plying their trade alongside the titans of the game? Or the sheer quality of the fare?

Batsmen topped the shopping lists during the initial import drive, in demand for their punter-friendly smash and dash, but as more competitions entered the market and the out-of-towner quota was reduced so the fast men moved in. Each of the eighteen hurlers selected by the West Indies for Test duty over the past fifteen years (up to and including the first Test against Australia in November 1992) have been signed by a county at one stage or another, although Milton Small never got as far as playing for Hampshire. All of which explains why, until 1989, Desi had yet to tread the county boards. During his first tour of England, David Gower intimated that Leicestershire were interested in signing him, but the club opted for Andy Roberts instead. After that, not a squeak, until the winter of 1988–9, when two suitors popped up. With Steve Waugh likely to be included in the Australian Ashes party for the following summer, Somerset were on the lookout for another foreign acquisition. So, too, were Middlesex, for whom the highly popular Wayne Daniel had just retired after twelve seasons' unstinting service. Then, on 15 January, the London county's kindly, unassuming, much-loved St Vincentian opener, Wilf Slack, collapsed and died of a heart attack while batting in the Gambian capital of Banjul.

The news filtered through to the West Indian camp shortly after they had touched down in Sydney for the second of the WSC finals. Capped three times by England – and never when he was in form – Slack had the sort of nature that made you feel you had made a friend for life as soon as you shook his hand. Desi was no exception. 'When I heard I went straight to Malcolm's room. I couldn't believe it. Slackie and I had been drinking together in Holders Hill only a few weeks earlier. It was very distressing because he was such a nice, genuine guy. "Bet you play for Middlesex now," said Malcolm, and he turned out to be right. Somerset approached me too but ultimately plumped for Jimmy Cook.'

Mike Gatting needed no persuasion that this was a smart move for his county. 'We were already talking about Desi even before Slackie died. I'd heard enough, seen enough, and with Angus Fraser coming through and other good seamers like Neil Williams, Norman Cowans and Simon Hughes in the side we certainly didn't need a bowler. From the few meetings we'd had he seemed very personable, a nice guy, very dedicated. He was proud of his game and I thought he would fit in well. Funnily enough, the first time we played against each other was at Lord's in 1980, my first Test in England, and he made that 184. I can remember him hitting a lot of shots through the leg side. My initial reaction was that he wasn't in the West Indian mould. He was there to play the anchor role, act as a counterpoint to all the strokeplayers, get stuck in.

'Gordon was more naturally gifted, whereas Desi had to work harder. His style wasn't particularly pretty but he was good for West Indian cricket because he was solid. You could tell he desperately wanted to make the position his own. He was very combative, and obviously there to stay. He struck us as a very good leg-side player but he didn't seem to play spin very well and we always felt Embers could tie him down, although that is far from the case now. Back then we tried to bowl off-stump and just outside at him and hope to get him early on. There was a feeling that you could get him lbw early on, but it was a bit different when we went back to the Caribbean that winter because the ball doesn't seam as much out there. The difference between him and Viv, Lloydy and Gordon was that we felt we could bowl to him. We didn't fear him smashing the ball about. He's certainly changed a hell of a lot since then. He has opened up his stance a bit, realizing that he has to keep his left shoulder pointing more towards mid-on, as a result of which he plays straight more consistently. After his first season with us he attributed his failure to get that shoulder round as the source of his problems. It was something he could get away with in the leagues.'

Gatting, unsurprisingly, holds the Fabulous Bajan Boys in high esteem. 'The best opening partnership of my time, no question. All the praise is justified. But the main reason was that, fine batsmen though they were, they were *allowed* to play together, which is something that the West Indies selectors deserve credit for. All right, so they don't have 250 players to choose from, and if they're lucky there are three or four opening candidates at any one time, but people should be able to pick a side and stick with it, instead of giving up on players too soon. Of course, it also helps being part of a successful side. When you have four quick bowlers of the quality of Roberts, Holding, Marshall and Garner it generates a lot of confidence in the batsmen. Desi and Gordon obviously practised against them in the nets, and I should think that every bowler after that must have seemed a lot slower and a sight less threatening.

'Because I was concentrating so hard on my own game in the early eighties, trying to prove myself, I didn't get to know Desi as well as I would have liked, knowing him as I do now. Having said that, I did think he was one of the more approachable members of the West Indies team and that became increasingly clear in subsequent series. It might have helped me to have talked to him. I know the people who had played with him in the leagues had a very high opinion of him.' It was no different at Middlesex. For much of the time since the club began its revival under Mike Brearley in the mid-seventies there have been as many as five black mainstays – Daniel, Slack, Williams, Cowans and Roland Butcher. The prejudices Desi might have faced at York- shire, to cite the most obvious example, were non-existent.

'He's one of the biggest mixers of all time,' chunters Gatting. 'He winds people up horribly. He's one of those characters who keeps the dressing room lively. We've had a very split team in racial terms since I've been at the club, but Wayne [Daniel] didn't worry about it and Desi certainly doesn't. He would fit in anywhere. We don't see a lot of each other after play because he pops off to Southampton to see his family and I'm very busy, but, generally speaking, we get on very well. Our outlooks are very similar. We've both been given the gift to play cricket and we want to use it to the best of our ability. Not everyone gets given that gift. That's why his enthusiasm has never surprised me. I consult him on the field because I want to keep him interested, make him feel part of things, and because he has so much experi- ence to impart. He always wants to chip in, offer advice. His biggest contri- bution, though, has been his keenness to talk to the youngsters, especially Mickey Roseberry. He's been a godsend to him. Mickey obviously had the talent but he wasn't coming on as quickly as he should have. Now he had Desi to talk to, to ask him how he would play certain bowlers, how he coped with the quicks, how he approached the start of an innings. One year with Desi was magnificent for him. The best way I can express what Desi has done at Middlesex is to cite the way Mickey has gone from a struggling batsman to a player on the fringe of Test recognition inside three years.'

Accompanying Desi on the flight from Barbados in April 1989 was David Maynard, the second young player for whom he had arranged sponsorship, this time with a St James travel agent instead of Caribbean Connection. His task was to select the most promising youth player in St James, whose passage would be paid by the agency. Maynard took the shortish hop from Heathrow to Chelmsford. At first, Desi was booked into the Clive Hotel amid the leafy groves of Belsize Park, a mile and a half from Lord's, but soon moved into a converted apartment in nearby West Hampstead. There was also a home in Hampshire, an investment he had made a few years previously on the same modern estate in Chandler's Ford where Marshall spent his summers. This was where the next branch of the Haynes clan would be raised. Dawn Jennifer, a spunky receptionist at the Barbados High Commission when Desi met her during the 1984 tour, had moved from Barbados to Edmonton with her family at the age of two. The pair lived together for a number of years, taking care of Kayoade, Dawn's son from a previous relationship, before finally getting spliced at the end of the 1990 season. Kayoade, who is fast approaching his GCSEs, has taken Desi's name and now has a brother and sister, Gemilatu, going on five, and Omotunde, three next birthday.

Desi arrived in London in early May at the end of a sapping if glorious winter. The delay was necessitated by the West Indies' 3–0 defeat of India, a gross mismatch of a series in which the visitors' only draw came in the first Test in Guyana, where four days were flushed away at the international venue closest to the Equator. The second Test at Bridgetown was immensely more satisfying for the hosts, particularly Greenidge, who made what was, incredibly, his first Test century at Kensington, a statistic that some explained by pointing to the antipathy many Bajans held for this converted Berkshire Basher and the consequent effect this had on his confidence when batting in their archly critical presence. Desi disagrees: 'People in Barbados love Gordon, but perhaps he never realized it.'

The panther-like Ian Bishop, a born-again Christian from Trinidad with a classical, full-bodied action, had taken 6 for 87 in his first complete Test innings to restrict India to 321 first time round, and when Marshall's nap hand dispatched them for 251 on the fourth afternoon, sending him past Gibbs's West Indian record of 309 victims, Desi sparked an undemanding chase for 196. Casting aside those self-imposed handcuffs, the unbeaten 112 that resulted was his most vibrant five-day effort since that maiden series against Australia, clean, calculated strokeplay bringing 11 fours and three sixes and hastening him to a bravura 100 off 128 balls, his quickest and most spirited century at this level. On a Trinidad turner where the match, paradoxically, turned on Marshall's 11 for 89, he pulled out the long handle again, wading in to the off-spin of Arshad Ayub to make 65, one of only three 50s in four complete innings. Walsh then prospered in his home town of Kingston, his 10 wickets deciding the outcome of a contest marred by a thirty-five-minute riot triggered by Richards's disgusted reaction – *not* towards the umpire responsible – to being adjudged caught behind off Kapil Dev. A

discordant cadenza to a winter rich in contentment, the sense of world
supremacy enhanced by a 5–0 victory in the one-dayers to which Desi supplied
the dream topping, an unconquered 152 liberally sprinkled with six sixes and
10 fours that *Wisden*, rarely given to hyperbole, dubbed 'rumbustious'.

Weariness, forgivably, was in evidence as Desi's normally implacable concentration faltered midway through the summer of 1989. There was no hint
of it, though, when he made his Middlesex début against Surrey at Lord's in
the Benson and Hedges Cup, a sturdy 59, the only half-century of the game,
earning him the Gold Award. Nor on his Championship début against Hampshire, whose de-Marshalled attack were fair game for an authoritative 67.
Nor, for that matter, on his NatWest Trophy début against Durham, when
an 83, nearly double the next highest innings of a low-scoring affair, brought
the Man of the Match award. For the world's most consistent one-day batsman – his 1066 runs in limited-overs internationals during the winter had
flowed at an average of 62.71, remarkable figures in a form where a mean of
40-plus was going some – it was the least his new employers expected. In
June he totted up 412 runs in the space of four Championship outings,
including the only 50-plus score of the match when Nottinghamshire came
to HQ, a feat that won him the Middlesex Player of the Month award as
well as his county cap. But before the month was out he had begun a run
of four Championship ducks in five visits to the crease, including a pair
against Lancashire, two of the seven home blobs in a lively Lord's debate
that saw Middlesex succumb for 96 and 43.

On the same supine Uxbridge square that Steve Waugh had scorched a year
earlier, an unbeaten 206 against Kent – the first double-century of Desi's career
and the basis of an opening stand of 361 – followed by another unbowed 100
against Essex and another 300-plus stand, this time with his captain, Gatting,
brought a total of 353 runs for once out. The remainder of the first-class
campaign was less bountiful, 335 runs at 33.50. In the Refuge League, 196
runs at a shade over 21 illustrated the difficulties he experienced in adjusting
to the Sunday biff and bang, a bat-and-ball encounter bearing only a passing
resemblance to the real thing but a devilishly hard – some say the hardest –
pot to win.

The non-stop exotic cabaret that is the lot of the modern international
cricketer was finally taking its toll. With the exception of a six-week break
between coming home from England and setting off for the Champions
Trophy in Sharjah, Desi had been on the road since the first Test in Delhi
barely eighteen months ago, managing fleeting glimpses of India, Guyana,

Trinidad, Barbados, Jamaica, England, Ireland, Scotland, Wales, the United
Arab Emirates and Australia in the process of participating in 20 Tests and
40 one-day internationals. 'Desi handled the ups and downs well,' says Gatting. 'He reasoned that in county cricket you would have more bad days than
good ones. We had a wettish start to the season, the wickets were seaming
and he had a spot of trouble in May but he worked at it and finished with
what anyone else might consider a good season. By the standards he set
himself it was merely goodish. He probably just got tired at the end.'

Naturally enough, Desi stirred himself for the big occasion, hooking Marshall to the Southampton boundary from the first ball he received in the
NatWest Trophy semi-final *en route* to a matchwinning 80, an innings ranked
by Gatting as the best hand he has ever dealt for Middlesex. There was
another 50 at Lord's, the only one of the contest, but the bespectacled,
bookish-looking Neil Smith, son of M. J. K., levered Simon Hughes over
the long-off fence to seal a shock four-wicket win for Warwickshire. 'The
whole thing was a learning process,' Desi acknowledges. 'I found out how
to adapt to different forms of the game, how to cope with the toing and
froing: 60 overs one day, 55 another, 40 the next, three-day games starting on
a Wednesday, four-day ones on a Tuesday. The travelling, needless to say,
was wearying, but I liked the competitive atmosphere that goes with playing
for Middlesex because they were so used to being in the running for one
competition or another. Reaching the NatWest final was a real kick: I was
planning what to do with the money long before Smith started flogging
Yosser [Hughes].'

The following year the balance between bat and ball swung too far the
other way. Goaded into action by the way the seam-up plonk merchants were
making hay on verdant pastures, the counties voted in two fundamental
changes when one might have sufficed. The proud, 15-stitch seams of yore
would now be humble, undetectable rims, while the pitches all had to be
beige-coloured, ideally with a hint of apricot. In an inordinately sunkissed
summer by local standards, bowlers wore their socks off for scant reward
(Neil Foster's 94 wickets were 19 more than the next best; only four managed
50 at under 25) and batsmen filled their boots as never before (a record 428
first-class 100s, three of them triples and 29 plain doubles; 20 averages of 60
or higher). All season long the arguments raged, the vast majority adamant
that the imbalance between bat and ball was now both ludicrous and intolerable. 'The county authorities fiddle around with the rules too much,' Desi
asserts. 'They must understand that what goes around comes around rather

than worry so much about the balance between bat and ball. Let things evolve.'

Desi made merrier than most, racking up 2346 first-class runs at 69 with eight 100s, two of them accomplished before lunch, one of which he expanded into a career-best 255 not out off 355 balls against Sussex at Lord's, this on a day when the other nine Middlesex batsmen to reach the middle mustered 160 between them. A gold-leaf scorecard, signed by the author, now rubs shoulders with mementoes from Hendren and Compton in the Middlesex Room. Knocks of 80, 131 (at Hove, surprise, surprise) and 64 were instrumental in steering Middlesex to the quarter-finals of the Benson and Hedges Cup, where they were surprisingly ambushed at Taunton, an eventual total of 1434 one-day runs at 65.18 finding him 103 clear of Cook at the top of the pile as the Seaxes landed the Refuge Cup. With eleven 100s and 3780 runs at 67.50 in all competitions, he claimed a proud bronze behind Gooch's 4186 at 93.02 with eighteen centuries and Cook's 3939 at 66.76 with thirteen three-figure scores. In a worthy tribute, he was named as the Britannic Assurance Player of the Year for his catalytic part in Middlesex's pursuit of their sixth Championship pennant in fifteen seasons. *Wisden* normally guards the identities of its Five Cricketers of the Year as if they were Oscar winners; guessing this one was a bit like predicting Brando would get the nod for Vito Corleone.

Desi's third county season, though less memorable, had its own highs. There was the obligatory mammoth effort against Sussex, a flawless 177 at Hove when it looked for all the world as if he could go on indefinitely, indifferent to bowlers, pitch or mental fatigue. But for playing on via a mis-hook he probably would have done. This time, though, it was the Sunday slap 'n' tickle that caught his fancy. Though 78 shy of Tom Moody's 1991 record, the 839 runs (average 69.61) he ransacked in the Sunday League was the single most influential factor in his county leaving the extant record for dead by winning their first twelve games, a run that ultimately led to them lifting the 40-over crown for the first time. 'Because there were so many gaps in the field,' says Gatting, 'Desi didn't expect to get out. He just enjoyed himself. All I would tell him was, "bat 40 overs." He and Mickey [Roseberry] always gave us fantastic starts, so much so that we hardly ever got past No. 7 in the order.'

Desi always thought he would prosper in the county game. 'I can remember Ian Gould standing behind the stumps while I was batting for West Indies against Sussex a few years back. "Think you'd enjoy county cricket, do you?"

he kept saying. "Think you'd do well?" I said I did. It was a challenge. It was also important for my development as a cricketer. I would be playing every day, facing different kinds of bowlers on different kinds of pitches. I couldn't help but benefit. And don't tell me English batsmen don't benefit from playing our fast bowlers. By the same token, the overseas professional is not simply there to learn about the game but put something back in. Maybe that is why I was well accepted from the very start. I like to think it was my approach, my open-mindedness, the fact that I was always willing to play the role of teacher. It's selfish to play in a side without passing on your expertise to colleagues. I get some stick in the West Indies dressing room for the way I advise Mickey Roseberry because he might play against us one day, but my response to that is to say that when I'm in England I'm playing for Middlesex, not the West Indies. I certainly don't see it as any betrayal.'

Back, then, to Roseberry. A record-breaking schoolboy batsman during his Houghton-le-Spring youth, he had been hailed as a budding star at sixteen, those blond, cherubic features plastered over the pages of the Sunday colour supplements, statistical achievements in the halls of academia proffered as proof of greatness in the making. Not for the first time, expectation exceeded the early reality. Gatting believes this owed much to the fact that, instead of going straight into second XI cricket, he was content to concentrate on his A levels at Durham School and carry on plundering his peers instead. A wayward, irregular member of the Middlesex middle order until 1988, he had yet to make 1000 runs in a season when the retirement (temporary, as it transpired) of John Carr left open an opening berth in 1990. In the 1989 edition of the *Cricketers' Who's Who*, Roseberry made no bones about where he stood on the desirability of imported labour: 'The position on overseas players should be tightened up, as it has got well out of hand.' Three years later he was the joint highest accumulator in the country with 2044 first-class runs at 56.68, rightly gaining selection for the England A tour to Australia. Beside the joys of fathering Jordan, a bonny daughter, Roseberry attributes his advance to Desi.

That stance on imports, needless to add, has undergone something of a reassessment. 'Before Desi came to Middlesex I had the impression that not all overseas players performed as they should. You could bring in three or four English players for the kind of salaries they get. And they didn't help with coaching. I knew you had to have one in order to compete but I wasn't absolutely sure they were worth it. Then Desi arrived and made me alter all those preconceptions. He's been very helpful to me and wonderful in the dressing room. He always comes to the barbecues. He just gets stuck into the food and has a good time. He mucks in. Mind you, I still think we're mugs. Our players don't play in the Sheffield Shield or the Ranji Trophy yet we welcome their players with open arms. It's crazy.'

Desi and Roseberry first crossed paths, and barely at that, when Desi was playing in the leagues. If the older man failed to notice the teenaged Gatting lookalike, the reverse was far from true. 'The first time we met properly was when Durham Schools toured Barbados a couple of years later and Desi came along to watch one of our games. "Hello," he said, "pleased to meet you." A true gent, though not on the golf course. His handicap – two – is too high for the player he is. I'm a sixteen to eighteen handicap and I've beaten him twice, which gave me great pleasure to report back to the boys. He wants us to play off scratch, just so he can win a few more quid. Even before you met him you always had this indelible impression of that big, wonderful smile and that bubbly manner. He really is like that. He really is a noble, happy character, but he's also very competitive, a great competitor. If a bowler says something to him, he'll have a go back. There is no racism that I am aware of in county cricket and, in any case, Middlesex have had a mixed dressing room for years. Desi calls himself "nigger". We nicknamed him Budgie because he talks all the time. Never stops.'

One regular feature of that 1989 season was Desi's contradictory attitude to the fine system introduced to punish any Middlesex latecomers. Many was the time when a tardy player would sneak in on tiptoe only for Desi to catch him bang to rights and demand he cough up the requisite pound or two. He was once observed lurking behind a pillar in the Uxbridge pavilion, waiting to leap out to claim another unsuspecting victim. 'He wouldn't pay the fines himself, of course,' recalls Roseberry. 'In fact, we stopped the whole exercise because of his reluctance. He was late out on the field once but his excuse was that he was the overseas player and, in any case, he was getting old.

'When Desi joined us I was batting down the order. I was quite happy with my form and the direction I was going, but my progress with Middlesex had been slow. To be fair, I'd struggled. It had taken me a couple of years to make any runs in the second team, and although I never lost confidence, it was the concentration thing I found so difficult, keeping going for long periods. In 1989, John Carr and Ian Hutchinson were both dropped and I moved up the order. I didn't think to approach Desi because I didn't know him, but he was very forthright and he came to me, just as he did to all the other young players. It wasn't so much technical advice he offered as a willingness to talk about the game, about his attitude to batting, to running quick singles, to fast bowlers. He would encourage me by saying things like, "Nah, he can't bowl." We developed a brilliant understanding between the wickets. The number of times he gets off the mark with a quick one is unbelievable. We don't even call. We just look and go, that's it. I did him twice in 1992 and twice in 1990, and each time it was my fault. It makes such a difference when you've got someone like that at the other end with that enthusiasm because scoring singles is crucial to an opening partnership. It breaks up the field, drawing fielders in, then pushing them out, keeping them guessing.

'One particularly valuable lesson Desi has given me concerned mental preparation. He feels you should start thinking about batting towards the end of an innings, while you're still in the field, and I've found that to be a worthwhile strategy because it means adjusting your thought processes earlier, getting in the right frame of mind. He's also a great confidence booster. At one stage I got out hooking three times in four innings, which is something that should never happen at Uxbridge, so I asked Desi what I should do. He told me to carry on because hooking was generally a good earner for me. These things happen, he said, but I shouldn't lose faith. In 1992 he said that if I didn't get on the A tour he would strip off and streak round Lord's. Lord's, thankfully, was spared.'

Perverse though it may sound, Roseberry's most disappointing liaison with Desi was also their most productive, a stand of 306 against Essex in 1990. 'We were 61 short of Barlow and Slackie's county record – and I got out to Foster first ball after tea. I'd like to have broken that record and that was the perfect chance: you don't get many opportunities to bat with someone like that who makes it possible. He made 220 not out that day and batted brilliantly, fantastic concentration. No matter how good you are you need hunger, and Desi certainly has that. He says he's not interested in records, and he doesn't seem to be either, but he is certainly interested in his average. His presence has also made Gatt feel he has something to beat – and vice versa. I tend to remember his one-day knocks better. In games like that you are generally watching the play more carefully because things happen quicker, and the best innings I've seen from him was the century he made against Lancashire in the 1990 NatWest semi-final at Old Trafford. The rain kept the match going for three days, and he was still in on the third, smashing Akram all over the place. He is a very correct player, very straight, a good worker of the ball, runs it down to third man a lot. We don't talk about cricket a great deal at Middlesex – I don't know if that's just us or professional teams in general – but I think we should discuss it more often. Desi is a big one for having team meetings before away games when we're all staying together, assessing what happened during the day and deciding on a plan for the next one. Four-day cricket should enable more time for that.'

Arguments over the pros and cons of a full four-day programme were a constant source of angst as English cricket prepared for its 1993 reformation. Throughout it all, the most fervent advocates cited one seemingly indisputable advantage. The growing tendency for Championship games to be settled by barter and a third-day panto offended Desi's notion of what constituted a proper contest, just as it had so many of us reporters tearing up our notebooks and launching into ritually scathing rhetoric. 'I didn't agree with all those declaration bowlers one bit, but then when the wickets are as good as they have been over the past three summers I don't think three days are enough to prove that one side is better than another. Somehow a way has to be found to suit the players and the county treasurers, but you must also ensure that you don't bore your public. Four-day cricket will be very good for English players as a grounding for Test matches, but I can see the spectators being bored to death. You can picture the scenario. One team will bat first, make 250 for 2 on the first day, declare after tea on the second, then their opponents will spend another day trying to avoid the follow-on. After that the captains will do their level best to cram two innings into the last four sessions. What the four-day game will definitely do for the better is to allow more time for planning and practice, because, up to now, there has been no time for the coaches to actually coach. Don Bennett has coped well at Middlesex, but he had to work out mutually suitable times with each member of the side.

'The point is, so long as the other competitions provide the members with some form of consolation, it probably doesn't matter whether the Championship is less than enthralling for them. As for the other changes brought in by the Murray Report, I know I'm far from alone in resenting the noon starts on Sundays, in my case because it means that I can't lie in or go to church. I'm not sure that making the NatWest and the Benson and Hedges almost indistinguishable is a good thing either. The TCCB might have been more imaginative with regard to the 55-over game, throwing it open to European sides like Holland and Denmark or perhaps turning it into a regional tournament, North versus South, Midlands versus the West, that sort of thing. Having said that, the balance between limited-overs and first-class cricket is now just about right.'

When Richard Hadlee left Nottinghamshire, many took umbrage at his vituperative condemnation of the English county pro. 'There is an enormous amount of mediocrity in English cricket,' he grumbled. 'A lot of very average players are making their living out of the game when really they shouldn't be in it.' He was probably lucky to become Sir Dick after that parting billet doux. While declining to go quite so far, Desi has his doubts too. 'The mood can sometimes be too relaxed, but what bothers me is that the nature of the circuit breeds a degree of negativity, of selfishness. It is possible, after all, to build a worthwhile career without playing for your country, something which is alien to West Indians on a practical basis, let alone a philosophical one. There are so many players to whom the biggest worry is whether their contract will be renewed, which cannot be conducive to the team effort.'

Desi's current two-year contract is due to expire at the end of the 1993 season. He is now as much a part of the fixtures and fittings as Wayne Daniel was before him, and would dearly love an extension. Whether he is offered one, unfortunately, is beyond his control, since Middlesex's most pressing need is for a strike bowler. Ricky Ellcock's spinal condition forced him to retire in 1992; Fraser's hip problems threaten the career of the most dependable English seamer since Brian Statham, Hughes has gone to Durham and neither Cowans nor Williams is exactly in the first flush of youth. In the event of the county opting for an overseas flame thrower – of whom there is a severely limited supply – Desi would happily entertain advances from elsewhere in the shires. Demanding though it is, the county circuit keeps the edges sharpened and the competitive juices flowing, ideal ingredients for anyone determined to keep his career going for as long as possible. There are worse ways to spend the off-season.

12

King for a Day

'Who needs the pressure?'
Desmond Haynes on captaining the West Indies, September 1991

He had a point, of course, but he didn't really mean it. Not completely, anyway. On the morning of 23 March 1990, when Desi sauntered out to the middle at the Queen's Park Oval to toss up with Allan Lamb, he was fulfilling the ambition of every West Indian from Anguilla to St Vincent, albeit by default. Within eight months Viv Richards's troublesome nether regions had permitted him to go a stage further. Named as captain for the tour of Pakistan, the likeliest pretenders to loosen the Caribbean stranglehold, he presided over a side that lost all three one-day internationals and then the first Test in Karachi by a numbing eight wickets, yet returned home a hero by splitting the three-match rubber 1–1. With Richards having announced his intention to relinquish the captaincy following the 1991 visit to England, the accession seemed clear cut. By September of that year, however, the picture had grown cloudier. For an English journalist less than privy to the machinations and thought processes of the West Indies Board of Control, sharing a cab with Desi at the end of that tour afforded the first indications that the vice-captain was not, after all, the anointed heir. While the logic of the pressure argument was irrefutable, the eyes betrayed more mixed emotions. Unbeknown to me, Clyde Walcott, the president of the board, had telephoned Desi in Chandler's Ford a few days previously to inform him that Richie Richardson would captain the West Indies that winter.

To discover why Desi was overtaken it is first necessary to trace his drive

into pole position, a journey that began with his appointment as captain of
Barbados and vice-captain of the West Indies for that 1989–90 season. The
latter honour soon yielded an appetizer for life at the sharp end. On the final
day of the third Test (in reality the second, the Guyana instalment having
been washed out), the West Indies, already one down in the series after
surrendering their 29-match unbeaten record against St George, faced apparent defeat when Wayne Larkins and Graham Gooch set off shortly after the
start in pursuit of 151. Pluvius intervened at 73 for 1 and when he finally
relented, England, captain *hors de combat* with a broken left hand, needed 78
from 30 overs, the outfield a squelchy, treacherous, unfit morass. Play continued for an hour after the scheduled close, yet only 17 overs were bowled
before bad light prevailed, England teetering on 120 for 5. The visiting scribes
waded into Desi for masterminding the go-slow, although few harrumphed
quite so loudly during the next Test when Lamb conducted a similarly funereal
march in a bid to stem the West Indian run flow. Unethical perhaps, yet
scarcely revolutionary. 'It required little skill to bowl as wide as he did at the
finish,' Jack Fingleton had written after seeing Trevor Bailey save the Leeds
Test of 1953 by keeping up a steady line a foot or more outside leg, 'but he
did the necessary job.' This, note, from a man whose compatriots had thus
been denied.

Gooch admitted that, had he been the fielding captain in those circumstances, he would almost certainly have taken the same tack. But was this a
pre-meditated policy or did the conditions compel it? 'If we'd been playing
in England I don't think we would have restarted because of the state of the
outfield,' avers Courtney Walsh, well versed in such matters through his
yeomanry service for Gloucestershire. 'Bishop couldn't run in. If he had tried
to do so he would have damaged himself. Luckily, it was drier from my end.
There was no policy to slow the rate. We didn't want to rush in because of
the run-ups. We were at a disadvantage. Yet we might have won in the end
if we'd managed to squeeze in a few more overs.'

Although he cannot deny a degree of malice aforethought, Desi confirms
that his hands were tied. 'The conditions were appalling, the worst I've ever
encountered for a Test match. There is no way we should have come back
on. I have a lot of respect for Ian Bishop, a deeply religious person, so when
he told me that he couldn't bowl, I knew how risky it was going to be. We
had to restart because the umpires said so, but I believe the TV people forced
them into it. It was the first time an England tour of the Caribbean had been
televised live round the world and they were anxious for some action. But

how could the cameras pick up the wetness? It was sad that I got so much stick for slowing the game down. When I came off at the finish I thought, well, at least I've tried to play the game. Then, when I got back to England I started receiving all sorts of nasty letters and comments. I'm happy to say that the England players said they would have done exactly the same in my position. Nobody likes to lose a Test match. It was my first one as captain, after all, and it meant a lot not to lose.'

Desi's image in England shed some more lustre when the next day's papers provided visual evidence of the intemperate climax. There he was, embroiled in an animatedly frank exchange of views with Alec Stewart, whose chatty, assertive manner belied his inexperience at international level. By his own admission, Desi had been sniping away at the cocky Cockney. 'If you are going to use psychology to upset a batsman you shouldn't swear, but if a player is inexperienced and he's going to let it get to him, tough luck. I didn't think Alec could handle the short stuff so I told him he'd get a lot of it. That's all. I wasn't abusive, not like the Australians. You shouldn't go on like that for long, and I didn't, but neither do I think cricket should be played in silence.'

Silent was about the least appropriate adjective one might use to describe the remainder of the series. At Kensington, a superlative blast of five wickets in as many overs from Ambrose earned the equalizer with less than half an hour's daylight to spare, Desi having played his part with 109 in the second innings, leaping with unbridled joy to high-five Logie upon reaching three figures for the third time in a Bridgetown Test. Another neighbourhood boy, Best, had even more fun, stroking an impressive maiden Test century, though, sadly, he was unable to capitalize, breaking a finger and missing the next Test. Between times, Richards, restored to fitness, incensed the English guardians of propriety. Taking off on a lap of honour when Rob Bailey looked, from the imperfect perspective afforded the slip region, to have been caught behind – the ball had in fact deflected off his hip – Richards was accused over the World Service airwaves by Chris Martin-Jenkins of coaxing umpire Lloyd Barker into giving the Northamptonshire batsman out. Richards's reaction, 'maybe a bit dramatic', he later accepted, was plain and simple 'cheating' according to the BBC correspondent. Even the locals, the least sensitive in the Caribbean on the colour issue, held such assertions to be racist. Martin-Jenkins withdrew the 'cheating' claim and apologized to Barker, who issued him with a writ for defamation for alleging that he had 'cracked under pressure'. Desi was sceptical. 'I don't believe we've got that much power.

How guys appeal shouldn't matter, anyway. What about the way Lillee used to crouch in front of umpires and bellow in their faces? We shouldn't tell people how to appeal. It's how they react when the umpire goes against them that counts.'

Richards was the reluctant centre of attention once again when the series was decided in Antigua. After Bishop (5 for 84) had kept England down to a mediocre 260, the Fabulous Bajan Boys shredded the errant visiting bowlers for 228 in 51 overs before the close of the second day, going on to set a new West Indian first-wicket record with 298, Desi's second highest Test score of 167 spanning nine hours of economic batsmanship. Having started the winter with an indifferent showing in Sharjah, he had collected centuries against England and Pakistan during the West Indian drive to the runners-up slot in the one-day Nehru Cup, blipped again in the first two Tests as Gladstone Small administered a duck in successive games, and ended on the upswing, heading the five-day averages with 371 runs at 53. Ambrose and Bishop stitched up the innings victory and the rubber, extending Richards's record unbeaten run as captain to 10 series.

By then, regrettably, he had let himself down badly. Asked by James Lawton of the *Daily Express* why he had apparently made a V-sign towards his buddy Lamb on the third day, Richards, less than delighted at being quizzed on a rest day, pointed out that the gesture had been aimed at a section of the crowd. Lawton, Richards later told his ghost writer, 'persisted with his stupid questions' and duly felt the lash of King Viv's tongue, threats and all. 'Richards Blows His Top', screamed the front page splash the next morning. Richards, who had warned Lawton that he would come looking for him if the story ran, clambered up to the press gantry to give the columnist a word or two of advice. To make matters worse, he chose to do this at the precise moment he should have been leading his team on to the field. Even his staunchest supporters had to blanch at this pointless exercise. Heroes should be above such ill-conceived actions. When he began referring to himself in the third person singular, as the less than cuddly-sounding 'Vivi', this merely hardened the impression of a man with distinct hubristic tendencies.

Desi was sympathetic none the less. 'The whole thing was planned to upset Viv. His reaction was not the right one, but things had been building up. People wanted to get him because he was the symbol of our dominance. The British press contingent was huge by then, which didn't help. They'd brought in reinforcements after England's victory at Sabina, but we ruined the plot by winning on the two best batting strips. Curtly's spell at Kensington turned the tide and, by the time we got to Antigua, we thought they had played their best cricket. England had gained in confidence, making the series more competitive, so it was a good series for West Indian cricket.'

In some senses, the regional captaincy was even more fraught than Desi's dalliance with the top job, for these were recessionary times in Barbadian cricket. When it comes to furnishing the Caribbean with cricketers of world-class calibre, Barbados, with the slimmest population among the senior islands to draw on, has more than done its bit. Up to March 1987, 55 of the 198 players selected to represent the West Indies in Tests, a relatively whopping 27.78 per cent, had sprung from the loins of this tiny eastern member of the brotherhood. Occasionally, predictably, resentment has surfaced, Carlisle Best for one detecting 'a little antagonism' towards the Bajan sector of the West Indies team. The tide of selectorial favour, too, seems to have shifted else-where, with only one Bajan being introduced to the Test team between 1987 and 1992. Ezra Moseley, furthermore, was a ripe thirty-two when he made his bow in 1990, which means that, until Anderson Cummins made his début in 1993, no Bajan born since independence had claimed his apparent birthright. In the B party that toured Zimbabwe in 1989, horror of horrors: not a single Bajan in sight. While a quintet participated in that 1990 series against England, only two were chosen for the 1992–3 tour of Australia.

The treatment recently meted out by the West Indies selectors to Roland Holder, Philo Wallace and Cummins has given rise in certain quarters to suggestions of a sort of Bajan-GAJT, a fiendish plot hatched by Guyana, Antigua, Jamaica and Trinidad to diminish the Bajan influence. As alibis go, the American cultural invasion, spearheaded by Michael Jordan, Super Mario and Bart Simpson, is even less credible since this is a debilitating factor throughout the Caribbean. More pertinent is the decline in bats-manship, a development unimpaired by the fact that sixteen-year-old school-boys are still able to test their embryonic skills against the Marshalls and Cumminses in club games. In part, many Bajans contend, the deterioration is attributable to soggy, inadequate club pitches. Traditionally, local matches have been staged in the rainy season, partially in deference to the sugar harvest, mostly because grounds tend to be bone dry, cracked and essentially unplayable during the first six months of the year. The Barbados Cricket Association, profitability guaranteed by its scratchcard Instant Money Game, may be the best administered and wealthiest of the individual Caribbean boards, but economic reality means that covers are not so much thin on the ground as invisible, rendering crease survival something of a lottery.

That Desi, Sobers, Nurse, Hunte and the three Ws all coped pretty well would seem to puncture such a theory, yet the pitch issue certainly holds true at national level. In the late seventies, fed up with the plethora of run-jammed stalemates, not to say eager to derive the maximum benefit from Marshall, Garner, Daniel, Clarke and Moseley, the Kensington Oval authorities began to leave grass on their strips. Naturally enough, while this secured a succession of Shell Shield triumphs – eight in eleven years between 1976 and 1986 – many of the younger batsmen, technique exposed, courage relentlessly challenged and confidence pricked, were a bit miffed. By the time Kensington was restored to its customary pristine self in the late eighties, the damage had been done. It should therefore come as no surprise to learn that, while a dozen of the Bajans who made their Test débuts between 1948 and 1978 had run up 118 centuries between them by the end of 1992, only two of those brought in since – Best and Collis King – have reached three figures, and even then only once apiece. In Desi's view, however, this apparent fall-off is only a comparative one. 'Thanks to the youth programmes that evolved during the early eighties other nations in the Caribbean were on the rise: ours had yet to bear fruit. Now it is. We won the West Indies youth tournament a couple of years ago and there is still a lot of talent there. It's just taking time to come through. Kids no longer play under the streetlights as we did. There are a lot more alternatives open to them now apart from cricket, which was all we had. Their role models are more likely to be footballers now. But the schools are still playing the game and we just have to ensure we protect our youth programme. I am certain that the people who describe me as the last great batsman to come out of Barbados will prove to be wide of the mark.'

Desi, nevertheless, inherited the reins against a discouraging backdrop, one mitigated only slightly by the one-point margin separating Barbados from winners Jamaica in the 1988–9 Red Stripe. Neither did it help that the Leeward Islands, with six Test players in their line-up, had now assumed the invincible mantle. For the first time, Barbados endured a fourth fallow season in a row, the Leewards cruising to their first regional title on the back of five wins and an unprecedented 100 per cent record after getting off to a flyer by winning at Kensington. According to Best, who had captained the side the previous season but harboured no grudge, respect for the new skipper was automatic. 'When he led us against the Leewards it was the first time he had entered a field at the head of a team, but his experience made it easy for the players to accept him, even if it did take a little longer for the press and public. As a captain, his authority as a performer commanded respect, and in the end he became a very good captain. He didn't offer me any commiserations at losing the job because neither of us were aware of any sense of competition. Marshall wasn't interested and, as I understand it, the vote was a narrow one in Desi's favour.'

Keith Holder, who has edited the sports section of the Barbados *Sunday Sun* since 1974 and first met Desi when the latter was in the Barbados Youth XI, recalls the hostile reception accorded the new captain by the local media. 'There was a lot of criticism because he seemed too defensive. He lost his first game and then, after the draw against Jamaica, one commentator said he would have been hard pressed to give him one out of ten for his tactics. That really angered Desi and in the end the last three games were won.' Despite a century against Trinidad, Desi mustered only 177 runs from his other eight innings, giving him a disappointing average of 35.62. From a Bajan perspective, happily, there were signs of a revival to nourish. Runners-up once more, Barbados also came second in the one-day Geddes Grant Shield final. Something to build on.

The brickwork started in earnest in 1991, though not before Desi had underlined his credentials for a higher calling. With the speed and swing of Waqar Younis and the leg-spin of Mushtaq Ahmed putting the final touches to the House of Imran, Pakistan on their own turf constituted as testing a proposition as any in the game. Since 1964 they had lost a mere three of their 70 home Tests, and now they boasted their strongest collective yet. Desi won the toss at Karachi and enjoyed a memorable opening day from a personal standpoint, his third successive Test 100 completing a full set of three-figure scores against each of the West Indies' opponents. Batting throughout that first day for 113, he was trapped early next morning by Wasim Akram for 117, only six less than his charges would aggregate between them. A lopsided scoreboard – Salim Malik 102, Shoaib 86, Imran 73 not out, the obliging Mr Ex Tras 48, eight other contributors a combined return of 36 – produced a Pakistani lead of 84. Desi strove to combat the irrepressible Waqar with 47, but a total of 181 was nowhere near sufficient to tax the hosts, who coasted cautiously to the 98 needed.

Just as they had when the sides last met, the West Indies counter-punched with venom. With the seamers obtaining sharp movement through the air and off the pitch, Malik's 74 was the one score of note on the first two days at Faisalabad, only 110.2 overs being needed to dispense with the first two innings. When Pakistan reached 145 for 4 midway through the third day, 120 on, a fascinating duel was in store, whereupon Marshall bowled Malik for 71, then shunted out Javed, Imran, Akram Raza and Waqar in the space of a dozen deliveries. Defending 130, Wasim Akram made short work of Desi, who drove the first ball of the West Indies second innings to cover to glean his tenth and, briefly, unhappiest Test duck, but Richardson's unbeaten 70 sealed a seven-wicket waltz fifty minutes after tea. The tourists maintained the whip hand in Lahore, where Hooper's classy 134 and five wickets apiece for Ambrose and Bishop, fast emerging as the new Garner and Holding, engineered a first-innings lead of 172. At 110 for 4 on the final morning, Pakistan, chasing an unlikely 346, were in trouble, but the series was saved by the stickability of Imran and nightwatchman Masood Anwar, the débutant off-spinner. Not for a decade had a touring side come so close to downing Pakistan.

Desi basked in the glow. 'I received so many letters and telegrams from the board congratulating me on how well I'd captained the side, how I'd brought on Hooper and Brian Lara, how I'd shared the series against the odds and so on. I loved the challenge. We held a training camp in Barbados before flying out and that helped us prepare mentally. I tried to instil in the players who had never been to Pakistan before the need to be in total control and not worry about the umpiring decisions. It wasn't a case of being negative but realistic. They had to accept that they were going to get a few bad ones and that they shouldn't let that get them down, that their captain would support them. I promised that I would write in my report, where applicable, that they played well in the circumstances. In the end, fortunately, there were few problems in that area. The senior players were all very supportive and helpful. I outlined my plans to each of the bowlers – who was going to bowl the long spells, who the short ones – so when I handed over the ball to them they were aware of what they were expected to do.'

To expect a tour of Pakistan to draw a blank on the controversy scoreboard would be naïve, and this was no exception, even if the umpiring, for once, was blameless. Upon arrival in Pakistan, Desi was going through his messages when he came upon a handwritten note from Martin Crowe, who had just led an acrimonious tour there by New Zealand. So infuriated had Crowe and his men been by what they had perceived as ball-tampering, that one of the Kiwi seamers, the modestly gifted Chris Pringle, staged a one-man protest by picking the seam and disfiguring the surface of the ball in the third Test at Faisalabad, taking 7 for 52, his best five-day haul by the proverbial mile. Ian Taylor, the New Zealand manager, accused the hosts of doctoring the ball so as to obtain extra swing, Intikhab Alam, his opposite number, described the claim as 'rubbish', Waqar's adjective was 'bullshit' and the home board denied everything. In his missive to Desi, Crowe wrote that, after a couple of overs' use, the ball had been swinging inordinately. This, he accepted, was mainly because of the quality of the Pakistan seam attack, but he also felt that interference with the ball had honed their cutting edge.

Desi soon found himself in agreement and complained, both to the press and the West Indies board. He was ready to issue a statement after the first Test but refrained from doing so until the end when he and the tour manager, Lance Gibbs, both registered their displeasure. Imran dismissed the charge as 'ridiculous', although the fact that Waqar had been a member of the Surrey side warned the previous summer for such nefarious practices appeared to negate the Pakistan captain's claim that his bowlers had been given a clean bill of health by county umpires. The then secretary of the Pakistan board, Arif Ali Abbasi, stated that, at the end of the first Test, he had shown Gibbs the balls used by both teams and that 'The manager agreed that the ball used by the West Indians was in a much worse condition than the one used by Pakistan.' It was, Imran and his comrades insisted, the roughness of the arid, grassless, usually debris-strewn Pakistani outfields that made all balls prone to damage. There was even some guff about Pakistani sweat having different propensities. Mudassar Nazar, the Pakistan B coach, convinced that the tourists were the main culprits, was more honest: 'The outlawed practice of roughing up one side of the ball to enhance swing must be eradicated in Pakistan.'

The issue, without doubt, was complex, and remains so. Defacing the ball is neither innovative nor even the sole province of the seamer. Had not the spinners of the past quite brazenly rubbed the new ball in the dirt to erase the shine and make it easier to grip? Nor is cricket the only sport wherein altering the state of the ball is advantageous, baseball having had its fair share of offenders down the years. Developments of the past few years, however, have conspired to put the ruse back in vogue. One eminent county captain responded to the featherbeds and slim seams of 1990 by advocating that bowlers should be encouraged to indulge in a bit of creative resculpting in order to even the score. Ted Dexter, the chairman of the England selectors, said that might not be a bad idea if it encouraged a return to the lost art of swing. As recently as the autumn of 1992, in the wake of Surrey's £1000 knuckle-rap from the TCCB for four infractions of Law 42 (5) and Lamb's original £5000 fine for accusing the Pakistan bowlers of the same offence, Desi's Middlesex colleague Angus Fraser conceded that the majority of county

seamers had done likewise. Desi feels this is nothing to be proud of. 'It's been
going on in some form or other for years and you should be fined heavily if
caught, simple as that. Otherwise, the next thing you know players will be
buying flannels with sandpaper flaps.'

The second flare-up occurred during the second Pakistan innings at Lahore.
In a near-replica of a previous incident involving Sylvester Clarke, Walsh was
struck by an orange thrown from the crowd and apparently blew his lid. 'He
grabbed a stump and seemed intent on searching out the spectator concerned,'
ran the report in *Wisden Cricket Monthly*. 'Walsh was restrained by Ambrose,
then skipper Haynes came up and told the Jamaican to go to the dressing
room for a while to cool off. He returned ten minutes later. Haynes's prompt
action may have prevented an ugly incident, and showed his mature approach
to the captaincy.' Very flattering, but was there any truth in it? Not according
to Walsh. 'Somebody threw something and it hit me in the back. I was
bowling at the time and I couldn't lift my right arm. Desi asked me if I was
OK and I said I was all right but that I couldn't carry on because of my arm. So
I went off for some ultra-sound treatment. Dennis [Waight] said something in
the vertebra had come out of place. From what they saw people interpreted
that I'd lost my temper and Desi had sent me off to cool down, but I would
never lose my temper on the field.'

Desi tells a similar tale. 'Walshie showed me the swelling on his back and
suggested he went off for treatment. He was very upset, understandably so.
Not until a couple of months later did he tell me that that Pakistani correspondent had thought he'd been sent off.' An apology appeared a full seven
months later, in the August issue of *WCM*: 'We accept that there is no truth
in any such suggestion [that Desi had ordered Walsh to the sin-bin] and that
he left the field only for treatment to a blow received from an object thrown
by a spectator. We also accept that Mr Walsh did not, as alleged in the
report, seem intent on searching out the spectator involved with a stump.'
If blame could scarcely be attached to the magazine, the correspondent concerned deserved a Booker Prize nomination at the very least.

Reverting to regional concerns, youth, Desi decided, held the key to a
Barbados resurgence. As a consequence of this, a clutch of the eight thirtysomethings who dominated the side in 1990 were discarded, the still capable
Thelston Payne, who earned his solitary cap behind the stumps during David
Gower's tour of 1985–6, and Franklyn Stephenson among them. In the latter's
stead came Andy Cummins, twenty-four, wiry and hasty, who proceeded to
take more wickets (23) than any other fast bowler in the Red Stripe Cup,

including Richards, Richardson and Keith Arthurton in the space of an hour. Philo Wallace, an ebullient if headstrong young opener, carved Ambrose, Baptiste and the emerging Kenny Benjamin for 135 off 191 balls to set up victory over the Leeward Islands. Sammy Skeete, who had spearheaded the Young West Indies attack in the 1987–8 Youth World Cup, worked up a full head of steam to claim 21 victims in his first full season. Greenidge, Marshall and Moseley provided the seasoning and only one total in excess of 300 was conceded as Haynes led his country to four wins out of five and 72 points, all but double that of the runners-up, Trinidad and Tobago. The homecoming parade at Grantley Adams Airport was one for the scrapbook.

The man who lit the fire, though, was the captain, whose personal contribution read as follows: 3, 40 not out, 21, 122, 21, 125 not out, 113, 146, 63 not out. In averaging 109 he racked up 654 runs and four centuries in all, both competition records. Privileged to have viewed it from the other end of the pitch, Best, who made one himself that day to play a full hand in a matchwinning second-wicket stand of 237, rates the unbeaten century against Trinidad as the best he has seen Desi play. 'Given that we had been set 280 against an attack led by Tony Gray and including the spin of Dhanraj and Nanan, to win by nine wickets in those circumstances was incredible. To all intents and purposes, that clinched the Red Stripe Cup.' In Keith Holder's estimation, the captain of 1991 was a supercharged version of the 1990 model. 'I saw a different Desi. Having the opportunity to captain the West Indies in Pakistan clearly helped and he came back extremely confident. One of the hallmarks of his leadership for me was that he let the younger players have their say, instilling confidence in them.'

With Richards about to embark on his final tour at the helm, these, one might reasonably have imagined, were indeed persuasive reasons to appoint Desi as the fifth full-time West Indies captain since Worrell's retirement, a period in which England, for one, used up no fewer than seventeen. At thirty-five, he was coping with that persistent back condition and otherwise displaying not a hint of wear and tear. The technique, zest and desire were all intact. Now he had imposed himself as a leader of men.

The opposition, encouragingly, was limited. At one juncture in the late eighties, Roger Harper had been Richards's dauphin, but his off-spin and self-belief later crumbled. Greenidge had been tried and found wanting and, in any event, fitness and age counted against him. Brian Lara, a product of the best grooming Trinidad could offer, was the long-term bet, but his career was still in its pre-pubescence. The chief threat was Richardson, Richards's

Antiguan protégé. A destructive bat on reliable wickets, it was his thunderous 182 off 242 balls at Bourda that had turned the West Indies around after a sluggish start to the so-called 'World Championship' series against Australia. England, though, remained a bugbear. On two previous tours in 1984 and 1988 he had been so discomfited by the seaming ball that his 614 runs had arrived at an average of barely 25. If this constituted a tick in the minus column, it also contributed to another: a diffident, reserved air that failed to convince the outsider that here was a figure with either the self-assurance or strength of personality required to marshal the disparate nationalities and so sculpt the whole expected, even in a time of flux.

The millstones that are part and parcel of this occupation cannot be under-estimated. For all the success that has attended Lloyd and Richards, and, to a lesser extent, Sobers, the onus on the West Indies captain weighs heavier than it does on any of his counterparts. Respect, fear even, have been far too hard-earned to be relinquished. Every victory in the middle is another blow to the white supremacists, but there can never be enough victories: there is still so much ground to make up. It's too late to stop now. The rise to power has been too recent for complacency. With vast chunks of the area blighted by economic strife and its partner in disaster, rising crime, the demand for consolation has risen, the level of public expectation soaring in inverse pro-portion to the quality of life beyond the boundary. As the nearest approxima-tion to a leader of a united Caribbean, the captain of the West Indies carries a burden far above his station. Who needs the pressure, indeed? That Desi possessed the wherewithal to bear the strain nevertheless appeared self-evident. The early spring of 1991, however, would prove to be the apex in the progress of his application.

Desi, as may have been deduced by now, is a soul riven by two distinct forces, between playing up and playing the game and standing up for his, and his team's, rights. These forces should not be opposing ones, yet all too frequently they are precisely that. Perhaps the best (or worst?) example of this was the Worrell Trophy series of 1990–91. The West Indies Cricket Board has reputedly recorded no fewer than nine counts of unsatisfactory behaviour on the debit side of Desi's account, the most conspicuous of these occurring during that rubber against Australia, itself the cumulation of years of simmering mutual dislike and arguably the most unpleasant confrontation ever to scar a square. For many, the root cause of the fractiousness was the determination of Allan Border and his tourists to wrest their hosts' undisputed if unofficial world title by hook or crook. They opted for the crooked route, the forked tongue scam. Convinced that sledging – aka the science of verbal abuse, copyright Ian Chappell and Ray Illingworth – was not only a valid weapon but a powerfully unsettling one to boot, they nagged, niggled, scratched and scraped at their opponents' self-control until the itch grew into a weal and festered beyond tolerance. The sound of snapping patience crackled throughout the domain, spreading like wildfire.

Black consciousness uppermost as always, Richards alienated many admirers with an ill-advised statement about his team being an African one ('African Caribbean people,' he later elaborated, 'include all the different nationalities of the Caribbean'). To him, it all boiled down to a lack of respect. 'If you don't understand a people's culture you won't understand the people at all. Some people look at you and remember you as just being a slave. Some don't see the progress that has been made: that we have broken those particular chains. One is looking forward to us joining hands and living together but some people don't want it that way. On cricket circuits you will get "black bastard" or "jammy black so and so". It's crazy. Some of them really look at you out there like you should be hunted. But I can tell you, no man is going to hunt me in this day and age. I take up the pursuing first.'

The jury is still out on Richards, the paranoia lobby trading licks with those who believe his tirades to be justified. We will cite the case of Marge Schott, the owner of the Cincinnati Reds baseball franchise who, besides referring to 'money-grubbing Jews' and maintaining that 'Hitler was good in the beginning but went too far', once called the club's outfielder, Dave Parker, a 'million-dollar nigger'; the racist comments flung at Jeremy Guscott, Ellery Hanley, 'Syd' Lawrence and sundry other black sporting Britons; the jibe Allan Border cast at Joel Garner after receiving a bouncer in Kingston; the 'racist' behaviour which the Sri Lankans claimed to have experienced at the hands of the Australians in 1990; the cry of 'No. 57, Pilau Rice' an equally frustrated Ian Botham directed at Essex's Karachi-born all-rounder, Nadeem Shahid, in front of Worcester Cathedral; of the Headingley oafs who have hounded Richards himself. The list is as endless as it is reprehensible.

Racially motivated or not – and, given their track record with the Aboriginals it would not be entirely out of character had that been the case – the Australian tactics resembled the advanced stiletto technique employed by the skilful, inappropriately named Italian hit-man, Claudio Gentile, during football's 1982 World Cup. Time and again, the sly, unscrupulous defender would subtly rake a stud or three across the back of Diego Maradona's calves, pull a sleeve, grasp a clump of hair, allow a knee – or, for variety, a shoulder or elbow – accidentally to follow through a foot too far. The plan worked to perfection: Argentina's Maradona, the game's foremost exponent, physically taunted, frustrated to breaking point and increasingly ineffectual, eventually lashed out and was sent off. Italy edged the holders 2–1 and went on to lift the trophy. Sport at its least sporting.

The West Indies proved less susceptible than Maradona and his forgivably gullible cohorts, refusing to allow anger to dilute the single-mindedness of their intent. Stung by a 4–1 loss in the one-day rubber, they rebounded to sew up the Test series in four games, the turning point coming in Georgetown via an exhilarating run-a-ball salvo of 297 by Desi (111 off 221 balls with 17 fours, his sixteenth five-day 100) and Richardson (182 off 242, including 106 in a session). In the space of 70 overs, this record second-wicket stand for West Indies against Australia, erasing the pair's own mark, rendered the final outcome only a matter of time.

The appreciation of the Bourda crowd, never a favourite of Richards, was in marked contrast to their behaviour during the one-day international. Incensed by the captain's 'African' statement, the East Indian majority backed the Australians to the hilt. Walsh was hit on the hand by an unidentified projectile thrown from the Lance Gibbs stand, Richards complained to the local board and the police went in search of the guilty party. As they were doing so, a bottle hurtled towards Desi from the opposite end of the ground. Seeing it fall well short, he picked it up without fuss, deposited it on the safe side of the boundary and carried on as if nothing untoward had happened. He was somewhat more demonstrative when Mark Waugh later guided him to the pavilion with some choice directions following a contentious leg-before verdict. So tense was the atmosphere that Richards and Border took to shouting at each other during the tea interval, the former aggrieved that his counterpart had exercised his right to strike for four a delivery that plopped out of Phil Simmons's hand and rolled down the track.

Wound up tighter than a posture bedspring, the victors did not forgive their verbal tormentors. During the Australian second innings at Bourda, Dean Jones had his middle stump bent askew by Walsh, tucked his bat under his arm and headed for the pavilion, oblivious to umpire Clyde Duncan's no-ball call. Border, standing in horror at the non-striker's end, exhorted him to regain his ground, but by the time the confused batsman reacted, Hooper, fired up by the smell of victory, was on his way from gully, ball in hand. Summarily uprooting a stump, he led a vehement appeal. The Buddha-esque Clyde Cumberbatch, wobbling at square leg, raised his right index finger in ignorance both of Law 38 (2), which states that, if a no-ball has been called, 'the striker cannot be given out unless he attempts to run', as well as Law 27 (5): 'The umpires shall intervene if satisfied that a batsman, not having been given out, has left his wicket under a misapprehension that he has been dismissed.'

A case for the video replay/third umpire? Not according to Desi, a firm non-disciple. 'It makes no sense having umpires if you're going to use replays. You may as well have robots. I don't even agree with them for assessing run-outs. There has to be some give and take between us and the umpires. They're going to make mistakes. They're only human, after all. Having said that, I don't think players should help them. Cricket is a mortgage-paying business. I don't believe you should walk unless captains are willing to call you back, and how often does that happen? Let the umpire make the decision, for good or bad. As soon as you show any sign of inciting the crowd by your reaction you know you'll be slapped with a heavy fine. I do favour a panel of the best umpires, changing the members every couple of years and using the others in one-day games to give them a feel of what's required. As the excellent standard in county cricket proves, if you umpire regularly you get better. Equal representation is not important: quality counts.'

Knowing full well that his side would assuredly have followed suit, Jones did not expect to be recalled (subsequently asked whether he would have recalled an opposing batsman, he smirked, saying he drew the line at answering hypothetical questions). Rules forgotten, politesse all but discarded in the heat of an ugly battle, Hooper and his kinsmen rejoiced as Jones trudged away. At the end of the game, he sought out Richards to congratulate him on his team's victory and was genuinely surprised when his invitation to share a couple of bottles of Red Stripe was brusquely rejected. 'After being abused by a guy,' Richards reasoned, 'you don't expect him to come over and say, "How are you doing? You want a Toohey's?" You don't do things like that. When I draw the sword, I draw the sword. When I draw it, that's it. It's the way we are brought up. You don't come and call me all sorts of things and then expect to come up and put your hand on my shoulder telling me that we are the best of friends. Forget about it.'

When the series was wrapped up, Richards lit an immodest cigar, went to the press conference in the Sir Garfield Sobers pavilion at Bridgetown and denounced the Australian coach, Bobby Simpson, who, it transpired, had been getting up his nose since he first encountered the abrasive New South Welshman, then the Australian captain, during the 1977–8 Worrell Trophy

series. Simpson, it should be added, had long been one of the West Indies'
most vociferous critics, and although he had not been at Bourda when Jones
was so unchivalrously run out, he questioned the morality of the dismissal.
A bit rich that, thought Richards. In his opinion, 'Simmo' was 'a moaner
and a bad loser . . . a very sour sort of guy. I've seen him over a number of
years and seen the way he operates. I may say that I'm not the greatest lover
or greatest admirer of Bobby Simpson. You treat people as you are treated.'

After Australia had gained a consolation win at St John's in the fifth Test,
Clyde Walcott was moved to berate both sides for abusing the spirit of healthy
competition. 'It needed to be said,' Desi asserts, 'but he should have identified
the problem. It was up to the individuals concerned, but while we tried to
keep things even-tempered, they stirred the pot. What really bothered me
was that if the positions had been reversed, i.e. we had behaved badly in
Australia, the outcry would have been far greater. It was suggested that
Australia decided retribution was in order after Walshie had hit Waugh
and McDermott when Jamaica played them. Australians complain because a
batsman got hit? I doubt that very much.'

Reclining in the petite pavilion at rain-spattered Horsham last summer,
Jones, an aggressive, strutting presence on the field for Australia, Victoria
and now Durham, garrulous if scampishly charming off it, gave the ruckus
short shrift, dismissing it as par for the course. 'When Viv made that personal
attack on Bob [Simpson] we couldn't believe it. Why have a go at him?'
While pointedly refusing to deny his side's indulgence in verbal warfare, Jones
was adamant that there had been no racial connotations: 'We never used the
word "black" once.' What a relief.

It was at Kensington, of all places, that Desi became immersed in the most
publicized altercation of the series. The tension that April morning as 12,500
Bajans thronged their capital packed enough kilowatts to illuminate half the
island. Before long, the home boys were 22 for 3. A proud and recent recipient
of his country's Silver Crown of Merit (the post-independence OBE), Desi
had just been joined by his captain. Having inched his way to 10 in 17
overs he removed his bat from the line of an inswinging delivery from Craig
McDermott, so clearly that Richie Benaud immediately felt entitled to assure
his armchair audience that the ball had struck the batsman high on the inner
thigh. Ian Healy, the provocative Australian wicket-keeper with the weasely
smile, sprang to leg, swallowed the deflection and launched the ball skyward.
The slip cordon exulted as one.

This was all arrant nonsense to Desi, who promptly indicated to the fielders behind the wicket that the ball had in fact brushed his shirt. Healy piped up again, suggesting in less than ambiguous terms that it was not Desi's place to be submitting evidence for the defence. At this, Desi took off his helmet and walked slowly toward his tormentor, bat cocked in a horizontal plane above his right shoulder. Jabbing the blade in Healy's direction as if about to prod this decided nuisance in the chest, he suggested they reconvene after play was done, preferably with pistols around dawn. 'Healy responded by blowing him a kiss,' reported that perceptive, fair-minded Australian journo, Mike Coward, 'as Richards ambled down the pitch and touched gloves with Haynes in a powerful show of solidarity.' The gauntlet, unsurprisingly, was never picked up. 'Healy is a difficult man to ignore,' I was advised by one West Indian alumnus.

That injudiciously raised bat, invoking as it did unpleasant visions of Javed Miandad's dust-up with Lillee, was untimely to say the least. For the first time, an Australian tour of the West Indies was being transmitted across the world. Millions saw an exchange the like of which had not been witnessed, ooh, not since the Duleep Trophy final in Jamshedpur a couple of months previously. On that occasion, Rashid Patel of North Zone had aimed a head-high full toss at West Zone's Raman Lamba, then unsheathed a stump and proceeded to assault the batsman with it, instigating a full-scale riot complete with burning covers. Desi tendered his apologies in the *Sunday Sun*: 'Healy used abusive language to me and I am sorry if it looked as if I was protesting because he appealed. It was just a matter of showing Healy where the ball hit me on my shirt but then he started cursing me. It was not that I was trying in any way to make a scene and I apologize to the fans and people of Barbados.' Greenidge, happily, was soon overshadowing everything, striking a Test-best 226 eleven days before his fortieth birthday. For the sixteenth and final time in a Test, he and Desi prepared a three-figure entrée.

'It all started in Guyana,' Desi asserts, referring to his initial *tête-à-tête* with Healy during the second Test. 'I said to him that I saw nothing wrong with appealing at everything, but if you appeal when you think a batsman is not out, then when the umpire gives him not out you shouldn't be carrying on the way he had been during that match. I told him he should take the good with the bad, but I'm not sure he understood what I was saying. When we got to Kensington, what with all the hype that was swirling around and the way everyone was worked up, it all came to a head. There's no way I'm going to quarrel with a keeper about appealing. People appeal all the time when I'm batting. But what was nasty about the incident was that when I indicated to the slip fielders that the ball had hit me just above the thigh, Healy said, in less than respectful fashion, "Let the umpire do the job." I was in Barbados, my home, in front of my people, and that made it harder to take and easier to snap back. It looked as if I was about to go after him when I took my helmet off – Wes Hall has since made us more aware of the care that needs to be taken with the cameras around, but live cameras in the Caribbean was still a new phenomenon then – but that was done purely to let him hear what I had to say. Besides, I'd have been mad to hit him during a game. I find these guys have a lot of chat, but get them on a one-to-one basis and it's a different thing entirely. At the same time, TV is so close but it relies on vision rather than sound so it can often distort. Take an incident during the 1992 World Cup. Richie [Richardson] was discussing field placings with Benji [Winston Benjamin]. To look at Benji's hand movements it looked as if he was arguing with his captain. The point is that TV is there. We can't avoid it.'

To Holding and many other West Indians, not least the board and selectors, the spectacle afforded by the Haynes–Healy charade was distasteful, whatever the provocation. Threatening Australians with execution by willow was Javed Miandad's game. All the same, the Jamaican, who covered the series as a member of the Channel Nine commentary squad, was not altogether surprised by his former teammate's outburst. 'Desi does have that happy-go-lucky aura about him, forever jovial, forever cracking jokes, but he's always serious about his cricket. He's a strong character too, and sometimes he can get over-emotional. And there was a lot going on in that series, on and off the field. You didn't have to hear what was being said to know that: you could tell from the body language. But that's always been the Australian way, getting under your skin, trying to put you off your game. I didn't mind that so long as it related to the way I played. If someone said I couldn't bowl for toffee I could take that, but I draw the line at abuse, racial or otherwise.' That national aptitude for getting under skins was neatly summed up when the West Indies played the Prime Minister's XI in Canberra the following year. One of the touring officials asked a minister whether the new PM, Paul Keating, a far from reticent Pom-basher with scant respect for decorum in the presence of royalty, had ever trod the greensward himself. 'I don't know if he could bat or bowl,' the visitor was informed, 'but he'd be bloody good at sledging.'

To the relief of all concerned, relations were almost uniformly cordial when the West Indies toured England a few weeks later. Richards made it plain from the start that he saw the Test series as an antidote to the acrimony of the Worrell Trophy, and so it proved. The game was the thing, and the ensuing debate, thankfully, was as even (and even-tempered) as any between the sides in their sixty-three-year debate. That said, had not Bishop (back) and Greenidge (knee) both been prevented from taking part, it is difficult to imagine that the West Indies would not have prevailed.

As it was, Gooch's magnificent solo of 154 inspired England to draw first blood at Leeds while rain ruined the second Test at Lord's. Desi, who had missed his team's 0–3 thumping in the Texaco Trophy with back trouble, won his hundredth cap at Trent Bridge, scene of his first notable knock in England eleven years before. While this had become, if not commonplace, then certainly an increasingly accessible landmark, the twelfth player and fourth West Indian to reach it was inexplicably short-changed. Neither David Norrie nor Scyld Berry mentioned it in *Wisden*. Richard Hutton in *The Cricketer* and Richard Lockwood in *The Cricketer Quarterly* were equally remiss. *Wisden Cricket Monthly* offered a picture caption and a statistical note but nothing in David Frith's match report. Desi had the last laugh, scoring his 2000th run against England during the unbowed 57 that helped reel in a nine-wicket win, maintaining the West Indies' unbeaten record at Nottingham, an unbroken stand of 114 with Richardson, his ninth of 100 or more with the Antiguan.

Richardson at last gathered his first Test century in England at Edgbaston, where Patterson's 5 for 81 set up Hooper and Richards, who finished proceedings with an imperious six into the pavilion off Richard Illingworth, securing a seven-wicket win. The captain was chaired from the field as he ended his tenure with an unprecedented record of twelve series without defeat. The Oval brought anti-climax for him, if not the spectators. Galvanized by the return of Botham, England totalled 419, whereupon the West Indies batsmen, with one noble exception, harked back to the rashness of Madras and Sydney, wafting instead of grafting against the spin of the local Artful Dodger, Phil Tufnell, who took the last six wickets for four runs in 33 balls either side of lunch on the third day. Desi was alone in possessing the rigour to counter the threat, albeit unsuccessfully, of the West Indies' first follow-on against England for twenty-two years and forty-eight meetings, carrying his bat for 75 in four and three quarter hours: the fifth time he had batted throughout a Test innings. There were a further 43 second time round, supplemented by another Richardson ton, but with 143 to get, England muddled home by five wickets to square a memorable series.

Desi's reflections are mixed. 'I don't know why my hundredth cap was hardly mentioned, but perhaps that just shows the extent of the media's interest in the game. The West Indies board later presented me with a commemorative plate but it was all a bit low-key. I went out for a meal in Nottingham with some friends by way of celebration, but there was no sense of being let down. What did disturb me was that no one wrote how good the series had been. It was a tremendous tussle, one of the best and fairest in recent memory, but the media didn't seem particularly interested. When reporting the game I believe you should let the public know that there is a lot of good going on too. There are several people who don't write things because they fear it won't be accepted in today's market, but sometimes you have to write from the heart, use your views and make a contribution to the world, instead of just taking. As for the Oval, I think our minds were distracted by the thought of going home. We just didn't bat well, although Tufnell deserved full credit.'

Not long afterwards, Desi informed the selectors that he would not be available to go to Canada and Sharjah in October. In sore need of a rest, he wanted to spend some time with Dawn and the kids, take a holiday, shut off. Not for a moment did he envisage this having any effect on his taking over from Richards. A long winter of one-day fast-food fare was on the menu, culminating in the World Cup in Australia and the inaugural Test in Bridgetown against South Africa. For a thirty-five-year-old body, a bit of R and R, surely, was not too much to ask. Unfortunately, this was the escape hatch the board and selectors had been seeking. 'People feel that I didn't get the captaincy because I didn't go to Sharjah, but my view is that if they were going to make me captain they would have asked me to lead the side there. I didn't know when they were going to choose the new captain and I certainly didn't imagine there to be any risk in my not going. I do feel, however, that they thought I was too old for the job. That, at least, was what was hinted when Clyde Walcott rang me in Hampshire to tell me that they had appointed Richie for the whole winter. Why did he call me? He didn't say that I had been under consideration or why they had selected Richie ahead of me. I'd like to know whether all those telegrams of congratulation I received from the board after Pakistan counted for anything. It was a massive disappointment, an extremely hurtful experience. I can't express it more strongly than that. I was only thirty-five. It was wrong to put a time span on my career. Unless, that is, they had plans for me to play on for only a couple more years. Why? Lloydy, Viv and Gordon all played on into their forties.

'What I would like to know is, why did they lead me on? Why make me vice-captain and not Richie? He could have gained knowledge and gone into the job with some experience behind him. In my case, it was a waste of time making me vice-captain if I wasn't going to succeed Viv. And I thought I was. Did that statement about ball-tampering in Pakistan upset them? Maybe that was a factor. Healy? Bad behaviour? I couldn't believe they were reasons. All sorts of thoughts went through my head. It is a pity that the board operate in such a secretive way, but what about the time they criticized me for secrecy over Packer? On the other hand, although I was very hurt, I was quite relieved in some respects because I would have had to answer for the omission of Viv, Gordon and Dooj from the World Cup squad. I'll say it again: who needs the pressure?'

Richards had expressed his eagerness to gain selection for the World Cup as a humble member of the infantry, but his haemorrhoids were still causing discomfort and he felt no compunction to prove his worth by playing in the Red Stripe Cup. The selectors, however, had ruled that consideration would only be given to those who did. Greenidge, meanwhile, announced his retirement from 'all first-class cricket under the aegis of the West Indies Cricket Board', a pointed response to being omitted from the Sharjah and Australian tours. 'It has become evident', he acknowledged in a statement, 'that the policy of the selectors and/or West Indies Board is to infuse the West Indies with a limited number of younger players while, at the same time, dispensing with some of the older players. Such a policy is in the best interest of West Indies cricket but I regret that it was not clearly expressed to me prior to the sudden and disappointing act of exclusion from the team.'

Out, at a stroke, went the two best batsmen to make their débuts for the West Indies in the seventies, together with another formidable servant, Dujon, goose cooked by a waning bat as well as Father Time. In his case, as well as those of the other two, there appeared to be another reason. Dujon, after all, was the shop steward, Greenidge the disgruntled bod at the back and Richards ... was Richards, King Vivi. West Indian cricket, moreover, was up to its neck in financial grief. The much-hyped deal with Mark McCormick's IMG stable had brought fees for interviews and TV coverage, but little more. The team had no sponsor. The secretary of the board, Steve Camacho, was already talking about the death of the five-Test series in the Caribbean. With their respective dollars the weakest in CARICOM, Jamaica and Guyana were in danger of falling by the wayside. Overseas goodwill, seeping away all the more readily in the aftermath of that imbroglio with Australia, was all-important.

Richards in particular embodied an era of tumult that had to be consigned to history.

'There was a bit of a demolition job after the Australians had gone home,' says Greenidge. 'It seemed as if people were sent in to be a hit squad. It was rather foolish, sheer nonsense in fact, to get rid of Viv. If you look at the World Cup it looks as if the opposition went in with their confidence booming. They felt they could beat us. There was no real depth of experience. All we can do is hope this is not going to cause too many disruptions to West Indian cricket. You must wonder how much honesty is in the minds of the people who make these decisions. They have no regard, no feelings whatsoever. There's still animosity towards us even now. You would not be far wrong to call it jealousy.'

Greenidge still believes Desi's insistence on taking a break was probably what cost him dearest. 'He was the right person. He did a fine job in Pakistan and he'd done a very fine one for Barbados. Perhaps where it fell apart was him not going to Sharjah because the selectors didn't want to give the captaincy to Richie then take it away. I don't know, I wasn't on the scene, no one tells me anything. Reading between the lines I don't think he was treated fairly. It was hard on him. And although the boycott of the South Africa Test was mainly due to Andy Cummins not playing, the unrest may have been compounded by Desi not getting the captaincy. On the other hand, he didn't do himself any favours.'

Steve Camacho affirms this. 'The one constant theme in Desi's career has been his unbridled enthusiasm for the game, his delight in his own success and that of the team, but the unfortunate thing is that it was a policy decision to start rebuilding. It was decided to appoint a captain for Sharjah, Canada, the World Series Cup in Australia and then the World Cup, and unfortunately Desi was not available for the first two tours. He didn't make himself available for the captaincy. I have no way of knowing, if he had made himself available for Sharjah, whether he would have been named as captain, but he certainly ruled himself out of consideration by declining to go. The idea of naming a captain for the long term has worked for us over a long period of time. Only time will tell whether we have burdened Richie Richardson.' None of which explains why Desi was not advised of the ground rules in advance.

There is no doubt in Clive Lloyd's mind that Desi was the best candidate to replace Richards. 'He's that sort of cricketer. He can get people to do things for him. He's also a very astute person who knows the game well. I was told he did a marvellous job in Pakistan and it was all a little unfortunate because I thought our cricket would have risen to another plane had he been given the captaincy after Viv. If the reason was that the selectors wanted to break up the old guard then that is a very prejudiced view. If a guy has played in 100 Tests he's obviously a dedicated player and, as we like to say, Desi had no previous. He's a kind chap, he helps people. He also speaks his mind, which is very important. I couldn't think of a better player to lead the West Indies, even if it was for just an interim period. So, yes, I think he was treated badly.'

Lloyd, furthermore, is even more convinced than Desi that the memory of the Packer Pack still exerts a powerful influence on the West Indian establishment, a charge that Camacho, not unnaturally, refutes. 'Like elephants, people never forget and it is quite obvious to me that the selectors and the board, the Establishment essentially, have not forgotten the Packer situation. This is so silly because we could only ever have played for the West Indies. We won trophies for the West Indies, put them at the pinnacle, and the selectors and all those around them took all the accolades. We didn't mind because we are servants and we are paid to do a job. We were dedicated servants. So if something is coming your way, then it should be given to you. I feel very bitter that Desi didn't get what was coming his way. Sharjah? Surely these are such petty things. Better to give a young guy a chance in those circumstances. After all, it wasn't a major tour. Of course, the Establishment may have been looking for an excuse not to make him captain, but I find that very strange – and very disappointing.'

While Holding rejects the Packer theory – 'as far as I was concerned, the board was never unhappy with us' – he is anything but certain that the nomination of Richardson was the right one. 'In my opinion, the board decided that Desi would not be around for long enough, although I personally think he has it in him to play at the highest level for another three years, and that he was unsuitable because, like Viv, he had been involved in a few onfield conflicts and the feeling was that some sort of Snow White figure was needed. At the time, to be honest, I thought it was a good decision. Now I'm not so sure. A few things have happened under Richardson, notably the way in which Desi and Marshall were treated during the World Cup, that have made me reassess that judgement.'

Informed of his recall by England a few days earlier, a decidedly good-humoured Mike Gatting, himself a victim of selectorial peccadillo not so long ago, offered his twopence worth at the Oval last September. 'I was very surprised when Desi got passed over. He had two or three more years in him as a Test player and I thought he could have given Richie more time to establish himself as vice-captain. I thought there would be a strong lobby for Richie because he was at a goodish age [twenty-nine] and had had a lot of international experience, but I still thought Desi would get the nod. He would have been good for Richie, and it would have been a lot easier during a rebuilding stage for him to have done the job. Maybe the authorities were trying to sever that last link with Packer. That business with the over rate in Trinidad may have been a factor but everyone would have done the same in his position. Who needs the pressure? We all think like that. It goes with the job. Captaining your country is an honour and I think Desi would love to have done it for longer than he did, but that's how we protect ourselves, by saying we don't need the pressure. I should know.'

Our final witness is Tony Cozier. 'Desi carried the side well in Pakistan and I took it for granted that he would succeed Richards, especially since the board is not inclined to rock the boat. But the incidents with Healy and Stewart were fresh in the board's mind and, having had no control over Richards, they were wary of appointing another captain with a very strong personality, another one they couldn't control. Richardson was the opposite. He had no blemishes. He'd even recalled Nasser Hussain to the crease when England were over in 1990. It was a question of a change of image. The problem was not Packer *per se* but how that experience made the players more independent. The board is absolutely clueless. There's no man-management. Most, if not all, of the members were happy when the Richards era came to an end. He embarrassed them. But sad ends to great careers in the West Indies are nothing new. Roberts and Gibbs both went out bitter. There should have been some glowing tributes. Instead, the players were allowed an opportunity to vent their anger. On reflection, I still think Desi would have been the right choice. The captaincy has certainly affected Richardson's personality and batting. It wouldn't have done that to Desi.'

Realizing that none of this had anything to do with Richardson, Desi dispatched a congratulatory telex to the new captain's Antiguan home. 'I've always got on well with Richie, as I have done with everyone I've ever played with. I told the press that I'd support him. I felt I was still an important member of the side and I wasn't going to let any of this get in the way of that. Gus Logie was then promoted to vice-captain but when he was injured in a nasty car accident I was offered the job at short notice. I accepted it because I wanted to show my support for Richie. There was no thank-you. Then, just before the Test against South Africa, Gus was injured again. Again

I was offered the vice-captaincy. This time I turned it down, although of course, if Richie had gone off and asked me to take over I would have. I just felt that the board could have sent me a little note, saying thanks for stepping in before, making me feel I was wanted, recognizing that I was a player with a wealth of experience who deserved to be treated well.'

13

Era's End

'Be proud of your ancestry and upbringing. Teach youngsters that
with hard work, dedication, education and training, they can
overcome their underprivileged environment.

Turn your cricketing success into something tangible for your
country.

There are great players and players of great innings. Great players
are consistent. Form is temporary, but class is permanent.

Take your place in history, as you are examples to the human
race and worthy ambassadors for the West Indies.'

Concluding summary of a handout entitled *The Cricketer as an
Ambassador*, prepared by the Barbados Minister of Tourism, the
Hon. Wes Hall, and distributed among the members of the West
Indies tour party bound for Australia at the Kensington Oval,
Barbados, on 21 October 1922

'DIVORCE DRIVES CHEERS STAR TO SUICIDE BID'. A misty Monday
morning, 26 October 1992, 9.05 a.m. In the plush lobby of the Excelsior Hotel
at Heathrow Airport, Curtly Ambrose peruses a copy of the *National Enquirer*,
fresh from a ten-day training camp in Barbados and looking for all the world
as if he has been poured into those overly snug jeans. Ian Bishop, devout
Christian, walks by and glances disapprovingly at his comrade's choice of
reading matter. 'I haven't got to the good bit yet,' proclaims Ambrose, not
quite suppressing a boyish titter. A paunchy middle-aged autograph hunter
lurking among the pot plants spots them and rushes over as discreetly as

possible, briefcase under his left arm, the *Sun* clutched in his right fist. Soon they are joined by Richie Richardson, dapper in maroon tracksuit and shades. Brian Lara, his time almost nigh, hovers inconspicuously, clearly self-absorbed. World Cup stardom was all very well, but will this be the tour in which he makes his name in the serious game? Anyway, how many English cricket fans would recognize him? Familiar faces are sparse all round. For the first time since the trip to England in 1973, the West Indies are embarking on an overseas Test mission without at least one of Messrs Richards, Greenidge, Marshall and Dujon. Next stop, the Land of Oz.

The new regime, of course, had begun a year earlier, prematurely and poorly. Richardson's charges lost three of their four games against India and Pakistan in Sharjah, were eliminated from the World Series Cup in Australia after failing to win any of their first five matches, and then stumbled by an innings to a less than daunting Australian XI. Philo Wallace's cutlass had twirled a few imaginations, as had Andy Cummins's whippety pace, but there was little else to compensate. The World Cup was not exactly being approached with confidence. The tourists then flew home, where they dispersed for a month to play for their respective islands in the Red Stripe.

Having reluctantly passed the Barbados captaincy on to Roland Holder because his Australian commitments precluded him from everyday involvement – 'people said it was because I was piqued about not getting the West Indies captaincy, but that's wrong: I'd love to have done it' – Desi marched out to the middle at Kensington with Wallace on the second day of the match against the Windward Islands, a point or three to prove. Matching his vivacious junior partner stroke for stroke, he took part in a stand of 136, then rode on into a personal sunset, amassing 246, his highest score in the Caribbean. He smoothed the way to victory again in the next game against the Leewards, hitting 136, then flew back to Oz, 410 runs stashed away in the swagbag. Let our diarist pick up the trail:

Melbourne, 22 February:
First match tomorrow. I am surprised with the arrangements. The economic crisis here is making the Australian Cricket Board hungrier than ever. We started with a dinner in Sydney with a simple bill of fare – nothing to match the occasion – and a speaker who insulted all the players. We signed about 350 bats but didn't get one as a keepsake for ourselves. Thank God the itinerary is fairly good in terms of air

miles. I understand the Sri Lankans and Zimbabweans have already complained about theirs. Why is it that the only method the authorities have arrived at to assess the best team in the world involves white balls and floodlights – when only about three countries actually play with either? As with the coloured clothing, I guess it's all about big bucks. I'm not making excuses for our recent poor performances in the World Series Cup because when we first went to Australia and used a white ball we were brilliant. Me? I feel in good form after those runs in the Red Stripe. In fact, I am batting as well as I have ever done. One-day cricket can sometimes come as a release, particularly for me. Not this time.

Melbourne, 23 February. West Indies (221–0; D. L. Haynes 93 not out) beat Pakistan (220–2) by nine wickets:
A very convincing win to start with. Bowled well, fielded well and Brian Lara did a splendid job as my partner, an unusual role for him. All the other guys in the order are moaning about not getting a chance to bat. Bit unlucky not to get a hundred, although there had been talk of trying to get me one. Winning more than atones. Felt like the West Indies of old, a good feeling.

Melbourne, 27 February. England (160–4) beat West Indies (157; D. L. Haynes c Fairbrother b DeFreitas 38) by four wickets:
Very disappointed. Didn't play to the best of our ability, particularly the batsmen. Felt a bit hard done by when I hit DeFreitas hard but straight to backward square leg, but Brian, Richie and Carl made 10 between them. Must look at ways to improve the middle order. Suggested changing the order and getting the in-form batsmen in earlier and let them use up most of the overs. Fell on deaf ears. Put England under pressure early on but couldn't maintain it. At least we lost to a good side.

Brisbane, 29 February. West Indies (264–8) beat Zimbabwe (189–7) by 75 runs:
Back playing up so feet up for me. Curtly too. We expected to beat these guys easily. Brian, Carl, Richie and Keith [Arthurton] all played well but still don't think we batted well as a whole because we didn't really capitalize on the great start given us by Phil Simmons, who was playing in my place. We should have had over 300. No one said anything about that and, as usual, the bowlers brought home the bacon.

Yet we eased off by refusing to bowl them out. We won, so that's all that matters, but we should be looking to improve our run rate in case that's needed to decide who qualifies for the semi-finals. About to take off for New Zealand. Arrival scheduled for 1 a.m., practice at 10.30 a.m., a mistake. Before fixing the time, couldn't someone have tried to see whether it could be arranged for the evening? The manager, Deryck Murray, didn't try. Then again, he doesn't have a clue about what West Indies cricket needs. He is hard to talk to, refuses to countenance any views outside the captain's. I was involved in selecting the World Series Cup team but at no stage did he agree with any view I offered. Everyone looks tired and jaded and we haven't even left the tarmac.

Christchurch, 5 March. South Africa (200–8) beat West Indies (136; D. L. Haynes c Richardson b Kuiper 30) by 64 runs:
Worst game in years. Manager spoke about this being more important than any other game in the competition but I believe they are all equally important at this stage. Richie said as much when he played down the significance of the occasion to the press. It was the first official match between our countries, but getting the points and improving our run rate was the aim, although of course there was no way that we could countenance defeat against the newcomers. Our chief objective was to reach the semi-finals, not to make a political statement. Richie played it down to ease the pressure, but it didn't seem to work. Bowled very well to restrict them but again batted poorly. Bouncy wicket: got bashed on the right index finger three times and had to retire hurt. Probably best to have gone to hospital for X-rays but Meyrick Pringle reduced us to 19 for 4 and I returned while there was still hope. Preparation inadequate: a wasted morning practice session beforehand when an evening session would have been of far more use. The pressure was on from all angles and we buckled. Now for some more.

Auckland, 8 March. New Zealand (206–5) beat West Indies (203–7; D. L. Haynes c & b Harris 22) by five wickets:
Whole side dispirited by performance against South Africa. We were the better team here but we arrived a bit low and practice was disturbed by the weather. Crowe put us in and continued his ploy of opening with Dipak Patel's off-spin. We had a slow start, Patel tied us down and although Brian and I put on 65 and he played well yet again, the middle order failed to push the score along. The wicket was slow and

low and once again I suggested changing the batting order, but nothing came of it. Still felt we could defend 203, but Greatbatch came out and swiped the bowlers off their line and got away with it. We still had a chance because they kept losing wickets. We could, in hindsight, have tried to stop Crowe scoring and bowled out the rest, but we didn't and we lost. Now we have to win our final three games.

Wellington, 10 March. West Indies (195–5; D. L. Haynes c Manjrekar b Kapil Dev 16) beat India (197) by five wickets after target reduced to 194 in 47 overs:
At the team meeting yesterday, Murray said that the way I was batting was not acceptable unless I made a 100. That must be the most inane statement I have ever heard in my fourteen years as a pro. He could have sent a message to me when I was batting asking me to push it on a bit. Instead he is implying that I'm not giving 100 per cent to the team. It's a matter of respect. I am not involved in the team plans and I should be. So should Malcolm, who is unhappy about being sent out to the boundary and being ignored, but Murray won't allow it. He is trying to get rid of both of us, but that is another story. So to the latest chapter. We had to win and played like it. Even without Malcolm we bowled well and fielded well, again, and, if anything, the rain delay – and prospect of more – helped us because it made us more positive. The new rules meant that the side batting second were at a disadvantage when it rained: we lost three overs, but our target only went down by four runs, and we knew that it would get even stiffer if it rained again, which looked likely. Brian and I put on 57 in less than seven overs before I went, caught driving. Brian, in my view the find of the tournament, played very well, as did Phil until he holed out, but by then the weather had cleared and Carl and Keith saw us home. Still upset about the manager's remarks. Back to Oz.

Berri, 13 March. West Indies (268–8; D. L. Haynes c Tillakaratne b Ranatunga 38) beat Sri Lanka (177–9) by 91 runs:
Out in the South Australian countryside, where people are nice and friendly. Had to travel all day to get here and arrived dog-tired, but minds focused on the job. Brian, for once, did not get a start, but Phil and I made up for that by adding 66, particularly Phil, who made a typically rugged 110. Yet again we failed in the middle order and didn't make 300 as we should have, and we should have gone after it because our run-rate isn't good enough. Bowled fairly well but the wicket was

flat and slow and we had to suffer some odd wide calls. Richie failed
again, run out for eight: it is very important for him to perform because
that would boost the middle order. Fancy New Zealand in the semis
because I know we can beat them.

*Melbourne, 18 March. Australia (216–6) beat West Indies (159; D. L. Haynes
c Jones b McDermott 14) by 57 runs:*
It was a big shock to me when Malcolm didn't play against India or
Sri Lanka, but to leave him out against the Aussies was a big blow.
How can a player with his ability and experience not be included for
a match like this? It just proves the lack of respect and knowledge our
tour selectors have been showing. The Aussies, much to everyone's
joy, are out already, but we needed to win to go to Sydney for the
semi-final against England. Unfortunately, we again showed no sign
of professionalism. There was no discussion of team problems, no
planning. The bowlers didn't discuss their feelings about the opposition
or what line they were going to bowl. We celebrated Roger Harper's
birthday instead. Food and drinks nice, timing wrong. At the pre-game
meeting I ask the captain whether he is happy with my batting in the
first 15 overs or whether he might like someone to play a
Greatbatch-type innings. He says he is happy, that I should play it as I
see it. The meeting was a waste of time. There was no explanation
why Malcolm had been left out – and we all knew that that sore ankle
was not it: he was fit. Boon and Moody put on 107 but Boon was
lucky not to be given out after clipping one down the legside to David
Williams, only for Mr Reporter to give him not out. He went on to
make a good century but Australia failed to build on that solid
foundation, Border failing again, Jones and all the other main batsmen
struggling to get going. It was a good batting track and we needed
around four an over. Brian and I started the ball rolling with some
fine shots but I didn't last very long, hitting a McDermott full toss
straight to Jones at backward square. Brian continued his lovely form,
another gem. But where was the support? We ended up losing badly to
a side low in morale and fight. Once again the batsmen failed miserably
yet still we stuck by the same order and refused to drop anyone. We
went in with the same six or seven in every game. How could that be?
Brian must be congratulated for adapting so well, but he was the only
one of us in form.

Holders Hill, 28 March:
Viv, Dooj and Gordon should have been there. They were fit enough
and good enough, and that is all that should matter. Why couldn't the
rebuilding have started after the World Cup? Wish I knew. The
manager only made matters worse. I felt he was trying to be divisive.
He thought I was disruptive because I'd been rejected as captain, that
I was trying to pull the players away from Richie. Why would I do that?
Lloydy should have done that job instead of Murray. He could have
helped Richie because he'd been through it all himself, but the board
probably thought he leaned towards the players too much. The
relationship between the board and the players has never been very good
in my time. The World Cup as a whole? The worst aspect was the fact
that a team could be allowed to play all their games by day, as New
Zealand did, while the rest play at night on faster wickets and bigger
grounds and have to do all the travelling. Still, although Pakistan were
worthy winners – and to think we beat them more easily than we beat
Zimbabwe or Sri Lanka – New Zealand must be congratulated for
coming back so well after their poor display against England prior to
the tournament. It was a great transformation, a clever one too, what
with the way Crowe used Patel. Shrouding everything else is Malcolm's
retirement from international cricket, a great loss to the West Indies, a
player with so much knowledge to use and pass on, so much to
contribute. I believe Murray set out to get Malcolm and me because he
was trying to protect his job. He saw us as threats instead of people
who could forget personal feelings and be objective for the team's sake.
It was hurtful to see the way Malcolm was pushed into the outfield,
far from any sphere of influence. Then again, I was out of it too.

The West Indies slunk home, all but ignored. There were inquests, of course,
notably a radio discussion involving Sobers, Holding and Greenidge, but
there were also other items on the agenda. Jamaicans were contemplating a
battle for the Prime Minister's chair renounced by Michael Manley.
St Lucians, too, were readying for an election. Trinidadians were awaiting
the results of a hearing into the validity of an amnesty granted to 114 Muslims
charged with offences related to an attempted coup two years earlier.
Guyanans were preparing to fall in line with the rest of the Eastern Caribbean
territories – by turning their clocks back an hour. The Bajans, meanwhile,
were grappling with the country's worst economic blight since independence.

In one Holetown supermarket, there was no sugar to be had, unless, of course, you were a tourist with the cash to splash out on a sack of the stuff. The industry itself, riven by union disputes, was importing labour from Guyana to cope with the harvest. Union battles proliferated, government buildings were decaying. The UN representative Besley Maycock wondered whether the plight of the public services stemmed from the haste to embrace independence and the consequent decision to throw the baby out with the bathwater.

His big complaint [reported the *Sunday Sun*] is that the gaping holes which have emerged are still with us, years later, creating 'bad attitudes' and disciplinary problems. Essentially, he thinks if necessary there must either be a marriage between the tried and true methods of doing things, or the introduction of fresh approaches which work effectively.

The West Indies selectors faced a similar dilemma when they convened to nominate a squad for the three one-day internationals and that historic Test against South Africa, membership of the club restored and now about to do what they had never deigned to do before. Marshall was no longer an option, Logie was injured and the World Cup had been a good few beats short of a bar. What they came up with was the biggest posse of tenderfoots the West Indies had called into action for aeons. Desi, Patterson, Walsh, Ambrose and Richardson apart, six members of the Test XI that ultimately assembled at Kensington on 18 April had collected thirteen caps between them. David Holford, to no great astonishment, displaced Murray as manager.

The one-dayers were horribly one-sided, the hosts winning by 107 runs, 10 wickets and seven wickets. Simmons smashed two centuries and Lara continued with an unbeaten 86 at Port-of-Spain, where he and Desi (59 not out) gobbled up a target of 153 inside 26 overs. The unabridged game promised greater competition between two teams in transition. In their captain, Kepler Wessels, briefly an Australian but now firmly clutched to the bosom of his forebears, South Africa possessed a doughty batsman and redoubtable competitor. In Allan Donald they had the fastest white quick treading the boards, in Peter Kirsten a grizzled old campaigner with a few yarns still to spin, in Adrian Kuiper the Botham of the Veld. In seamers Tertius Bosch, Richard Snell and Pringle, the man who gave the West Indies the World Cup willies, there were three right arms of promise, guided by the most talented of all the exiles, Mike Procter. Their opponents recalled Walsh, his scratchy fielding and batting deemed surplus to World Cup requirements, and turned to Jimmy Adams, a Goweresque left-hander from Jamaica who had displayed a penchant for stylish suicide during the West Indies A team's summary execution of their English counterparts. Then, when Hooper's fractured finger forced him to pull out at the eleventh hour, enter Antigua's Kenny Charlie Griffith Benjamin, whose bounce, hostility and use of the crease had done justice to his self-detested middle names. The third new cap was Trinidad's pint-sized David Williams, so long Dujon's patient deputy and deserving of the gauntlets even if his batting couldn't hold a candle either to the Dooj's delicious insouciance or even the well-meshed technique of the flashy Grenadian gloveman, Junior Murray. For Richardson, this was the real thing.

There might have been a potential fourth new cap had the selectors had any nous. Andy Cummins, a lean local lad, had been the West Indies' most penetrative bowler in the World Cup as well as their joint top wicket-taker in the recent one-dayers, yet he was excluded from the Test thirteen. To Bajans this was the last slap. Even if they had no intention of playing him, a questionable if acceptable stance given Benjamin's irresistible form against England A, would a place on the bench have been too much to ask, just for the experience? It would certainly have pepped up the doleful ticket sales. Come the morning of the match Bridgetown was divided unevenly between commemoration and condemnation. The latter had nothing to do with the tourists, who had been welcomed warmly wherever they went in the Caribbean, nor even the price of admission, too high for the poorly publicized A Tests but now fixed sensibly to accommodate the shallow of pocket. What it did reflect were the slights heaped upon the collective Bajan ego by the spurning of Desi, Greenidge, Marshall and now Cummins. A boycott was organized, only 3000 turning up on the opening day and even fewer on the rest, barely 500 bothering to trot along for the admittedly unexpected climax. Estimated losses ran into six figures, sterling not dollars, joining the record £300,000 deficit from the previous season. Richardson, a convenient symbol of unpopular change, the man who took our Desi's job, was roundly, if ludicrously, booed.

What ensued spelt out why the West Indies remained supreme at the highest, most demanding level of the game. For all the politicking and bickering, for all the break-up and make-up, for all the apathy and antipathy, the cast was all right on the night, albeit not before some heartstopping pauses. The dignitaries almost outnumbered the punters, yet despite the dearth of atmosphere Desi and Simmons batted like millionaires, sending boundaries scudding across the blotchy outfield to add 99 at better than a run a ball. Snell, however, dismissed both in the space of nine deliveries shortly before lunch, Desi edging to slip, and the complexion of the innings altered abruptly on an amiable pitch, only Arthurton's bubbly 59 enlivening the descent before the elongated tail went limp, the last six wickets going down for 22.

For the best part of the next nine hours Andrew Hudson held court, becoming the first South African to score a century on début *en route* to a game if colourless 163. Adams's seemingly innocuous left-arm spin then provoked a slither from 279 for 4 to 345 all out, a far from decisive lead of 83, yet the Slough of Despond beckoned all the same by the first over after tea. Richardson, Simmons and Desi – caught behind off Snell for 23 after seeing Donald's second ball nudge his off stump without disturbing the bails – had all gone with the arrears still 15. Arthurton and Lara hit back with an alliance of 52 but it was Adams who breathed hope into despair, confounding memories of previous laxities with fibre and determination to solicit 99 for the last three wickets. Needing 201, rather more than had appeared likely, South Africa lost Hudson and Mark Rushmere in Ambrose's first four overs but closed in comfort, Wessels and Kirsten plugging the dyke with aplomb to adjourn on 122 for 2.

Twenty minutes before lunch on the final morning it was all over, if not quite in the manner anticipated. Cutting the ball this way and that in addition to accepting the odd donation from a wearing pitch, Walsh took 4 for 8 in 11 overs, and four of the first five to fall, striking the most telling blow in the third over by having Wessels expertly pouched by Lara, the diving, solitary slip. Aided by the breeze from the same southern end he had rumbled in from two years earlier to destroy England, Ambrose gusted through the lower orders to finish with 6 for 34, but this time the Kingston Kernel had been the principal safecracker as eight wickets descended for 26 in an hour and a half of script-scrapping. Joy unconfined, impending disgrace averted, Richardson and his men linked hands, forgot that only a crowded disco's worth of devotees were dishing out the applause and went on a lap of honour, the West Indies' outstanding run at Kensington now extended to 28 Tests, 57 years and 11 successive victories. A tradition maintained, in every sense.

Desi savoured the taste of victory with a satisfied smack of the lips. 'I wanted to win that Test more than any I have ever played in. It had nothing to do with politics. I wanted to beat them badly because it was their first Test in twenty-two years and I didn't want people scoffing at us. Throughout my career there had always been so much talk about the great cricketers they

had produced, the Pollocks, Procter, Richards, Van der Bijl, all those guys
who missed out. It was another challenge for us. Most of the members of
the side are religious and each day someone would lead the prayers before
play – me one time, Bishop another, Williams another. We were looking to
the Lord for guidance, always of a general sort, never specific. You don't pray
for 500 runs. Not that it seemed to be doing much immediate good: after
four days we were basically done for, although I did think that their lack of
experience might tell. On the night before the final day Walshie agreed to
do the donkey work and bowl into the breeze, allowing Ambrose to slip
himself at the other end. They had such a weak batting line-up that we
thought that if we could get Wessels out there might be a glimmer of a
chance, and so it proved.

'I wasn't happy about the boycott. People should have supported us but
they didn't and we all felt let down, particularly me as a Barbadian. To give
them their due, people in Kensington were unhappy, which is why they booed
Richie. A lot of things had been boiling up: the captaincy situation, the way
Barbados players were being treated by the selectors, the economic situation.
One friend said that even if I was on 90 he still wouldn't come along. The
selectors should have put Cummins in the squad, but even if they didn't feel
he was ready for Test cricket, they could still have picked him and then
dropped him on the day. A simple solution and one that might have had a
placatory effect.'

Instead, the West Indies Board of Control was left to count the cost and
make efforts to win back public trust. At its AGM in Antigua in May, Clyde
Walcott was unanimously returned for another two-year term as president,
David Holford and Richardson, respectively, were named as manager and
captain for the next winter's tours of South Africa and Australia, Rohan
Kanhai as assistant manager (cricket) for 'an as yet unspecified period'. A
coach at last. Each of the participants in the Northern Telecom youth tournament, furthermore, would be provided with a coach financed by the board.

The most significant appointment was that of Edward Hallam Cosmo
'Teddy' Griffith, a business executive from Barbados with a classics degree,
'to form and chair a specialist committee to devise a strategic plan covering
the Board's operations over the next five years'. Son of Herman Griffith, one
of the first great Caribbean pace bowlers, Griffith was himself a left-handed
opener, making the very first century in Shell Shield cricket after emigrating
to Jamaica, where he stood on the management board of the Jamaica Cricket
Association before returning to Barbados in 1978. This was not, as far as he

was concerned, a commission of inquiry, but an advisory body. Suggesting that the game had 'not been as aggressively marketed as some other sports in the Caribbean itself and certainly not on an international basis,' he conceded that this was 'a serious problem we'll have to address'.

His main theme, it seemed, was conciliation. An 'outreach programme' conducted by his committee would draw on the expertise of delegates from all corners of the Caribbean, from local boards to players and umpires. At its first meeting, Griffith outlined their 'perceptions of the strengths and weaknesses of the Board and of West Indies cricket and of the opportunities and threats that exist ... We went to get feedback about how they [the delegates] see certain things that the public at large or the press may have been articulating. If our views are radically different from what we are hearing from other people, that is the thing we have to be very finely attuned to because if those signals start coming, then something is really quite wrong. Our antennae have to be up.' In response to 'certain misconceptions', Walcott and his colleagues also felt obliged to release letters the board had sent to Richards, Greenidge and Dujon, congratulating them on their outstanding contribution to West Indian cricket.

There was more than one reason why Desi's form faltered at the start of the 1992 county season. For one thing, the winter had brought seven first-class innings and three times as many of the limited kind (for the record, he made 516 runs at 73.71 in four first-class fixtures and 734 runs at just over 38 in 21 one-day internationals), so getting in occupational mode was never going to be easy. Neither was forgetting the rancour of the past few months. A bulwark in the Sunday League and Benson and Hedges Cup, he endured a sketchy start in the Championship, frequently vacating the crease when well set and making only one century before mid-August.

'I was frustrated, mentally tired, disappointed in the way the World Cup had gone, sorry for my friend and colleague Ricky Ellcock, who had been forced to give up the game early because of a back injury. I was sad that Malcolm had been allowed to retire on a bad note, sad at the way Viv, Gordon and Dooj had finished. It made me feel that my turn was next. I was desperate not to go out as they had. I wanted to go out with a smile on my face. The upshot was that my concentration suffered and I kept on getting out in the seventies and eighties. I find it very relaxing playing county cricket, and it was nevertheless a consolation and a comfort to be back with Gatting and the guys. They'd had a disappointing season in 1991, so to win the Sunday League was very important for the Middlesex supporters. They do a lot for the county and for cricket, and they had had to put up with a lot. I was sorry to see Mark Ramprakash go through the wringer, but he's only young. He'll come back. By having a winter off he has had a chance to get his act together. He is a very competitive person who expects a lot of himself. As the years go on, as I'm sure he will discover for himself, you learn to live with things you once couldn't accept.'

27 January 1993. As befits the prettiest of all Test gardens, the Adelaide Oval has had its fair share of prize blooms. In 1961, 'Slasher' Mackay and Lindsay Kline, Australia's final pair, kept Hall, Sobers and Gibbs at bay for the last 100 minutes to salvage an unlikely draw. Eight years later Paul Sheahan and Alan Connolly survived the last 26 deliveries to deny the West Indies in similarly suspenseful fashion. This, though, was something else. With 186 needed to win the fourth Test and thus the series, and two full days at their disposal, Australia had lost four wickets immediately after lunch to sink to 74 for 7 courtesy of an awesome spell from Curtly Ambrose. Justin Langer, a shrimp of a left-hander making his Test debut, had led a recovery, but when his 4¼-hour stint in the sentry box ended half an hour after tea, 42 were still required with one wicket standing. Slowly, surely, Tim May and Craig McDermott, both paid-up rabbits, had contrived to whittle the target down to two, accompanied with increasing gusto by the strains of 'Waltzing Matilda' reverberating around this intimate, idyllic ground.

The clock creeps towards six o'clock. In lopes the spidery frame of Courtney Walsh for the penultimate ball of the day. McDermott flicks the ball off his legs at an angle of about 45 degrees. Australian hearts leap while those of Caribbean origin plunge into their boots. After all, the only obstruction barring the ball's path for 50 yards is within point-blank range. Even more fortuitously, this crouching duck is impaired by a pair of creaking knees which are due to celebrate their thirty-seventh birthday in a couple of weeks' time. There is certainly enough force and timing in the shot to reel in at least one of those two runs. After thirteen years without losing a Test rubber, the West Indies are not so much staring down the barrel as about to give it a big French kiss. To widespread astonishment, however, Desi summons enough strength for one last spring. Diving to his left, he intercepts and clasps the ball. No run. Walsh, cucumber-cool, ambles back, biding his time. It is only the 79th over of the day, but who cares about slow over rates? In lopes the Jamaican once more, pinging the ball in just short of a good length. As it rises towards McDermott's throat the batsman tries to take evasive action, but the missile is homing in too fast and brushes a glove, then his helmet. The fielders are airborne long before the gift arrives at its final desti-nation, gleefully pouched by wicketkeeper Junior Murray. The West Indies have prevailed by one run, the closest winning margin in 1,200-plus episodes of a 116-year-old soap called Test Cricket. Had Desi fluffed his lines, we might have had the third tie of the entire run. Proof of the tension came in the shape of several holes in the dressing room walls, for which the South Australian Cricket Association blamed Caribbean boots and demanded A$1000 in compensation.

Duly galvanized, the West Indies wrapped up the fifth Test in Perth with something of the old swank and swagger, Ambrose conjuring up a wondrous spell of 7 for 1 on the opening day and Australia caving in before lunch on the third to concede the series, 2–1. If the Worrell Trophy presented to Richie Richardson was a replica, the original having apparently been mislaid somewhere in the Caribbean, there was no doubting the authenticity of the talents responsible for quelling a spirited Australian rebellion.

As the bubbly bubbled, even Ambrose overflowed, breaking his five-year silence with the non-Caribbean media to announce that, contrary to rumour, he intended to stick with this Test lark for a while yet, 'because when you are on top it feels grand'. Desi's discoloured right cheek struck the only minor chord. In going to pull Jo Angel, the strapping new Australian paceman, he had misjudged the bounce. Thinking the ball was there for the shot, he pulled from the throat, just as he always did. Instead, it rose higher, hammering on the grille of his helmet, which in turn forced its way into his cheekbone. The blood seeped from the resulting cut with sufficient profusion to concern Allan Border, who advised Desi to go off. The victim was more reluctant. 'I wanted to go on. I'd been struggling all tour but that day I was picking up the line and feeling better.' All the same, for the first time in 108 Test matches, Desi was compelled to retire hurt.

He resumed his innings the following day, although it was not until the end of the game that he was certain there was no fracture. It had been a painful series all round, certainly Desi's worst in a five-match rubber. His first four innings yielded 8, 1, 7 and 5. In all, his eight sojourns at the crease brought 123 runs at 15.38 and not so much as a solitary fifty. At Melbourne Merv Hughes bounced one off his forearm and into the stumps. At Sydney an off-break from Greg Matthews trickled off the face of the bat, dribbled through his legs and just about had enough puff left to disturb the bails. His best knock, a sparkling 45 on the first morning at the WACA, was cut short by a stumping, only the fourth time in 187 Test innings he had been so dismissed. He had played a full part in spurring his side to the World Series Cup, yet even that was tarnished by a £160 fine in Brisbane. Pausing at the crease upon being adjudged caught behind by his old sparring partner, Healy, Desi was punished, according to the match referee, Donald Carr, for slamming his bat into the ground 'in an obvious show of dissent'.

Even so, to speak to Desi that Monday afternoon was to hear a contented soul. Amid the glow of one of the most stirring of all comebacks, there was no thought of himself, merely delight at the success of the team. It had been a rocky journey, albeit an exhilarating one. Having hung on grimly to save an enthralling first Test with two wickets remaining, the West Indies were routed in the second, transfixed by the leg-breaks of young Shane Warne. When Mark Taylor held a rebound off Ian Healy's gloves to dispatch Phil Simmons shortly before stumps on the second day of the third Test, Australia's mammoth first innings score was still 490 runs distant and a second loss beckoned. Instead, Brian Lara turned his maiden Test century into a stupendous innings of 277, the fourth-highest by a West Indian in Tests, the third-highest ever conceded by Australia. A week later, Pakistan were skittled for 71 in the World Series Cup. Halfway through the massacre, Murray and Simmons both decided to chase Wasim Akram's miscued hook and duly collided, the crack of cranium on cranium echoing sickeningly around the Gabba and sending the opener to hospital with a suspected fracture of the skull. The fears, happily, proved unfounded, and it was Simmons, hitherto erratic, whose characteristically rugged 80 in Perth turned out to be the highest individual score of the final two Tests. The gods were smiling again.

Fingering the swelling around his right eye, Desi reflected on a tour that had made Richardson's reputation as a captain, confirmed Lara as a young batting lord to rank with Tendulkar, and raised Ambrose to regal status. A tour that, above all, had demonstrated that the West Indies possessed enough mettle and sheer pride, even in a period of transition, to scupper the odds. For Pakistan, due in town in March, having Waqar Younis and Wasim Akram on the poop deck might still be insufficient to blow the Caribbean flagship out of the water. 'That was the greatest fightback I have ever been involved in, a terrific boost for West Indian cricket. The young players came through and it was a great boost for them to be in a winning side. The turning point came in Sydney. We simply demoralized them. Heading them on first innings after they had made over 500, on our unlucky ground!

'Lara's knock motivated everyone. Funnily enough, at the team meeting beforehand he was genuinely concerned about his inability to score a Test century. So all the batsmen took turns to say how they responded when they passed fifty, what mental processes were involved in staying there. I was sharing a room with Lara. He's a good lad, very confident, with a little bit of a selfish streak, very keen on his average. His driving off the back foot against good-length balls, always a sign of class, is superb. I took him for a Chinese lunch before the Sydney Test and he ordered Peking Duck. "No way," I said, "no duck before a Test," but he went ahead anyway. Bang goes that superstition. He has a very good future. In fact, I recommended him as vice-captain. We need to groom him, help him learn the job, prepare him to succeed Richie rather than let things drift as they did with Malcolm and myself.

'I was happy for Richie, too, because he had had to put up with a lot of criticism, and all that booing in Barbados last year. He is very positive, a good listener with a great belief in the team. Some of the guys were flustered by certain decisions, beginning with our first innings of the series when Lara was given out stumped even though Healy didn't have the ball, but Richie tried to keep us as cool as possible. "The whole world is watching," he would say. "There's no point in making a fuss."' Ambrose? 'For the past couple of years he has been the best fast bowler in the world, period. He's so like Hadlee because he bowls so straight. If you are not in form you'll edge him, and, even if you are, he always makes you play. He doesn't even bowl bad spells in the nets, never gives you anything to drive. For a while, though, he was bowling as he did in England last summer, without any luck, but he has enormous inner confidence. "One day," he assured me at one point, "it'll all come right for us." Well, at least it did for him. He never seems to worry. He turns off at six o'clock, then switches on again at 11. He doesn't really like the game that much. He is liable to get up one morning and pack it all in. He sees it as work, always saying "cricket's too hard".'

While it was visibly hard for Desi at times – 'I can't put my finger on it, other than that I was never in long enough to play myself back into form' – he was never in the remotest danger of being dropped. 'I thought about suggesting that one of the younger batsmen should play, but it was awkward being on both the tour and the selection committee. That said, none of the batsmen, apart from Lara, were really consistent, and the guys kept saying that Australia would have felt better without me in the side. You never make runs in the dressing room, so I always wanted to play. I informed the other selectors they would have to drop me, because there was no way I was volunteering.'

Adelaide? 'I've never played in a Test like it. I enjoyed it so much. I knew we would win on the evening of the third day. I was very disappointed with the way I had got out, and the way we had batted against Tim May, especially after Curtly had earned us a useful lead on a grassy pitch. I couldn't focus on the game at all, but then I walked into a bar and saw all these Australian players there, laughing and joking. They looked like the South Africans did on the fourth evening in Bridgetown. They thought they'd won already. After that, I told the guys I thought we would win. Even when May and McDermott were nearing the target I kept saying, "one ball, one ball". Some people thought I could have taken a bat-pad catch off May but I hadn't fielded there for a long time. Earlier in the match I had suggested that, since his hands were better than mine, Simmons, the normal bat-pad, should swap with me in the gully. By the end I'd been there all day and my knees were tired and hurting, but somehow I stopped that shot from McDermott. It felt good to make that contribution. Courtney was incredible, stopping, settling, taking his time, as if it were all a show. That match should be shown in the Caribbean for ever. It was the greatest thing to happen to our kids in years.'

Better still, although Border and Hughes were fined for dissent in Brisbane, the protagonists put a decade of sniping behind them. 'The relationship between the sides was much better, because of what had happened in the Caribbean last time, though having a referee certainly helped. Healy was the same as ever. He had an opportunity to start the tour with a fine gesture by admitting his mistake over that Lara stumping, but he didn't take it. I congratulated Border when he passed 10,000 runs, a fine achievement by a loyal servant who deserves everything that comes his way. No one wanted it to be about grudges and not speaking to each other. There is a lot of life after cricket.'

It is this philosophy, Clive Lloyd contends, that distinguishes Desi from so many of his peers. 'You don't hear people saying nasty things about him, in the dressing room or outside. He's a very nice guy. He respects what he does, respects his fellow professionals, wants to help people, especially in Barbados where they are not as fortunate as he is. I have the same attitude. We both came from low-income families and have earned everything we possess. It was hard for him because his parents weren't together and hard for me because my father died when I was twelve. We both want to make the world a better place.'

At the time of writing, Desi is about to board a plane bound for South Africa. It may only be a limited-overs do, but it represents the first official tour of the Republic by a West Indian party. 'I've *so* wanted to see the place,' he enthuses; 'a dream fulfilled.' Next up is a quick jaunt to Dubai, then home to face Pakistan, then back to Middlesex. Retirement? Too busy to name the date. He envisages himself studying, then maybe going into marketing or hotel management. He would dearly love to continue serving West Indian cricket, possibly as a selector. 'When I was in Sydney I made a list of all the equipment used at the SCG to show people back home. *We* should have that machinery, and the same expertise among groundsmen.'

When he does retire, Desi has no plans to return to Barbados straight away, at least not on a permanent basis: 'I want to stay away for a while so I can be missed for a while.' A smirk cloaks the seriousness of the sentiment. The game will undoubtedly miss him, but what has it given in return? 'A wider experience of life, a greater understanding of the culture of my people, a keener intelligence. In England, I can stand next to Erskine Sandiford, my Prime Minister, and I'll be recognized by more people than him. That's why I want to put something back in, and that's what makes it easier for me to do so. I thank everybody who ever helped me, and thank God that I never fell into bad company, that I was treated so well at Middlesex and, perhaps most of all, that I experienced the camaraderie of the game. I do fear for the future of Test cricket, however. The game must be marketed properly, and if that means giving the fielders baseball mitts so we can sell the one-day stuff to the Americans, so be it. That way the five-day game may yet survive.'

If the powers that be defend their realm with even a smattering of the devotion, pride and instinct for self-preservation with which Desmond Leo Haynes has protected his, the future of the finest of all trivial pursuits will assuredly be secure. If they remember to carry out their duties with the same smile in their hearts, that security will be deserved.

Appendix A

DESMOND HAYNES:
Born 15 February 1956, Holders Hill, Barbados

TEST CAREER
(up to end of 1992–93 tour of Australia; opening partnerships plus other notable stands in brackets)

1. v AUSTRALIA (Port-of-Spain, 3, 4, 5 March 1978) – WON BY INNS & 106
A 90 and 209; WI 405.
c Rixon b Higgs 61 (87 with Greenidge, 56 with Richards)

2. v AUS (Bridgetown, 17, 18, 19 March) – WON BY 9 WKTS
A 250 and 178; WI 288 and 141–1.
c Rixon b Higgs 66 (16 w Greenidge, 83 w Lloyd)
c Yardley b Higgs 55 (131 w Greenidge)
Series: 182 runs at 60.66

3. v AUS (Brisbane, 1, 2, 3, 4, 5 Dec 1979) – DRAWN
A 268 and 448–6 dec; WI 441 and 40–3.
c Marsh b Thomson 42 (68 w Greenidge)
lbw b Hogg 4 (2 w Greenidge)

4. v AUS (Melbourne, 29, 30, 31 Dec, 1 Jan) – WON BY 10 WKTS
A 156 and 259; WI 397 and 22–0.
c Hughes b Lillee 29 (46 w Greenidge)
9* (22 w Greenidge)

5. v AUS (Adelaide, 26, 27, 28, 29, 30 Jan) – WON BY 408 RUNS
WI 328 and 448; A 203 and 165.
c Lillee b Mallett 28 (11 w Greenidge, 104 w Richards)
c Marsh b Pascoe 27 (48 w Greenidge)
Series: 139 runs at 27.80

6. v NEW ZEALAND (Dunedin, 8, 9, 10, 12, 13 Feb) – LOST BY 1 WKT
WI 140 and 212; NZ 249 and 104–9.
c and b Cairns 55 (3 w Greenidge, 66 w Lloyd)
c Webb b Troup 105 (4 w Greenidge, 88 w King, 63 w Murray)

7. v NZ (Christchurch, 22, 23, 24, 26, 27 Feb) – DRAWN
WI 228 and 447–5 dec; NZ 460.
c Parker b Hadlee 0 (1 w Greenidge)
c Cairns b Coney 122 (225 w Greenidge, record WI opening stand v NZ; 500
    runs in 13th inns).

8. v NZ (Auckland, 29 Feb, 1, 3, 4, 5 March) – DRAWN
WI 220 and 264–9 dec; NZ 305 and 73–4.
c Edgar b Cairns 9 (10 w Greenidge)
b Troup 48 (86 w Greenidge)
Series: 339 runs at 56.50

9. v ENGLAND (Nottingham, 5, 6, 7, 9, 10 June 1980) WON BY 2 WKTS
E 263 and 252; WI 308 and 209–8.
c Gower b Willis 12 (19 w Greenidge)
run out 62 (11 w Greenidge)

10. v ENG (Lord's, 19, 20, 21, 23, 24 June) – DRAWN
E 269 and 133–2; WI 518.
lbw b Botham 184 (37 w Greenidge; 223 w Richards, 51 w Kallicharran; best by
    WI at Lord's at time: 8¼ hrs, 1×6, 27×4)

11. v ENG (Manchester, 10, 11, 12, 14, 15 July) – DRAWN

* = not out

E 150 and 391–7; WI 260.
c Knott b Willis 1 (4 w Greenidge)

12. v ENG (Oval, 24, 25, 26, 28, 29 July) – DRAWN
E 370 and 209–9 dec; WI 265.
c Gooch b Dilley 7 (15 w Greenidge)

13. v ENG (Leeds, 7, 8, 9, 11, 12 Aug) – DRAWN
E 143 and 227–6 dec; WI 245.
b Emburey 42 (83 w Greenidge)
Series: 308 runs at 51.33.

14. v PAKISTAN (Lahore, 24, 25, 27, 28, 29 Nov) – DRAWN
P 369 and 156–7; WI 297.
c Qasim b Nazir 40 (1 w Bacchus; 1000 runs in 22nd Test inns).

15. v PAK (Faisalabad, 8, 9, 11, 12 Dec) – WON BY 156 RUNS
WI 235 and 242; P 176 and 145.
lbw b Qasim 15 (39 w Bacchus)
lbw b Qadir 12 (22 w Bacchus)

16. v PAK (Karachi, 22, 23, 24, 26, 27 Dec) – DRAWN
P 128 and 204–9; WI 169.
lbw b Qasim 1 (19 w Bacchus)

17. v PAK (Multan, 30, 31 Dec, 2, 3, 4 Jan 1981) – DRAWN
WI 249 and 116–5; P 166.
b Imran 5 (9 w Bacchus)
st Bari b Qasim 31 (57 w Bacchus)
Series: 104 runs at 17.33.

18. v ENG (Port-of-Spain, 13, 14, 16, 17, 18 Feb) – WON BY INNS & 79 RUNS
WI 426–9 dec; E 178 and 169.
c and b Emburey 96 (168 w Greenidge)

19. v ENG (Bridgetown, 13, 14, 15, 17, 18 March) – WON BY 298 RUNS
WI 265 and 379–7 dec; E 122 and 224.
c Bairstow b Jackman 25 (24 w Greenidge)
lbw b Botham 25 (0 w Greenidge, 57 w Croft)

20. v ENG (Antigua, 27, 28, 29, 31 March, 1 April) – DRAWN
E 271 and 234–3; WI 468–9 dec.

c Downton b Botham 4 (12 w Greenidge)

21. v ENG (Kingston, 10, 11, 12, 14, 15 April) – DRAWN
E 285 and 302–6 dec; WI 442.
b Willey 84 (116 w Greenidge)
Series: 234 runs at 46.80.

22. v AUS (Melbourne, 26, 27, 28, 29, 30 Dec 1981) – LOST BY 58 RUNS
Aus 198 and 222; WI 201 and 161.
c Border b Lillee 1 (3 w Bacchus)
c Lillee b Yardley 28 (4 w Bacchus)

23. v AUS (Sydney, 2, 3, 4, 5, 6 Jan 1982) – DRAWN
WI 384 and 255; Aus 267 and 200–4.
lbw b Thomson 15 (37 w Greenidge)
lbw b Lillee 51 (29 w Greenidge, 60 w Gomes)

24. v AUS (Adelaide, 30, 31 Jan, 1, 2, 3 Feb) – WON BY 5 WKTS
A 238 and 386; WI 389 and 239–5.
c Marsh b Thomson 26 (12 w Greenidge, 60 w Richards)
c Marsh b Thomson 4 (7 w Greenidge)
Series: 125 runs at 20.83.

25. v INDIA (Kingston, 23, 24, 26, 27, 28 Feb 1983) – WON BY 4 WKTS
I 251 and 174; WI 254 and 173–6.
c Amarnath b Kapil Dev 25 (36 w Greenidge)
b Kapil Dev 34 (46 w Greenidge)

26. v INDIA (Port-of-Spain, 11, 12, 13, 15, 16 March) – DRAWN
I 175 and 469–7; WI 394.
c Kirmani b Sandhu 0 (0 w Greenidge)

27. v INDIA (Georgetown, 31 March, 2, 3, 4, 5 April) – DRAWN
WI 470; INDIA 284–3.
c Yashpal b Venkat 46 (89 w Greenidge)

28. v INDIA (Bridgetown, 15, 16, 17, 19, 20 April) – WON BY 10 WKTS
I 209 and 277; WI 486 and 1–0.
c Kapil Dev b Shastri 92 (98 w Greenidge, 122 w Richards)
0*

* = not out

29. v INDIA (Antigua, 28, 29, 30 April, 1, 3 May) – DRAWN
I 457 and 247–5 dec; WI 550.
c Shastri b Yashpal 136 (296 w Greenidge, then a record WI opening stand and still all-wicket record for WI v. India)
Series: 333 runs at 55.50.

30. v INDIA (Kanpur, 21, 22, 23, 25 Oct) – WON BY INNS AND 83 RUNS
WI 454; I 207 and 164.
c Madan Lal b Kapil Dev 6 (9 w Greenidge)

31. v INDIA (Delhi, 29, 30 Oct, 1, 2, 3 Nov) – DRAWN
I 464 and 233; WI 384 and 120–2.
c Yashpal b Kapil Dev 12 (44 w Greenidge)
b Shastri 17 (50 w Greenidge)

32. INDIA (Ahmedabad, 12, 13, 14, 16 Nov) – WON BY 138 RUNS
WI 281 and 201; I 241 and 103.
lbw b Binny 9 (16 w Greenidge)
c Patil b Sandhu 1 (4 w Greenidge)

33. v INDIA (Bombay, 24, 26, 27, 28, 29 Nov) – DRAWN
I 463 and 173–5 dec; WI 393 and 104–4.
handled the ball 55 (47 w Greenidge, 81 w Richards – fourth batsman to be so dismissed in a Test)
b Maninder 24 (4 w Greenidge)

34. v INDIA (Calcutta, 10, 11, 12, 14 Dec) – WON BY INNS AND 46 RUNS
I 241 and 90; WI 377.
lbw b Kapil Dev 5 (32 w Greenidge)

35. v INDIA (Madras, 24, 26, 27, 28, 29 Dec) – DRAWN
WI 313 and 64–1; I 451–8 dec.
b Maninder 23 (47 w Greenidge)
c Vengsarkar b Shastri 24 (38 w Greenidge)
Series: 176 runs at 17.60

36. v AUS (Georgetown, 2, 3, 4, 6, 7 March 1984) – DRAWN
A 279 and 273–9 dec; WI 230 and 250–0.
lbw b Hogg 60 (reached 2000 runs; 29 w Greenidge)
103* (250 unbroken with Greenidge, highest opening stand for WI v. Aus)

* = not out

37. v AUS (Port-of-Spain, 16, 17, 18, 20, 21 March) – DRAWN
A 255 and 299–9; WI 468–8 dec.
run out 53 (35 w Greenidge, 58 w Richardson)

38. v AUS (Bridgetown, 30, 31 Mar, 1, 3, 4 April) – WON BY 10 WKTS
A 429 and 97; WI 509 and 21–0.
b Hogg 145 (132 w Greenidge, 145 w Richardson)

39. v AUS (Antigua, 7, 8, 9, 11 April) – WON BY INNS AND 36 RUNS
A 262 and 200; WI 498.
b Lawson 21 (0 w Greenidge)

40. v AUS (Kingston, 28, 29, 30 April, 2 May) – WON BY 10 WKTS
A 199 and 160; WI 305 and 55–0.
b Hogan 60 (162 w Greenidge)
15* (55 w Greenidge)
Series: 468 runs at 93.60, heading averages.

41. v ENG (Birmingham, 14, 15, 16, 18 June) – WON BY INNS & 180 RUNS
E 191 and 235; WI 606.
lbw b Willis 8 (34 w Greenidge)

42. v ENG (Lord's, 28, 29, 30 June, 2, 3 July) – WON BY 9 WKTS
E 286 and 300–9 dec; WI 245 and 344–1.
lbw b Botham 12 (1 w Greenidge)
run out 17 (57 w Greenidge)

43. v ENG (Leeds, 12, 13, 14, 16 July) – WON BY 8 WKTS
E 270 and 159; WI 302 and 131–2.
b Allott 18 (16 w Greenidge)
c Fowler b Cook 43 (106 w Greenidge)

44. v ENG (Manchester, 26, 27, 28, 30, 31 July) – WON BY INNS AND 64
    RUNS
WI 500; E 280 and 156.
c Cowans b Botham 2 (11 w Greenidge)

45. v ENG (Oval, 9, 10, 11, 13, 14 Aug) – WON BY 172 RUNS
WI 190 and 346; E 162 and 202.
b Allott 10 (19 w Greenidge)

* = not out

b Botham 125 (51 w Greenidge, 63 w Lloyd, 82 w Dujon)
Series: 235 runs at 29.37; Over rates: Eng 13.4/hr, WI 13.5

46. v AUS (Perth, 9, 10, 11, 12 Nov) – WON BY INNS AND 112 RUNS
WI 416; A 76 and 228.
c Yallop b Hogg 56 (83 w Greenidge)

47. v AUS (Brisbane, 23, 24, 25, 26, 27 Nov) – WON BY 8 WKTS
A 175 and 271; WI 424 and 26–2.
b Alderman 21 (36 w Greenidge)
c Alderman b Hogg 5 (6 w Greenidge)

48. v AUS (Adelaide, 7, 8, 9, 10, 11 Dec) – WON BY 191 RUNS
WI 356 and 292–7 dec; A 284 and 173.
c Hughes b Hogg 0 (4 w Greenidge)
c Wood b Lawson 50 (4 w Greenidge, 76 w Gomes)

49. v AUS (Melbourne, 22, 23, 24, 26, 27 Dec) – DRAWN
WI 479 and 186–5 dec; A 296 and 198–8.
c Border b Lawson 13 (27 w Greenidge)
b McDermott 63 (2 w Greenidge, 51 w Gomes)

50. v AUS (Sydney, 30, 31 Dec, 1, 2, 3 Jan 1985) – LOST BY INNS & 55 RUNS
A 471–9 dec; WI 163 and 253.
c Wessels b Holland 34 (26 w Greenidge)
lbw b McDermott 3 (7 w Greenidge)
Series: 247 runs at 27.44.

51. v NZ (Port-of-Spain, 29, 30, 31 Mar, 2, 3 April) – DRAWN
WI 307 and 261–8 dec; NZ 262 and 187–6.
c Rutherford b Hadlee 0 (5 w Greenidge)
c M. Crowe b Chatfield 78 (10 w Richardson, 114 w Richards)

52. v NZ (Georgetown, 6, 7, 8, 10, 11 April) – DRAWN
WI 511–6 dec and 268–6 dec; NZ 440.
b Hadlee 90 (3000; 30 w Greenidge, 191 w R'son, record 2nd wkt for WI v NZ)
c Smith b Hadlee 9 (22 w Greenidge)

53. v NZ (Bridgetown, 26, 27, 28, 30 April, 1 May) – WON BY 10 WKTS
NZ 94 and 248; WI 336 and 10–0.
c Smith b Hadlee 62 (12 w Greenidge, 79 w Richardson)

5* (10 w Greenidge)

54. v NZ (Kingston, 4, 5, 6, 8 May) – WON BY 10 WKTS
WI 363 and 59–0; NZ 138 and 283.
c J. Crowe b Coney 76 (82 w Greenidge, 62 w Richardson)
24* (59 w Greenidge)
Series: 344 runs at 57.33.

55. v ENG (Kingston, 21, 22, 23 Feb 1986) – WON BY 10 WKTS
E 159 and 152; WI 307 and 5–0.
c Downton b Thomas 32 (79 w Greenidge)

56. v ENG (Port-of-Spain, 7, 8, 9, 11, 12 March) – WON BY 7 WKTS
E 176 and 315; WI 399 and 95–3.
st Downton b Emburey 67 (59 w Greenidge, 150 w Richardson)
39* (72 w Greenidge)

57. v ENG (Bridgetown, 21, 22, 23, 25 March) – WON BY INNS & 30 RUNS
WI 418; E 189 and 199.
c Botham b Foster 84 (34 w Greenidge, 194 w Richardson)

58. v ENG (Port-of-Spain 3, 4, 5 April) – WON BY 10 WKTS
E 200 and 150; WI 312 and 39–0.
c Botham b Foster 25 (58 w Greenidge)
17* (39 w Richardson)

59. v ENG (Antigua, 11, 12, 13, 15, 16 April) – WON BY 240 RUNS
WI 474 and 246–2 dec; E 310 and 170.
c Gatting b Ellison 131 (23 w Greenidge, 74 w Gomes, 54 w Dujon)
run out 70 (100 w Richardson, 61 w Richards)
Series: 469 runs at 78.16, topping aggregates and averages.

60. v PAK (Faisalabad, 24, 26, 27, 28, 29 Oct) – LOST BY 186 RUNS
P 159 and 328; WI 248 and 53.
lbw b Imran 40 (12 w Greenidge, 91 w Richardson)
lbw b Imran 0 (5 w Greenidge)

61. v PAK (Lahore, 7, 8, 9 Nov) – WON BY INNS & 10
P 131 and 77; WI 218.
b Tausif 18 (49 w Greenidge, highest stand of match)

* = not out

62. v PAK (Karachi, 20, 21, 22, 24, 25 Nov) – DRAWN
WI 240 and 211; P 239 and 125–7.
lbw b Imran 3 (14 w Greenidge)
88* (36 w Greenidge, 73 w Richardson)
Series: 149 runs at 37.25, best for either side.

63. v NZ (Wellington, 20, 21, 22, 23, 24 Feb 1987) – DRAWN
NZ 228 and 386–5 dec; WI 345 and 50–2.
b Bracewell 121 (150 w Greenidge, 10th 100+ stand in 58th Test, 58 w Gomes)
c Hadlee b Boock 13 (33 w Greenidge)

64. v NZ (Auckland, 27, 28 Feb, 1, 2, 3 March) – WON BY 10 WKTS
WI 418 and 16–0; NZ 157 and 273.
c M. Crowe b Hadlee 1 (7 w Greenidge)
6* (16 w Greenidge)

65. v NZ (Christchurch, 12, 13, 14, 15 March) – LOST BY 5 WKTS
WI 100 and 264; NZ 332–9 dec and 33–5.
b Hadlee 0 (2 w Greenidge)
c Horne b Chatfield 19 (4000 runs; 37 w Greenidge)
Series: 160 runs at 32.

66. v INDIA (Delhi, 25, 26, 28, 29 Nov) – WON BY 5 WKTS
I 75 and 327; WI 127 and 276–5.
c Lamba b Sharma 45 (0 w Greenidge, 53 w Benjamin; 3rd time last out, all but one run in boundaries)
hit wkt b Ayub 27 (62 w Green)

67. v INDIA (Bombay, 11, 12, 13, 15, 16 Dec) – DRAWN
I 281 and 173; WI 337 and 4–1.
c sub (Pandit) b Shastri 58 (55 w Greenidge)
0* (3 w Greenidge)

68. v INDIA (Calcutta, 26, 27, 28, 30, 31 Dec) – DRAWN
WI 530–5 dec and 157–2; I 565.
c Srikkanth b Kapil Dev 5 (13 w Greenidge)
c and b Shastri 47 (114 w Greenidge)

69. v INDIA (Madras, 11, 12, 14, 15 Jan 1988) – LOST BY 255 RUNS

* = not out

I 382 and 217–8 dec; WI 184 and 160.
c Kapil Dev b Shastri 13 (17 w Simmons)
lbw b Hirwani 6 (22 w Simmons)
Series: 201 runs at 28.71.

70. v PAK (Georgetown, 2, 3, 4, 6 April)–LOST BY 9 WKTS
WI 292 and 172; P 435 and 32–1.
c Yousuf b Imran 1 (7 w Simmons)
b Ijaz 5 (18 w Simmons)

71. v PAK (Port-of-Spain, 14, 15, 16, 17, 19 April) – DRAWN
WI 174 and 391; P 194 and 341–9.
lbw b Wasim 17 (1 w Greenidge, 54 w Richardson)
c Ijaz b Imran 0 (1 w Greenidge)

72. v PAK (Bridgetown, 22, 23, 24, 26, 27 April) – WON BY 2 WKTS
P 309 and 262; WI 306 and 268–8.
c Aamer b Mudassar 48 (18 w Greenidge, 79 w Hooper)
c Salim Malik b Wasim 4 (21 w Greenidge)
Series: 75 runs at 12.50.

73. v ENG (Nottingham, 2, 3, 4, 6, 7 June) – DRAWN
E 245 and 301–3; WI 448–9 dec.
c Downton b Jarvis 60 (54 w Greenidge, 75 w Richards)

74. v ENG (Lord's, 16, 17, 18, 20, 21 June) – WON BY 134 RUNS
WI 209 and 397; E 165 and 307.
c Moxon b Dilley 12 (21 w Greenidge)
c Downton b Dilley 5 (32 w Greenidge)
Missed third Test due to damaged hamstring after 72 successive appearances.

75. v ENG (Leeds, 21, 22, 23, 25, 26 July) – WON BY 10 WKTS
E 201 and 138; WI 275 and 67–0.
lbw b Pringle 54 (15 w Dujon)
25* (67 w Dujon)

76. v ENG (Oval, 4, 5, 6, 8 Aug) – WON BY 8 WKTS
E 205 and 202; WI 183 and 226–2.
c Richards b Foster 2 (9 w Greenidge)

* = not out

77* (131 w Greenidge, 64 w Logie)
Series: 235 runs at 47.

77. v AUS (Brisbane, 18, 19, 20, 21 Nov) – WON BY 9 WKTS
A 167 and 289; WI 394 and 63–1.
c Healy b S. Waugh 40 (135 w Greenidge)
30* (43 w Greenidge)

78. v AUS (Perth, 2, 3, 4, 5, 6 Dec) – WON BY 169 RUNS
WI 449 and 349–9 dec; A 395–8 dec and 234.
lbw b Hughes 11 (16 w Greenidge)
c Healy b Hughes 100 (0 w Greenidge, 103 w Richardson, 113 w Richards; first
    100 in 30 inns)

79. v AUS (Melbourne, 24, 26, 27, 28, 29 Dec) – WON BY 285 RUNS
WI 280 and 361–9 dec; A 242 and 114.
c Boon b McDermott 17 (68 w Greenidge)
lbw b Alderman 23 (38 w Greenidge)

80. v AUS (Sydney, 26, 27, 28, 29, 30 Jan 1989) – LOST BY 7 WKTS
WI 224 and 256; A 401 and 82–3.
c Boon b Hohns 75 (90 w Greenidge, 54 w Richardson)
c M. Taylor b Border 143 (17 w Greenidge, 111 w Hooper)

81. v AUS (Adelaide, 3, 4, 5, 6, 7 Feb) – DRAWN
A 515 and 224–4 dec; WI 369 and 233–4.
run out 83 (5000 runs; 19 w Greenidge, 167 w Richardson)
c Healy b Whitney 15 (21 w Greenidge)
Series: 537 runs (WI record in Aus) at 59.66; headed averages and aggregates.

82. v INDIA (Georgetown, 25, 26, 27, 28, 29, 30 March) – DRAWN
WI 437; I 86–1.
b Ayub 20 (41 v Greenidge)

83. v INDIA (Bridgetown, 7, 8, 9, 11, 12 April) – WON BY 8 WKTS
I 321 and 251; WI 377 and 196–2.
c Manjrekar b Shastri 27 (84 w Greenidge)
112* (14 w Greenidge, 128 w Richardson, 54 w Arthurton; 100 off 128 balls with
    11 fours and three sixes)

* = not out

84. v INDIA (Port-of-Spain, 15, 16, 17, 19, 20 April) – WON BY 217 RUNS
WI 314 and 266; I 150 and 213.
c Raman b Shastri 65 (33 w Greenidge)
c Shastri b Sharma 6 (17 w Greenidge)

85. v INDIA (Kingston, 28, 29, 30 April, 2, 3 May) – WON BY 7 WKTS
I 289 and 152; WI 384 and 60–3.
c Shastri b Dev 15 (1 w Greenidge)
st More b Venkataramana 35 (31 w Greenidge)
Series: 280 runs at 46.66.

86. v ENG (Kingston, 24, 25, 26, 28 Feb, 1 Mar 1990) – LOST BY 9 WKTS
WI 164 and 240; E 364 and 41–1.
c and b Small 36 (62 w Greenidge)
b Malcolm 14 (26 w Greenidge)

87. v ENG (Port-of-Spain, 23, 24, 25, 27, 28 March) – DRAWN
WI 199 and 239; E 288 and 120–5. Captain.
c Lamb b Small 0 (5 w Greenidge)
c Lamb b Malcolm 45 (96 w Greenidge)

88. v ENG (Bridgetown, 5, 6, 7, 8, 10 April) – WON BY 164 RUNS
WI 446 and 267–8 dec; E 358 and 191.
c Stewart b Small 0 (6 w Greenidge)
c Malcolm b Small 109 (13 w Greenidge, 67 w Richardson, 114 w Logie)

89. v ENG (Antigua, 12, 14, 15, 16 April) – WON BY INNS AND 32 RUNS
E 260 and 154; WI 446.
c Russell b Small 167 (298 w Greenidge, record opening stand for WI against
    all-comers)
Series: 371 runs at 53, heading averages.

90. v PAK (Karachi, 15, 16, 17, 19, 20 Nov) – LOST BY 8 WKTS
WI 261 and 181; P 345 and 98–2. Captain.
lbw b Akram 117 (4 w Greenidge, 73 w Richardson, 55 w Logie; 3rd successive
    Test century, completing set v all opponents)
c Yousuf b Younis 47 (47 w Greenidge)

91. v PAK (Faisalabad, 23, 24, 25 Nov) – WON BY 7 WKTS
P 170 and 154; WI 195 and 130–3. Captain.
lbw b Akram Raza 19 (26 w Greenidge)

c Raza b Akram o (o w Greenidge)

92. v PAK (Lahore, 6, 7, 8, 10, 11 Dec) – DRAWN
WI 294 and 173; P 122 and 242–6. Captain.
c Moin b Imran 3 (13 w Greenidge)
c Shoaib b Masood Anwar 12 (1 w Greenidge)
Series: 198 runs at 33.

93. v AUS (Kingston, 1, 2, 3, 5, 6 March 1991) – DRAWN
WI 264 and 334–3 dec; A 371.
b McDermott 8 (9 w Greenidge; retired hurt when 4 due to blow on toe from
   McDermott, resumed at 69–4 when Logie retired hurt)
c Healy b McDermott 84 (6000 runs; 118 w Greenidge)

94. v AUS (Georgetown, 23, 24, 25, 27, 28 March) – WON BY 10 WKTS
A 348 and 248; WI 569 and 31–0.
c M. Waugh b Border 111 (10 w Greenidge, 297 w R'son, eclipsing own all-wicket
   record v Australia)
23* (31 w Greenidge)

95. v AUS (Port-of-Spain, 5, 6, 8, 9, 10 April) – DRAWN
A 294 and 123–3 dec; WI 227.
b McDermott 1 (16 w Greenidge)

96. v AUS (Bridgetown, 19, 20, 21, 23, 24 April) – WON BY 343 RUNS
WI 149 and 536–9 dec; A 134 and 208.
c M. Waugh b Hughes 28 (17 w Greenidge, 50 w Richards)
c Healy b M. Waugh 40 (129 w Greenidge, 16th and last 100+ stand)

97. v AUS (Antigua, 27, 28, 29 April, 1 May) – LOST BY 157 RUNS
A 403 and 265; WI 214 and 297.
lbw b McDermott 84 (10 w Greenidge, 68 w Logie)
run out 33 (76 w Greenidge on latter's 40th birthday, 26th and last half-century
   stand)
Series: 412 runs at 51.50.

98. v ENG (Leeds, 6, 7, 8, 9, 10 June) – LOST BY 115 RUNS
E 198 and 252; WI 173 and 162.
c Russell b Watkin 7 (36 w Simmons)

* = not out

c Smith b Pringle 19 (0 w Simmons, 61 w Richardson)

99. v ENG (Lord's, 20, 21, 22, 23, 24 June) – DRAWN
WI 419 and 21–2; E 354.
c Russell b Pringle 60 (90 w Simmons)
4* (9 w Simmons)

100. v ENG (Nottingham, 4, 5, 6, 8, 9 July) – WON BY 9 WKTS
E 300 and 211; WI 397 and 115–1.
c Smith b Lawrence 18 (32 w Simmons)
57* (1 w Simmons, 114 w Richardson, ninth 100+ stand by pair)

101. v ENG (Birmingham, 25, 26, 27, 28 July) – WON BY 7 WKTS
E 188 and 255; WI 292 and 157–3.
c Russell b DeFreitas 32 (52 w Simmons)
c Hick b DeFreitas 8 (23 w Simmons)

102. v ENG (Oval, 8, 9, 10, 11, 12 Aug) – LOST BY 5 WKTS
E 419 and 146–5; WI 176 and 385.
75* (52 w Simmons, 60 w Lambert; carried bat for 2nd time)
lbw b Lawrence 43 (53 w Simmons, 54 w Richardson)
Series: 323 runs at 46.14.

103. v SOUTH AFRICA (Bridgetown, 18, 19, 20, 22, 23 April 1992) – WON
  BY 52 RUNS
WI 262 and 283; SA 345 and 148.
c Wessels b Snell 58 (99 w Simmons)
c Richardson b Snell 23 (10 w Simmons, 56 w Lara)

104. v AUS (Brisbane, 27, 28, 29, 30 Nov, 1 Dec) – DRAWN
A 293 and 308; WI 371 and 133–8.
c Taylor b Reid 8 (25 w Simmons)
c Healy b McDermott 1 (2 w Simmons)

105. v AUS (Melbourne, 26, 27, 28, 29, 30 Dec) – LOST BY 139 RUNS
A 395 and 196; WI 233 and 219.
b Hughes 7 (11 w Simmons)
c Healy b Hughes 5 (9 w Simmons)

106. v AUS (Sydney, 2, 3, 4, 5, 6 Jan 1993) – DRAWN

* = not out

A 503–9 dec and 117–0; WI 606.
b Matthews 22 (13 w Simmons)

107. v AUS (Adelaide, 23, 24, 25, 26 Jan) – WON BY 1 RUN
WI 252 and 146; A 213 and 184.
st Healy b May 45 (84 w Simmons)
c Healy b McDermott 11 (14 w Simmons)

108. v AUS (Perth, 31 Jan, 1, 2 Feb) – WON BY INNS & 25 RUNS
A 119 and 178; WI 322.
c Healy b Hughes 24 (111 w Simmons)
Series: 123 runs at 15.38

Appendix B

Statistics

(All figures correct up to end of the 1992 English season unless otherwise stated)

Honours: Wisden Cricketer of the Year, 1991; International Cricketer of the Year 1988–9; Britannic Assurance Player of the Year 1990; Middlesex Player of the Year 1990; Captain of West Indies four times; Captain of Barbados 1989–90, 1990–91.

TEST RECORD (TO 2 FEBRUARY 1993)

M	I	NO	RUNS	HS	AV	50	100	CT
108	188	21	6848	184	40.01	37	16	62

Bowling: 3–1–8–1; best figures: 1 for 2 v. Pakistan (Lahore, 1980–81 – Sarfraz Nawaz c Garner b Haynes 4).

COUNTRY-BY-COUNTRY RECORD IN TEST CRICKET

(h) = home; (a) = away

	I	NO	RUNS	HS	AVERAGE	50	100
v. ENGLAND (h)	21	2	1105	167	59.33	5	3
ENGLAND (a)	31	6	1070	184	42.50	7	2
v. AUSTRALIA (h)	20	4	1062	145	66.38	8	3
AUSTRALIA (a)	39	2	1171	143	31.64	6	2
v. INDIA (h)	14	2	613	136	51.92	2	2
INDIA (a)	18	1	377	58	22.24	2	–
v. PAKISTAN (h)	6	0	75	48	12.50	–	–
PAKISTAN (a)	17	1	451	117*	28.19	1	1
v. NEW ZEALAND (h)	8	2	344	90	57.33	4	–
NEW ZEALAND (a)	12	1	499	122	45.36	1	3
v. SOUTH AFRICA (h)	2	0	81	58	40.50	1	–
TOTALS	188	21	6848	184	40.01	37	16

RECORD AGAINST INDIVIDUAL COUNTRIES

	M	I	NO	RUNS	HS	AVERAGE	50	100
ENGLAND	32	52	8	2175	184	49.43	12	5
AUSTRALIA	33	59	6	2233	145	42.13	14	5
INDIA	19	32	3	990	136	34.14	4	2
PAKISTAN	13	23	1	526	117*	23.91	1	1
NEW ZEALAND	10	20	3	843	122	49.59	5	3
SOUTH AFRICA	1	2	0	81	58	40.50	1	–

MODES OF DISMISSAL IN TESTS (TO 2 FEBRUARY 1993)

Bowled 27
LBW 26
Caught (outfield) 63
Caught (wicketkeeper) 35
Caught and bowled 4
Stumped 4
Run out 6
Hit wicket 1
Handled ball 1

TOTAL 167

TEST PARTNERSHIPS WITH GORDON GREENIDGE

M	I	UNBROKEN	RUNS	HS	AVERAGE	50	100
89	148	11	6483	298	47.32	26	16

Record opening stands v. England, Australia, New Zealand and India. Averaged 50 or more in a series on eight occasions, best 136.80 v. Australia, 1983–4.

ONE-DAY INTERNATIONAL FIGURES

M	I	NO	RUNS	HS	50	100	AVERAGE	CT
203	202	25	7514	152*	46	16	42.45	49

Bowling: 5 overs, 0–24.

Most runs and centuries (Richards and Greenidge next best with 11 apiece) to date in one-day internationals.

* = not out

FIRST-CLASS RECORD

M	I	NO	RUNS	HS	AVERAGE	50	100
298	510	58	21,176	255*	46.85	113	50

Bowling:

Overs	Runs	Wickets	Average	Best
69.2	201	7	28.71	1–2

MIDDLESEX FIRST-CLASS RECORD

	M	I	NO	RUNS	HS	AVERAGE	50	100
1989	20	37	5	1446	206*	45.18	8	3
1990	23	39	5	2346	255*	69.00	7	8
1992	20	35	2	1513	177	45.84	10	3
TOTAL	63	111	12	5305	255*	53.59	25	14

Bowling:

	Overs	Maidens	Runs	Wickets	Average	Best
1989	6	3	13	0	–	–
1990	35	7	113	2	56.50	1–18
1992	2.4	0	5	1	5.00	1–2
TOTAL	43.4	10	131	3	43.66	1–2

* = not out

Bibliography

Beecher, Eric, *The Cricket Revolution* (Newspress, London, 1978)

Coward, Mike, *Caribbean Odyssey* (Simon & Schuster, London, 1991)

Doust, Dudley, *Ian Botham: The Great All-Rounder* (Cassell, London, 1980)

Gooch, Graham, *Testing Times* (Robson Books, London, 1992)

Griffith, Charlie, *Chucked Around* (Pelham, London, 1970)

Hoyos, F. A., *Barbados: A History from the Amerindians to Independence* (Macmillan Education, London, 1978)

Hunte, Conrad, *Playing to Win* (Hodder & Stoughton, London, 1971)

James, C. L. R., *Beyond a Boundary* (Stanley Paul & Co., London, 1963)

Jones, Brunell, *Cricket Confusion* (Sports News Service, London, 1978)

Manley, Michael, *A History of West Indies Cricket* (André Deutsch, London, 1988)

Marshall, Malcolm, with Patrick Symes, *Marshall Arts* (Queen Anne Press, London, 1987)

Richards, Viv, with Mick Middles, *Hitting Across the Line* (Headline, London, 1991)

Wisden Cricketers' Almanack 1929–92

Wisden Cricket Monthly

The Cricketer

The Cricketer Quarterly

Caribbean Cricket Quarterly

Index